one
£2
our pric
£8—00

C000158081

DEAN DWELLY
OF LIVERPOOL
LITURGICAL GENIUS

Alcuin Club Collections 90

"The laymen of Liverpool are giving you this great gift;
I sometimes ask myself if you will be able to use it."
Sir Frederick Radcliffe, 1924

"Liverpool Cathedral is known throughout the world.
It would, however, be an empty shell were it not for the uplifting
services which have brought life and colour, dignity and glory
to it. The man behind these services has been the Dean."
Bishop Clifford Martin

Dean Dwelly of Liverpool

Liturgical Genius

PETER KENNERLEY

Dedicated to four wise men:
John Elford, Noel Rawsthorne, Donald Gray, Simon Macaulay
who in different ways and at different times supported my work
on this book.

Copyright © Peter Kennerley, 2015
Alcuin Club Collections 90

First edition, 2015

Published by Palatine Books,
an imprint of Carnegie Publishing Ltd
Carnegie House,
Chatsworth Road,
Lancaster, LA1 4SL
www.carnegiepublishing.com

All rights reserved
Unauthorised duplication contravenes existing laws

ISBN 978-1-910837-02-3

Designed and typeset by Carnegie Book Production
Printed and bound by Nicholson Bass, Belfast, Northern Ireland

FSC
www.fsc.org
MIX
Paper from
responsible sources
FSC® C019241

Contents

Foreword by Justin Welby, Archbishop of Canterbury   vii

Apologia   ix

1   The establishment of a new cathedral in Liverpool   1

2   The development of a priest   35

3   Consecration   61

4   Canon Dwelly   89

5   The establishment of the deanery   121

6   Controversy   151

7   The liturgical artist   167

8   "The first human milestone"   203

9   Dwelly tradition: death mask or spirit   231

10   Cathedrals are the success story of the Church of England   257

Postscript by Simon Macaulay   283

Notes   289

Bibliography   301

The Alcuin Club

Founded in 1897, the Alcuin Club seeks to promote the study of Christian liturgy and worship in general with special reference to worship in the Anglican Communion. The Club has published a series of annual Collections, including *A Companion to Common Worship*, volumes 1 and 2, edited by Paul F. Bradshaw, a new edition of the classic text *Christian Prayer through the Centuries*, by Joseph Jungmann (SPCK 2007); *The Origins of Feasts, Fasts and Seasons in Early Christianity* by Paul F. Bradshaw and Maxwell E. Johnson (SPCK 2011) and, by the same authors, *The Eucharistic Liturgies: Their Evolution and Interpretation* (SPCK 2012); *The Cross and Creation in Christian Liturgy and Art* by Christopher Irvine (SPCK 2013), and most recently *Eucharistic Epicleses Ancient and Modern* by Anne McGowan (SPCK 2014). The Alcuin Liturgy Guide series aims to address the theology and practice of worship, and includes *The Use of Symbols in Worship*, edited by Christopher Irvine, and two volumes covering the celebration of the Christian Year: *Celebrating Christ's Appearing: Advent to Christmas* and *Celebrating Christ's Victory: Ash Wednesday to Trinity*, both by Benjamin Gordon-Taylor and Simon Jones. The Club works in partnership with GROW in the publication of the Joint Liturgical Studies series, with two studies being published each year. In 2013 the Club also published a major new work of reference, *The Study of Liturgy and Worship: An Alcuin Guide*, edited by Juliette Day and Benjamin Gordon-Taylor (SPCK 2013).

Members of the Club receive publications of the current year free and others at a reduced rate. The President of the Club is the Rt Revd Michael Perham, its Chairman is the Revd Canon Dr Donald Gray CBE, and the Secretary is the Revd Dr Gordon Jeanes. For details of membership and the annual subscription, contact The Alcuin Club, 5 Saffron Street, Royston SG8 9TR, or email: alcuinclub@gmail.com

Visit the Alcuin Club website at: **www.alcuinclub.org.uk**

Foreword

Justin Welby, Archbishop of Canterbury

PETER KENNERLEY is one of the few people who have seen the extraordinary wisdom and genius of Dean Dwelly, the first Dean of Liverpool, and my first predecessor in post.

Dwelly was introduced to me by Peter, and the more I have read of him (now quite a lot) the more I have seen how important it is that his contribution as a liturgist should be recognised more clearly.

We need to remember the era in which Dwelly presided at Liverpool Cathedral, either as *Ceremoniarius* and subsequently as Dean. He took on a Cathedral in the early stages of construction, in the immediate aftermath of the Great War. He saw its rapid advance through the twenties, and even through the thirties, during which period his capacity to raise money and to develop both the morale and the vision of those involved with the Cathedral was tested to its limits by the Depression. Despite that, enough money came in to keep hundreds of people in work and thus fed during the greatest economic crisis of the twentieth century, in a city harder hit than most. His success illustrates not only his liturgical but pastoral and missional skills.

Dwelly was not only a builder, but advanced steadily as a liturgist. In a traditional era, his creativity in the use of poetry, of music, of the commissioning of art, and in the use of the Great Space of Liverpool Cathedral sets him apart from his peers. To read the orders of service for Sea Sunday, or for other regular memorial events, is invariably moving and usually inspiring. It is said that when Dwelly was Dean 'normal evensongs' were the rare exception.

I suspect Dwelly had a low threshold of boredom, but the result was a remarkable creativity that resulted in a tradition open to liturgical innovation that exists to this day at Liverpool Cathedral.

Yet at the same time he was someone for whom the nature of the liturgy was centred around the value of the human being. Thus he invented the "Cross Guild", an association of ex-choristers who automatically became entitled to participate as servers on all Cathedral occasions, and who could come regularly, rarely or very occasionally, and still find that they had a role. This sprang from his sense that after years of service to the Cathedral through the choir, a chorister should not just be dropped at the end of his time.

Dwelly inspired me especially with the two questions that he often used to ask people when the planning of a service began. "What do you want to say to each other?" "What do you want to say to God?" These questions integrate pastoral care and liturgical purpose with immense depth and rigour. They bring those who are taking part in the service front and centre, and stop what can be a danger in most places where there are many exceptional services, that people become a necessary but inconvenient obstacle to the otherwise enjoyable business of liturgy. Dwelly was one of the great exponents of the Church of England tradition which is so strong in so many cathedrals that the liturgy relates to the people present, opens their eyes to the presence of God and draws the two together.

At the same time he was someone who saw the need of mission and the need of theological skill and catechesis. His colleague Charles Raven and he set up a service late on a Sunday evening, after the parish evensongs, that drew many with a mix of good sermons and popular hymns. It was in some ways the precursor to modern services of the word. The emphasis on time so as not to compete with the parishes, and on accessibility, together with the concentration on explanation of Christian truth all illustrate the depth and width of the care and skills of Dwelly.

Peter Kennerley has done a very valuable work in his studies of Dwelly. There are many questions to be raised about him and his work, he was certainly a complex character with faults, but in struggling with his humanity, as we all do, he set a pattern of Cathedral life and of liturgical skill that is an essential study. I strongly commend this book as material for reflection.

Apologia

THIS BOOK is an exploration of the influence of Frederick William Dwelly, the first Dean, on the worshipping life of a vast, newly established twentieth century cathedral in Liverpool. The book argues that Dwelly was responsible for establishing the style of public worship in Liverpool Cathedral, and way beyond, and that his influence is still discernible over fifty years after his death. It is argued that his was a liturgical genius commensurate with the architectural vision of Giles Gilbert Scott, the Cathedral Architect.

Liverpool's decision in 1901 to build a new cathedral on a previously unconsecrated site was a decision of great importance in the Diocese of Liverpool and in the history of the Church of England. No English cathedral had been consecrated on such a site since Salisbury in 1225. From the start it was clear that the cathedral was being built on a massive scale; it was to be the largest cathedral in Britain and the fifth largest cathedral in the world. Exactly twenty years after the laying of the foundation stone, the consecration of the cathedral in 1924 was an important historic event. The liturgy and styles of worship in this new foundation were to be of fundamental importance to the success of the cathedral venture and the consecration service itself was of major importance. The priest who devised the great service and went on to be Canon, vice-Dean and Dean and also to mastermind worship in the cathedral was Frederick William Dwelly. He was totally dissatisfied with "mangled Matins" and "mutilated Evensong" and was the initiator of the "special" service now such an important part of the worship and ministry of the English cathedrals. The importance of this phenomenon was highlighted in a leader in the *Church Times*, 12 August 2013: "… the emphasis on special services and events that target different sections of the community is a strategy that works". It had been a strategy central to the ministry of Liverpool Cathedral since the 1920s.

During my writing of *The Building of Liverpool Cathedral*,[1] I discovered the paucity of material available relating to Dwelly and my informal research and gathering of archive material used in this book began then. Despite the highly acclaimed work which Dwelly accomplished in the new cathedral, his work was not formally recorded and examined until the publication of my biography *Frederick William Dwelly: First Dean of Liverpool*.[2] The research for both of these books impressed upon me the need for a piece of research centred upon the influence

Dwelly had upon the worshipping life of the cathedral both during his life-time and after his death. He showed the diocese and the wider Anglican Communion how Scott's remarkable building could be used for worship that was dignified, imaginative and relevant for the thousands of people who attended services. Other cathedrals might quite justifiably have been seen as centres of learning, shrines of royal or national importance, unique ancient buildings, but Liverpool Cathedral would become famous as a vast and remarkable twentieth-century building which was brought to life by the character and quality of its public worship and was regarded as "the 'research' Cathedral of the Anglican Communion".

For thirty years Dwelly was responsible for all the services in the new cathedral and the traditions he established are still discernible today. His liturgical achievements are examined through inspection of the largely unexplored but extensive Dwelly archive – the service papers, letters, minutes, sermons, newspaper reports; the comments upon and assessments of his work by eminent contemporaries and by those who continued to work in the traditions he established and by the current practice in the cathedral.

Despite the shortage of standard bibliographical resources about his achievements, it is clear that Dwelly's work was known and admired by some of the great ecclesiastical figures of the day, and there is passing reference to him in some works by or about them. The fact that his work was highly regarded by some of the great figures in the Anglican Church in the second half of the twentieth century cannot be overlooked. Some of the most obvious names include Cosmo Lang, William Temple, Cyril Garbett, Colin Dunlop, Albert Augustus David, Charles Raven, Mervyn Haigh, Percy Dearmer, "Dick" Sheppard, Frederick Dillistone, Clifford Martin, Basil Naylor, Edward Patey, Alan Wilkinson, Gordon Bates. The recognition of Dwelly's ability by such significant names indicated the importance of a piece of research to examine his achievements.

A narrative, reportage mode of writing has been adopted partly because chronology is important in the developments of Dwelly's work. The narrative mode lends itself comfortably to the correlation of materials from various sources. The bringing together is of crucial importance in the process of exploration and analysis through which Dwelly's achievements as a liturgical artist can be evaluated. As can be seen from the chapter headings, the structure of this book is chronological but it is not a biography of Dwelly: the focus is upon his liturgical artistry and influence during his life time and after his death.

The twin foundation points in this study lie in the Dwelly archive materials which I have gathered and my own experience of the cathedral for sixty years. I have been Custos and Education Officer when I worked full-time in the cathedral for fifteen years. I know the building well and I know how it can be used. I have devised services and preached there. Although I remember Dwelly, I was too young to know him but I knew his successors – Frederick Dillistone, Edward Patey, Derrick Walters, Rupert Hoare and Justin Welby. I have been able to consult former Precentors: the Rt Rev. Gordon Bates, the Very Rev. Nicholas Frayling, the Very Rev. Ken Riley, the Very Rev. Mark Boyling. I did not know Harry Goss Custard, the first Organist, or Edgar Robinson, Choral conductor, but I know and meet their successors Noel Rawsthorne and Ronald Woan, and I am in contact with Ian Tracey, Organist and, until December 2007, Master of the Choristers. For ten years my office was the room which housed the almost unbroken collection of cathedral service papers from 1924 up to the present day. The room which served as Dwelly's war-time bedroom became my office.

Individual issues relating to Dean Dwelly's achievements are clustered around four main headings: personality, theology, liturgy, and artistry. Deliberately they have not been considered separately because they interweave in all his work. In terms of personality, his life exhibits a genius for friendship, kindness and generosity, a devotion to family and community, dynamism, adventurousness, dedication, strength, originality, powers of leadership and administration. In theology he was liberal, modernist, mystic, inclusive, and conscious of the transcendence and immanence of God. He was a liturgical genius; a creative artist, imaginative, master of design, skilled and elegant in his use of language, rich in his knowledge of poetry, talented in his use of symbolism, music, movement in a great space, and the designer of services relevant to the building and the particular congregations.

Although serious gaps remain, the archive material which I have been gathering is rich, varied and important. The Dwelly papers are not as yet in a public archive and they have been collected from a number of sources. The heavy use of primary source material is deliberate so that these important words are put into the public domain. It is the bringing together of such a wide range of varied material which lies at the heart of this study of a liturgical artist.

It was only when the book was nearing completion that I realised that the text needed illustrations, not only of some of the famous service papers but also of the cathedral itself both empty and in use during services. From my opening paragraph I have argued that Dwelly's liturgical genius was commensurate with the architectural vision of Sir Giles Gilbert Scott. Both archive and newly taken photographs will make the text and Dwelly's genius more meaningful to readers who have little or no experience of Liverpool Cathedral. I am grateful to Dean Pete Wilcox and the Chapter for allowing me to use material from the archives and grateful to several members of the Cathedral company who generously supported me with images to supplement my own photography.

"… an anachronism even when begun." Olive Cook

"The laymen of Liverpool are giving you this great gift: I sometimes ask myself if you will be able to use it." Sir Frederick Radcliffe

"The right use to be made of the cathedral foundation has long perplexed the Bishops, and constitutes a problem which none has yet succeeding in solving." Hensley Henson

"The practical requirements are few and simple, but appeal, both aesthetic and emotional, in the best sense of that much abused word, is an essential requirement, dominating all others." Giles Gilbert Scott

"The cathedrals are frequently characterized as being pockets of privilege, lethargy and decadence, inbred and self-centred, staffed by lazy and pompous clerics, little concerned with ordinary people or the hardships of their lives." Stanford Lehmberg

"Will Liverpool's new Cathedral be like York Minster, a cold and dead memorial of the past robed in the lifeless splendour of centuries that have gone but always void of contact with the life of today?" Catholic Times

"The cathedrals of ancient status seemed to be so dominated by established custom, so weighted with statutory obligations, as to be hardly capable of a fresh start: they had come to occupy a fixed position and are not easily moved from their routine." Charles Raven

The establishment of a new cathedral in Liverpool

ALTHOUGH in a radio broadcast in the late 1970s and quoted in *Liverpool Cathedral Bulletin* No. 99 Sir John Betjeman was to say, "Liverpool Cathedral is one of the great buildings of the world,"[1] Olive Cook was later to declare the building to be "an anachronism even when begun."[2] It is the largest cathedral in Britain, and fifth largest in the world at over 100,000 square feet. The cathedral stands in the estimation of many people alongside Canterbury, York, Durham, Lincoln, Ely and Salisbury in its architecture and its significance within the landscape but it is separated from these other great cathedrals by over 500 years. In the thirteenth century, the Christian Church was central to Western European society: by the twentieth century it was not and the largest cathedral was being constructed and established during 74 years of an increasingly secular age.

Before there can be any consideration of the life and work of the man brought to the cathedral in 1924 to prepare the service of consecration, Liverpool Cathedral has to be placed very briefly historically within its national and regional settings. The history of English Cathedrals corporately and individually from a variety of angles has been reported authoritatively by a range of writers, most recently Stanford Lehmberg.[3] These paragraphs are intended to do no more than place the foundation of Liverpool Cathedral within the general context of cathedral building in England so that the unique nature is clarified.

Archaeological evidence illuminates the world of Anglo-Saxon cathedrals, outlined by Tim Tatton-Brown.[4] The appointment of Lanfranc as Archbishop of Canterbury in 1070 was a landmark in the establishment of many of the great cathedrals existing today. By 1133 there were seventeen cathedrals in England: ten monastic cathedrals staffed by monks and seven secular staffed by canons who did not live under a monastic rule. After the dissolution of the monasteries, six new cathedrals were established in existing churches by King Henry VIII. After the establishment of the Diocese of Oxford with Christ Church as its cathedral in 1542, no new diocese was created and cathedral established until 1836, when a succession of parish or collegiate churches were upgraded to cathedral status. Such places as Ripon, Manchester, Newcastle, Sheffield, Derby and Portsmouth are known as "parish church" cathedrals and only those in Truro, Liverpool, Guildford and post-war Coventry were built from new.

By the time Liverpool achieved diocesan status in 1880, it had become a very rich and important sea port, gateway to the Americas, but the more distant past gave no suggestion of the rapid growth and change of fortunes experienced in the eighteenth and nineteenth centuries. There is not even a record of the settlement in Domesday Book of 1086. The whole of the north west was a desolate area. The estimated population on the whole sweep of land between the Mersey and the Ribble was two per square mile. The Hundred of West Derby stretched from Southport to Hale and eastwards to Wigan but the total population was no more than 3,000. In the words of local historian, Professor Ramsey Muir, "In Western Europe there were few more remote and isolated corners."[5] The only significant town and port in the whole region was the Roman town of Chester where an ancient Benedictine abbey had gained cathedral status in 1541.

On 28 August 1207, the settlement received its first charter from King John whose advisors had seen the possible strategic and economic significance of the tiny settlement protected by the River Mersey on one side and a tidal creek which provided safe anchorage for the small vessels bound for Ireland. Liverpool was not in the clutches of the powerful Earl of Chester. By 1235 a stone castle had been built and the little chapel of St. Mary del Key was in use by 1257 and the Church of Our Lady and St. Nicholas was built between 1355 and 1361. It was not until 1699 that Liverpool achieved the status of a parish, served jointly by Our Lady and St. Nicholas and St. Peter's. The population in 1296 was 168 families. By 1346 there were 1200 people; then came the first outbreak of plague and by 1565 the population had slumped to 700. Ramsey Muir pronounced the town during the fifteenth and sixteenth centuries to be both insignificant and decaying.

It was not until the middle of the seventeenth century that Liverpool's growth as a great seaport began. Once better communications with the rest of the country had been established by road, canal and railway, Liverpool was ideally situated geographically to become the centre of the trans-Atlantic trade. A cargo of American tobacco arrived in 1648 and sugar refining began twenty years later. Thomas Steers's Old Dock was constructed in the mouth of the Pool and in 1715 was opened as the first commercial wet dock in the world. By 1740, Liverpool had become the most significant port in the whole of Europe for its involvement with the slave trade. The town hall, to the design of John Wood, was completed in 1754 and much remodelling was undertaken by James Wyatt after a disastrous fire of 1795.The resulting building is of the highest quality: in the words of Joseph Sharples, "Among English civic buildings of its date, Liverpool Town Hall is probably second only to London's Mansion house in its richness".[6] Prosperity accompanied by civic pride became the hallmark of the whole spirit of Liverpool throughout the eighteenth and nineteenth centuries and the concept of a great new cathedral emerged during the period of Edwardian optimism at the dawn of the twentieth century.

There was little to mark Liverpool's cultural significance before the second half of the eighteenth century but in March 1753 William Roscoe was born. After little formal education, he went on to become one of Liverpool's most significant citizens of all time who exerted an astonishing influence on the whole cultural life of the town. His library was of national importance. He was

"One of the great buildings of the world." The foundation stone was laid in 1904 and the building was completed in 1978 despite two world wars and spiralling inflation.

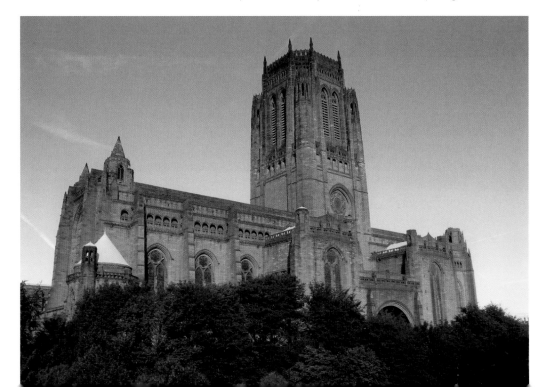

a lawyer, art historian, bibliophile, art collector, poet, botanist, politician deeply involved in opposition to the slave trade. He was a founder of the Liverpool Athenaeum Club which pre-dated the London club of the same name and he helped establish the Liverpool Botanical Gardens.

The buildings and port facilities of Liverpool from the late eighteenth century onwards can be interpreted as precursors of the plans to build the largest cathedral in Britain in the early years of the twentieth century. When Manchester was raised to diocesan status in 1848, a medieval collegiate church was upgraded to cathedral. Such a scheme was never going to satisfy the merchant princes of Liverpool. Prosperity was wholly dependent on the river. By the twentieth century there would be eight miles of docks. Between 1801 and 1824, the dock dues rose from £28,365 to £130,911. Jesse Hartley was appointed Dock Engineer in 1824 and was responsible for the massive developments in granite, brick and cast iron which remain such powerful features of the water-front even today. It is not irrelevant to relate Giles Scott's cathedral to Jesse Hartley's Albert Dock because of vastness and size and quality of design and workmanship.

Liverpool Cathedral cannot be contemplated away from the panorama of the city's nineteenth century architecture. Harvey Lonsdale Elmes's final plans for a building combining massive concert hall and law courts were to give rise to St. George's Hall, completed in 1856. It has been described by Nikolaus Pevsner as "the freest neo-Grecian building in England and one of the finest in the world."[7] The other civic buildings in William Brown Street – the Walker Art Gallery, Picton Reading Room, the William Brown Library and Museum create a magnificent welcome site to travellers arriving at Lime Street station: "this could be the finest civic parade in Britain".[8] To walk the area within a quarter of a mile radius of the town hall is to be convinced by the commercial prowess of Liverpool as presented through the quality of the buildings constructed as banks, insurance companies and the great trading houses. Of note must be the Bank of England, 1845, The Albany, 1856, Oriel Chambers, 1864, the Prudential Assurance building, 1886 and the White Star building, 1898. The great merchant figures started to see Liverpool alongside some of the great Renaissance cities of Italy. "The Italian Renaissance provided models for much mid-nineteenth century commercial architecture. Florentine palaces had an obvious symbolic appeal for Liverpool's merchant princes, as did those of Venice, the seat of a maritime trading empire."[9]

As Liverpool approached the seven hundredth anniversary of the granting of King John's charter it could justly claim to be the second city in the land and it handled a greater tonnage of cargo than the Port of London. The population rise over the previous two centuries had been steep: in 1700–5 it was 715; in 1801, 78,000; 1851, 376,000; and by 1901, 684,947.

In 1881 a charter was granted for the formation of a new university college which awarded degrees validated by the Federal Victoria University. In July 1903 a royal charter was granted, authorizing the university to award its own degrees under the name of the University of Liverpool. The prominent Victoria Building on Brownlow Hill led to the coining of the phrase "red brick university".

Liverpool has a poor reputation when it comes to preserving old churches but the nineteenth century saw the building of a number of particularly fine parish churches. Among the most significant Anglican churches are St. Mary the Virgin, West Derby, 1856, St. Margaret of Antioch, 1869, St. John the Baptist, Tuebrook, 1871, St. Matthew and St. James, Mossley Hill 1875, All Hallows, Allerton, 1876, St. Agnes, 1883. Though distinguished churches were built, Liverpool was still part of the vast diocese of Chester despite the fact that Chester itself as a city had faded from its Roman and medieval past. By the middle of the nineteenth century both Liverpool and Manchester had rapidly expanding populations and economies but they lacked independence from the distant, and one must assume, over-worked Bishop of Chester. The new Diocese of Manchester was carved out from Chester in 1848. The Liverpool Diocese was to follow on from the Bishoprics Act of 1878 after the city had raised ⊠100,000 to endow the new foundation, and the Bishop's throne was established in the old and cramped Parish Church of St. Peter in 1880, a building quite unsuitable for its new role and built on a site which made any extension to the existing building impossible and thought by the Rector of Liverpool to be "ugly and hideous".[10] An article in *The Graphic* magazine for 1877 declared it to be "perhaps, the ugliest and meanest building of its kind in the North of England".[11]

The establishment of a new diocese and cathedral at the start of the twentieth century was not an easy task because it was not in architecture alone that the already existing cathedrals differed. There was no simple blueprint to be followed. Right from the middle ages there was diversity. St. Paul's, Chichester, Salisbury, Wells, Exeter, Hereford, Lichfield, Lincoln and York are referred to as cathedrals of the old foundation and they were staffed not by monks but by secular canons. Canterbury, Durham, Winchester, Rochester, Worcester, Norwich, Ely and Carlisle were all great monastic churches staffed by monks living in a community under a strict rule. The first seven were Benedictine foundations and Carlisle was Augustinian. At the time of the dissolution of the monasteries, these nine together with five monastic houses at Gloucester, Chester, Bristol, Peterborough, Oxford, and for a short time, Westminster, became known as new foundation cathedrals. From 1542 to 1836 no further cathedrals were founded. Ripon, Manchester, St. Albans all existed originally as ancient churches with pre-existing functions and statutes and, though mostly new-built, Truro incorporated an old parish church. It is not surprising that on appointment as Bishop of Hereford in 1918, Hensley Henson remarked, "The right use to be made of the cathedral foundation has long perplexed the bishops, and constitutes a problem which none has yet succeeded in solving".[12]

Heritage and Renewal: The Report of the Archbishops' Commission on Cathedrals contains a short but significant chapter by Dr. Edward Norman on cathedrals and historical background. One aspect of his findings is particularly significant before any consideration of the building of a new cathedral: that is the lack of clarity over centuries as to the precise functions of a cathedral. The original function of every cathedral was without question in that the cathedral church was the place where the bishop had his official seat or throne – cathedra in Greek – and where the services of the church were celebrated daily. The standing of a bishop was enhanced if his cathedral housed some particularly important Christian relic such as the remains of Cuthbert and Bede at Durham, or Thomas a Becket at Canterbury. Such cathedrals became important centres

Liverpool Town Hall, a grade 1 listed building built between 1749 and 1754 and later rebuilt after a fire in 1795.

Saint George's Hall. Pevsner described it as the "finest neo-Grecian building in England." Building began in 1842.

of pilgrimage and attracted many donations. The medieval bishop gathered a range of secular functions and was often required to reside, not in his cathedral, but at court. In the absence of the bishop, the administration of the cathedral was largely the domain of the Dean and Chapter.

What appears striking is Norman's assessment that the functions of the cathedral were nebulous: "The functions of medieval cathedrals are not clear".[13] Even after the Reformation and Henry VIII's dissolution of the monasteries and the establishment of the new foundation cathedrals, "… no one took the occasion of the general upheaval of religion to ask what cathedrals were actually for … There was no suggestion that bishops should recover an immediate role in them, or that cathedrals might be regarded as centres of diocesan life".[14] It was the 1830s before reforming attention was focused upon cathedrals but even at that time Norman emphasizes the limitations of cathedral reform: "The real function was not an issue: reform was about the stewardship of their supposed wealth, not what cathedrals were for."[15] The Ecclesiastical Duties and Revenues Act of 1840 curtailed cathedral clergy by abolishing all non-resident prebends and rectoral sinecures. Most, though not all, of the cathedrals were limited to four residential canonries. There was clear reason for the establishment of the first parish church cathedrals at Ripon and Manchester through demographic developments particularly in the industrial north. But "as no one could agree about what cathedrals were for, it was scarcely to be expected that the new ones would be embodiments of ideological revision".[16] In Norman's view, it was not only the cathedral that lacked clarity of function but also the diocese: "The notion of the cathedrals as a focus of diocesan activity could hardly occur in a world in which the diocese itself had little activity to focus".[17]

Despite his doubts about the clarity of cathedral functions in the nineteenth century, Norman sees the nineteenth century as establishing much that is now recognised as important cathedral features. A professional music department now offers daily worship of the highest standards. Norman sees daily Choral Evensong as a Victorian invention. Professional attention began to be given to the upkeep of the fabric which had in many instances been neglected for centuries. Only during the nineteenth century did cathedral schools show themselves capable of offering high quality education.

Lehmberg opens his chapter on the eighteenth and nineteenth centuries with the most damning of sweeping statements:

> The eighteenth century is often regarded as being a low point in the history of cathedrals and, indeed, of the Church of England generally. The cathedrals are frequently characterized as being pockets of privilege, lethargy and decadence, inbred and self-centred, staffed by lazy and pompous clerics, little concerned with ordinary people or the hardships of their lives. Many deans and canons were drawn from genteel families and served for long periods of time with minimal duties, sometimes neglecting those obligations they did have.[18]

Such sweeping charges, though not refuted, have been opened to detailed scrutiny by Philip Barrett[19]. His lengthy account and 127 pages of bibliographical notes provide an important historical foundation for the examination of the establishment of new cathedrals towards the end of the century. The second half of the nineteenth century was a time of considerable development in all aspects of cathedral life. The Dean of Chester, J. S. Howson, edited *Essays on cathedrals by various writers* and in his introduction urged the need for fresh life to be breathed into cathedrals: "Nothing seems to me more adapted, with due modifications, to meet some of the urgent wants of our times, to bring new life out of old forms, and to animate and consolidate various existing agencies for religious good."[20] Howson had attracted a range of writers of considerable experience. Harvey Godwin wrote: "... the cathedral is a museum of curiosities, and the verger is the showman; you pay your shilling as you pay it at Madame Tussaud's and you see what you do see." He was dissatisfied with cathedrals in that they seemed "not adapted to Anglican services," and "Protestant worship rattles in them like dry bones in a coffin".[21] Westcott advocated cathedrals as the appropriate centres for theological studies and training for the priesthood; he saw them as feeding the intellectual and spiritual life of the diocese. Ouseley was highly critical about the intellectual and spiritual care of the young choristers who played so significant a role in the worshipping life of every cathedral: "badly schooled, badly cared for in morals and religion, snubbed, despised, slighted, and eventually sent forth into the world with no adequate provision for their maintenance."[22] Benson regretted that Bishops and their chapter members had tended to drift apart but believed that the attitude could be reversed. He was to go on to become Bishop and Dean of the new Truro Cathedral and published *The Cathedral: Its necessary place in the life and work of the church.*[23]

Liverpool is geographically close enough to Chester for the discerning to be aware of some of the severe problems faced by cathedrals in the nineteenth century. The Chester statutes remained unchanged from 1544. The Dean, Frank Bennett commented on the need for a cathedral to operate under modern statutes: "Obsolete statutes are a very awkward basis to work on and in many particulars they ought to be brought up to date."[24] Lichfield was the only cathedral in which Dean and Chapter, with the approval of the Bishop, could make alterations to their statutes. As late as 1927, the wholly unsatisfactory nature of the statutes governing many cathedrals was noted in *Report of the Cathedrals Commission.*[25] Of Chester, "New statutes are needed."[26] Of Wells, "It has no fully authorized body of statutes."[27] Of Durham, "The statutes need some revision."[28] Of Manchester, "The Caroline charter still governs the situation."[29] The 1840 loss of endowments at Chester and elsewhere had serious implications for almost all cathedrals. "The prominent feature of nearly all cathedrals in 1870 was their poverty."[30] Most cathedrals had a dean and four residentiary canons but each canon was in residence for only three months a year. Chester had only one house in the close for residence so there could only ever be one canon in residence. The same was true at York, Bristol, Llandaff and Ripon. There was no fund for the maintenance of the fabric and parts of the building were almost ruinous. Very poor provision was made for the housing and education of the choristers and there were only six men and twelve boys to sing all the daily services. The clergy were not well paid and as late as 1890 Worcester, Salisbury and Gloucester canons took only half stipend. The canons spent most of the year in their own parishes and these parishes were often widely spread throughout the country. In 1869 the records show the home residences of the four Carlisle canons: the closest lived fifty miles away, one lived in Northumberland, one in Hertfordshire and one in Devon. It is interesting to note comments made about the new Liverpool Cathedral in the Commission's Report:[31] "… we wish to state our general satisfaction with the vigour, the courage and the initiative displayed already in the young life of the cathedral. In many respects it will

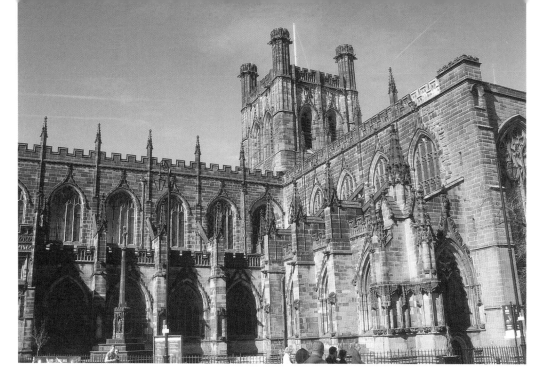

Chester Cathedral on the site of St. Werbergh's Abbey, part of a well-preserved range of monastic buildings.

naturally follow the best of the old traditions, but in others, and in perhaps a large number, it will break new ground, as indeed it has already done, with conspicuous success and ability." From the earliest days, Liverpool Cathedral was judged to be special.

Worshippers looked to the cathedrals to be able to offer high standards of worship accompanied by good and well-performed music but in many places statutes militated against this. There were lay-clerks with security of tenure for life despite their being vocally incapable of performing properly. In places statutes made no reference to choir rehearsals and lay-clerks refused to attend rehearsals. There were some distinguished musicians (such as S. S. Wesley) leading the musical life but, as late as 1880 under the chairmanship of Stainer, cathedral organists stipulated that choirs should be formed of twelve men and twenty boys; that the boys be properly boarded and educated and that the cathedral organist should have a stipend of £400 a year and a house so that he was not compelled to undertake outside teaching.

Relevant to the central focus of this study are some of Chadwick's comments in which he judges the Dean as the crucial influence in moving his cathedral forwards into a more healthy state: "… though the powers of Deans might be hedged, most developments of cathedral life grew from his initiative."[32] He cites the significance of Harvey Godwin at Ely, Church at St. Paul's, Duncombe at York, Lake at Durham, Plumptre at Wells, Goulbourn at Norwich and Bickersteth at Lichfield. Being eight months a year in residence meant that the Dean was the only chapter member with any real sense of continuity. Some Deans could over-rule canons, but some could not. Liverpool was not to have a Dean until 1931; up to that date, the Bishop carried out the duties of Dean.

At the end of his final chapter, Barrett is unequivocal in his judgments on the over-all health of the cathedral system:

> The revitalization of English cathedrals was one of the most impressive achievements of the Victorian Church … To reform an institution with such a long history is often harder than to make important new initiatives. That such notable progress was made in so many cathedrals in the closing decades of the nineteenth century is a remarkable tribute to the untiring energy of their chapters and staff, and also of their willingness to learn from one another. Such progress was founded on a growing perception of the distinctive role that cathedrals might have in the life of the Church;

Interior of Chester Cathedral: very small in comparison with Liverpool.

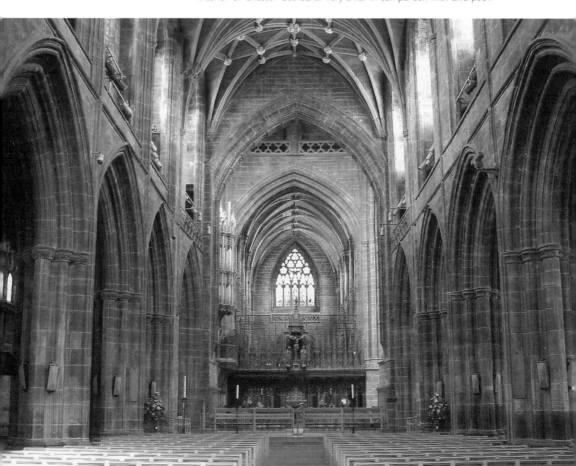

and the sustained enthusiasm that, for example, surrounded the building of Truro Cathedral shows that this perception was widely appreciated.[33]

The inadequacies of Church of England provision in the burgeoning centre of industrial development were clear. Nonconformity and Roman Catholicism were thriving and the parochial system was unable to cope with demographic change. A group of clergy and laity meeting in London in 1876 resolved that there was a need for a well-organised scheme to increase the number of bishops. Under Disraeli's government, bills were introduced to establish new dioceses at Truro and St. Albans in 1877, Liverpool in 1880, Newcastle, Southwell and Wakefield in 1888.

John Charles Ryle, a distinguished evangelical clergyman, was appointed to the see of Liverpool at the age of sixty four. In the opinion of Chadwick "Ryle of Liverpool was well known as one who thought the historic system of cathedrals to be a survival and a mistake".[34] In July 1880, Ryle was enthroned as Bishop of

The exterior of St. Peter's Church from 1885 to 1910 this building was the Pro-Cathedral.

The interior of St. Peter's looking towards the altar. The inadequacy of the cramped space as a Cathedral is obvious.

Liverpool in St. Peter's Church, Church Street, now designated pro-cathedral. It had been built in 1704 and Sir James Picton had described it as "large and commodious, but possesses few claims to architectural design".[35] The church was demolished in 1922 but from existing photographs the building appears cramped and certainly too small to function effectively as a cathedral.

It would not be right to censure Ryle for not embarking on the building of a suitably large cathedral at the start of his episcopacy. Though Liverpool might have become one of the richest and most successful towns in the country, it also had some of the worst slum conditions and grinding poverty anywhere in the country. Hordes of starving Irish families flooded the port after the potato famine. Families were herded into stinking courts and cellars and outbursts of cholera were so severe that Liverpool was forced, of necessity, to appoint Dr. Duncan as the first municipal Medical Officer of Health in the country. The Liverpool diocese extended way beyond the city boundaries and the new Bishop was determined that the Church of England be able to take on its pastoral responsibilities right across the diocese.

In 1881 he wrote,

> In Liverpool itself you have an enormous body of inhabitants connected with our docks and shipping and an incessant stream of emigrants from the Continent to America. You have smoky manufacturies and squalid poverty at one end of the city, and within two or three miles you have fine streets and comparative wealth. In Wigan, Warrington, St. Helens, Widnes and the districts round these places you have swarms of people employed in collieries, iron foundries, cotton manufactories, glass-houses and chemical works, Around Ormskirk, Sefton, Hale and Speke you will see admirable farming. In no part of England, perhaps, you will find such a variety of callings as all are followed with restless activity ..." if the Established Church of this country claims to be 'the church of the people' it is her bounden duty to see that no part of the people are left like sheep without a shepherd. If she claims to be a territorial and not a congregational church, she should never rest until there is neither a street, nor a lane, nor a house, nor a garret, nor a cellar, nor a family, which is not regularly looked after and provided with the offer of the means of grace by her officials.[36]

Ryle built new churches and mission halls, and raised the number of clergy because he felt such work to be more appropriate and urgent than the building of a cathedral.

However, in 1885, the Liverpool Cathedral Act went through parliament. A site, immediately to the west of St. George's Hall, was selected and a design by G. W. Emerson was accepted. The intricacies of the failure of this scheme

The Mersey Docks and Harbour Board building. The size and quality of a building like this ensured that Liverpool's new Cathedral would be a splendid building, worthy of the city which built it.

need not be examined here but Liverpool's initial failure to embark on the building of her Cathedral was to colour later deliberations. Having suffered one public failure, a second had to be avoided. From all that was said and written after the appointment of Francis James Chavasse as second bishop in 1900, there can be little doubt that he and his committees understood the essentials of the character and functions of the building they were planning. A letter was published from the Bishop, immediately after a meeting in the Town Hall at which the formal decision to build a cathedral was taken. The letter acknowledged the enormity of the effort which was going to be needed and considered that effort under three headings, a clear indication as to his priorities about the nature of the enterprise.

> The effort must be great. The Cathedral must be worthy of the Diocese. No thought of cheapness, no temptation to hurry must be entertained. It must be the best of its kind. It must be a fitting expression of the heartfelt homage and gratitude of rich and poor to the great and good God and Father of us all for all the countless blessings we have received at His Hands as a Nation, a Church, and as individuals. It must not be unworthy to rank with those great Cathedrals of the past which are the glory of our Country and of our Faith …
>
> The effort must be united. It must be the work of the whole Diocese, for the Cathedral will be the central Church and ecclesiastical heart of the vast net-work of towns and villages which lie between the Mersey, the Ribble and the Douglas …

The effort must be sustained. A Cathedral cannot be built in a day, perhaps not in a generation. Probably it must be raised piece-meal, as our fathers reared the Cathedrals in bygone days. The devotion of successive ages must extend, enrich and beautify its courts ...

The effort must be made with unceasing prayer. Spiritual work calls for spiritual methods. We must build to glorify God, not to magnify our Diocese or ourselves ...[37]

These four sentiments pronounced over a hundred years ago must have found a relevance in every generation whether or not the ideal has been attained. This was to be one of the great cathedrals of the nation if not of the world but there had to be constant checks on any sense of self-glorification. The diocesan significance of the cathedral was stressed as was the long-term commitment to such a project.

All the main speeches at the Town Hall Meeting were transcribed and were published by the Cathedral in 1901. The Bishop made the most significant speech of the afternoon and what he had to say must be seen as undergirding the whole cathedral scheme. Chavasse was not exaggerating when he spoke of the significance of their scheme:

> ... putting on one side St. Paul's Cathedral, which occupies the place of an older building, the Church of England has since the Reformation built only one Cathedral, and that in the remote and poor Diocese of Truro ... We have before us here in Liverpool a greater scheme than that of Truro. We are about, by God's help, to build a Cathedral in Liverpool, in a diocese four times the size of that of Truro, in the midst of a great commercial city, a city which, when the history of the world comes to be written, will be found commercially to rival the great commercial cities of Carthage, Tyre, Venice, and which we might say with perfect truth is far richer than any of them.[38]

These are not the words of a man suddenly glutted with a sense of his own power. He was being realistic in placing the scheme against a wider historical and geographical setting.

In direct visible and tangible terms he outlined his reasons for why a cathedral was needed.

> First, it will be a visible witness for God in the midst of the great city ... Why not something to speak for God in this great city as St. George's Hall speaks for our great municipality of Liverpool.

> Secondly, a Cathedral is needed for diocesan and popular services.

The Cathedral rising dramatically above the surrounding houses.

The Bishop reminded his listeners that to date in his short episcopate he had three times had to seek permission from the Lord Mayor to hold services in St. George's Hall because the pro-cathedral was far too small to accommodate a large congregation.

> Thirdly, we need a Cathedral which will express and deepen the spiritual longings and aspirations of many among us.

As example he refers to people's visits to Westminster Abbey or St. Paul's when on a visit to London.[39]

It will be interesting to examine to what extent after consecration and the appointment of the first Dean, the cathedral measured up to Chavasse's reasons for its very existence. These issues will be addressed in later chapters.

Panel from the Laymen's Window in the Nave. Sir Giles Scott is the second figure from the left above a representation of the original design for a Cathedral with twin towers.

The Town Hall meeting revealed the variety of feelings which existed over the choice of site but there was unanimity on the subject of the scale and grandeur of the eventual building. Lord Derby quoted Gladstone's words in 1892 when he became a Freeman:

> No doubt, it is a great work, because if such a community as Liverpool sets about the erection of a Cathedral, of one thing I am quite certain, and that is that it will be a Cathedral worthy of the country to which it belongs. I am sure that Liverpool, while it continues to amass wealth, will not fall behind in the concomitant necessary to redeem wealth from degradation – munificence.[40]

The Bishop himself was to put Liverpool and its plans into the context of Western European history

> We are about, by God's help, to build a Cathedral in Liverpool, in a diocese four times the size of Truro, in the midst of a great commercial city, a city which, when the history of the world comes to be written, will be found commercially to rival the great commercial cities of Carthage, Corinth, Tyre and Venice, and which we might say with perfect truth is far richer than any of them.[41]

These words are so expressive of the very spirit of Edwardian Liverpool,

Part of the massive interior space of the completed Cathedral uninterrupted by pillars so that people could see pulpit, lectern and High Altar.

a city at the very height of its powers and all this is reflected in the scale and grandeur of the Cathedral they were planning to build. It is interesting to be aware of three secular buildings being planned and built during the early years of progress on the cathedral. They are office blocks but office blocks built by Liverpool influence and money. In Pevsner's words, "They represent the great Edwardian Imperial optimism".[42] The Mersey Docks and Harbour Board Building, in essence a great office block, but also described as "a Renaissance merchant's palace with the dome of St. Peter's perched on top"[43] and "a secular cathedral of commerce"[44]. Indeed the dome had been designed originally as part of one of the plans for the cathedral. The Royal Liver Building, "an attention-grabbing monster,"[45] was being built at the same time as the Lady Chapel. It was far larger than the insurance company needed but it was to become an undeniably significant part of the water-front. The space between the two was filled by 1916 by the Italian Renaissance Cunard Building. These three buildings are indicative of the whole spirit of Liverpool during the first decade of the twentieth century. However sincere the cathedral builders might have been in their religious zeal, the cathedral project could never have remained untouched by the spirit of civic pride and an awareness of *civitas* was later to be revealed in the character of many of its great services which so clearly embraced so many aspects of the life of the city.

In retrospect, it is difficult to understand why the St. James's Mount site did not appeal to everyone. Those with vision realised that the site was ideal for the construction of a splendid cathedral capable of favourable comparison with great cathedrals of the past: "… it may be safely asserted that hardly any cathedral in Europe will possess such ample and undisturbed surroundings" (Cathedral Committee):

> The Cathedral Committee, by their purchase, have acquired the whole of St. James's Mount and Gardens and St. James's Walk, a space of 1,020 feet in length, and in its greatest breadth 248 feet, and there can be no doubt that its lofty and commanding position and the wide open space of its immediate surroundings, together with its admirable architectural possibilities, and the ease with which it can be reached from all parts of the City and Diocese, combine to make it not only magnificent, but almost unique among the Cathedral Sites of our land.[46]

The running of the competition to find the most effective plans, and the eventual acceptance of Giles Gilbert Scott's drawings have been narrated elsewhere,[47] but what is of relevance here is the part of the report by G. H. Bodley, and R. Norman Shaw, the assessors for the competition in 1903 and published in part in *Liverpool Cathedral, The Story of the Past, The Need of the Present, The Dream of the Future.*

> What we had to find was not the best or the most beautiful drawings, but the best idea and the finest conception. Many of the drawings are attractive, but we had to look much further than that – we had to look at the real effect of the building rising to its final completion; at the dimensions and proportions of the different parts, such as the piers and arches of the great nave; we had to look at the practical and feasible aspect of the designs; we had to look for a sufficiently original conception; we had to look for a fine and noble proportion combined with an evident knowledge of detail; lastly, we had to look for that power combined with beauty that makes a great and noble building.[48]

It is important to remember that when Scott won the competition he made considerable revisions to the original plans, and indeed he made continual modifications through the rest of his life. The most significant alteration of all was the substitution of one massive central tower, over 300 feet high, for the twin towers. Despite numerous changes of detail I believe the assessors' comment is still relevant because they were attempting to cut through detail to the fundamental principles of the great design. The cathedral captured the attention of the architectural world; 103 sets of plans were submitted for the first round of the competition and specialist journals devoted space to it. In 1902, a leading article in *The Builder* was entitled 'The Ideal of the Modern Cathedral' and is worthy of attention for the way in which it indicates the total change of function from medieval to modern cathedrals.

> Nearly all our medieval cathedrals were originally built as a portion only of a great clerical institution which, though, it has its survivals, no longer exists as part of our national life or of our nation Church. They were built for a worship carried on by the clerics in the choir, and not partaken in by the laity. The long nave was nearly useless except for occasional processions, but its grandeur, and that of the west front, were regarded in the light of an offering, an architectural praise of God. Now a modern cathedral is nothing of all this. It is not connected with a great religious establishment requiring a train of buildings grouped with it. It is not erected for the exclusive worship carried on by the clerical body on their own behalf. It is mainly a great church, principally built for the worship of the laity, with a service conducted by a limited number of priests ... The modern cathedral, then, is simply a great church, the mother church of the diocese, with a special official significance in that sense, but otherwise a church for public worship in the same sense as the parish churches.[49]

Scott contributed in July 1904 to a *Cathedral Souvenir* published by the *Liverpool Daily Post and Echo* and his sentiments are clearly in tune with much thinking about a new twentieth century cathedral: "... there is no concealing the fact that when a Cathedral is to be built of such vast proportion as that contemplated for the City of Liverpool, we have an event which is epoch-making in the history of English architecture. Liverpool is about to build a great church the like of which, in point of size, has not been equalled by any Cathedral Church in the United Kingdom."[50] Scott was aware that plans for a cathedral in the gothic style at the start of the twentieth century did not meet with universal approval but he made it clear that his work was no pastiche, or what he called "a medieval cathedral dished up". As his work on the Cathedral progressed, Scott was aware of the rise of modernism but he would have preferred the changes to have come about through evolution rather than revolution. As he said when President of the Royal Institute of British Architects in 1933, "I should feel happier about the future of architecture had the best ideas of modernism been grafted upon the best traditions of the past."[51] In theological terms, modernism was to become

Opposite Staggering view from the Corona Gallery above the Central Space.
The arch, with its twin to the west, are the largest Gothic arches ever constructed
This page View through from the Ambulatory into the main body of the building. Twin stairs on
either side of the Reredos lend themselves to impressive processions at the start of services.

clear when experienced within the walls of Scott's masterpiece. John Betjeman is unequivocal about the character and quality of Liverpool Cathedral.

> Liverpool Cathedral is one of the great buildings of the world. There is no doubt about that. I know that many people will tell you that its method of construction is the same as it was in the Middle Ages. But this does not prevent Liverpool Cathedral from being one of the great buildings of the world. It is superbly sited, and everywhere from as far away as the Welsh mountains, you can see from the central tower. The effect is massive and fortress-like from all angles. From all angles too, it composes into a noble skyline, dominating the city. Scott designed a modern cathedral. This was to be a building for vast congregations under a central space. The impression of vastness, strength and height no words can describe. No one who has been to Liverpool can say that we have lost the art of building Cathedrals. No one who has ever seen the huge crowd in this Cathedral's central space can say that a modern Cathedral has no use. Suddenly we see that the greatest art of architecture that lifts one up and turns one into a King, and yet compels reverence, is the art of enclosing space.[54]

The strength of feelings amongst the speakers at the Town Hall meeting in 1901 was supportive of a powerful, unignorable cathedral and, partly thanks to the choice of site, that was what Liverpool was to have. St. James's Mount is part of a sandstone ridge running north–south, roughly parallel to the river: the future cathedral was to dominate the skyline from so many parts of the city and particularly from the river and the water-front. Paul Johnson captures something of the audacity of Liverpool's architectural enterprise:

> The site chosen was magnificent and audacious, effectively dominating the arc of the vast city, and therefore demanding a silhouette of confident power and great size; the choice of the architect was audacious too. In 1901, Liverpool was bitterly divided on sectarian lines, and for the Anglican establishment to pick for this monumental work a twenty-two-year-old Roman Catholic demanded courage. But courage has been the keynote throughout the gestation of this cathedral. It took courage, for instance, for Giles Gilbert Scott to opt for Gothic at a time when the revival had lost much of its force, but Gothic organized on new principles which made radically different and dramatic allocations of space. It took courage, too, for him to make a decisive revision of his design after work had already begun.[55]

an important element in the worshipping life of the Cathedral community and will be examined in later chapters. It is interesting to note the awareness of modernism in architecture at this point because it will be seen to be paralled by modernism in theology and liturgy in later chapters. Gavin Stamp in "A Catholic church in which everything is genuine and good" in *Ecclesiology Today*, Issue 38, wrote, "Scott's own idea of modernism was expressed in a constant striving for simplicity and monumentality, eliminating unnecessary detail and delighting in broad surfaces." Stamp, architectural historian, and acknowledged expert on Scott cites an article in *The Architect & Building News* in 1930.

> At the same time his [Scott's] work is never startling in its novelty, and he is quite free from the modernist's vice of cleverness for its own sake. Yet his work is completely satisfying, full of life, originality and interest. He can be dramatic without brutality and gentle without sentimentality.[52]

It will be relevant to hold this statement in mind in later chapters which comment upon Dwelly's liturgy.

Scott indicated a number of qualities which were to him central to the architecture of a cathedral. These were the words he used when only the foundation stone was laid: it is interesting to relate these words to the completed building: solemnity, dignity, grandeur, simplicity, the "combination of strength and refinement". It is also interesting to relate these same words to the services which were devised for celebration within the cathedral and described in later chapters. In an anonymous article titled *The Need of a Cathedral* in the same souvenir, the author writes of the need for a cathedral and diocese to show evidence of its vitality. "By evidence is here meant not merely expression in stone or glass, but in the ordered ceremonial of the Cathedral service beautified by music; in influence which will radiate into every church in the diocese, raising the standard of taste, and promoting the feeling of reverence ..."[53] Rightly in 1904 the focus was upon plans, bricks and mortar and the raising of vast sums of money but it is interesting to note that even at this early point, the worshipping life of the cathedral is not neglected.

I am unaware of any evidence to suggest that Giles Gilbert Scott, Architect, and Frederick Dwelly, future Dean, met before the preparations for the consecration service in 1924 and yet there are significant parallels in their lives. They were similar in age and life-span, Scott 1880 to 1960 and Dwelly 1881 to 1957. They became close friends as revealed by their letters and by Scott's delight at being Dwelly's "house-guest" when he was actually living day and night in the Cathedral during the war. Scott provided the great shell which was to inspire and form the setting for Dwelly's imaginative liturgy. Dwelly's achievements are

Afternoon sunlight through windows on the south side of the Nave. The great Benedicite window by Carl Edwards. 16,000 square feet of glass. The figure of Christ in the fanlight is 19 feet high.

Courage is a word which will arise again when the first section of the building was ready for consecration and courage and adventurousness were to become features of the services devised by the first Dean.

Scott's early plans had twin transept towers between chancel and nave. Whether he changed his mind about this scheme for interior or exterior reasons is unclear but undoubtedly one massive central tower flanked by eastern and western transepts and then by chancel and nave makes a strong statement on the landscape. It was an overall shape Scott enjoyed because Cambridge University Library with its central tower is a 1930s version of Liverpool Cathedral. Johnson commented on the change: "The effect of the change externally was that the central tower, firmly based on its long, high plinth, seems to have the whole of Liverpool, not normally a subordinate city, at its feet, and brings to mind … the palatine absolutism of Durham." The exterior of the building is worthy of much further comment but as it is the inside of a church which is more relevant to a liturgist, I will curtail further examination of the exterior features.

The most prominent feature of the interior of the cathedral is its massive size at over 100,000 square feet. The tower arches at 107 feet are the highest

Gothic arches ever built. The under-tower vault reaches to 175 feet, the choir vault to 116 feet and the nave to 120 feet. The whole building is 619 feet long. It is now the fifth largest cathedral in the world. Almost more significant than the dimensions is that the cathedral feels vast at least partly because there are no pillars blocking the worshipper's view of pulpit and high altar. Until late in the building programme, Scott retained the possibility of a stone choir screen. One of the archive photographs c.1920 shows a springer arch within the pier of the chancel arch. The stone was not hacked out until Scott finally abandoned ideas of having a screen. A twentieth century cathedral had no need of a screen to demarcate the priestly area, shielded from the eyes of the laity. The Chapter House and the Lady Chapel, though connected to the east end of the main building are clearly separated by levels and doors so enabling them to be used as independent areas for smaller numbers.

Scott was constantly modifying details in his design. It might be interesting to hold this fact in mind when years later the Dean was constantly modifying and refining the details of the cathedral's liturgy and patterns of worship. The most significant architectural modification was the abandonment of plans for twin transept towers in favour of one massive central tower. This decision made a considerable enlargement of congregational space. Scott recorded his comments on the changes in *The Morning Post*, 19 July 1924:

> The space at the Crossing between where the twin towers were to have been was not large enough on plan for a tower of the size I required, and so a large tower was planned further west, with another set of transepts to balance the composition. This had the advantage of providing a large Central Space which was lacking in the original competition design.[56]

The actual square under-tower area added to the twin crossing spaces between the arms of the eastern and western transepts provided an area of 15,180 square feet. The shift from twin towers to central tower meant that the ground plan of the main building was symmetrical and so the building, in the Gothic style, acquired an overall Classical quality. Scott had interesting comments to make about Gothic and Classical qualities.

> One may take it broadly that in Gothic the verticals dominate the horizontals, while in Classic the reverse is the case. Now for some reason, which I have not been able to discover, verticality of expression seems more suggestive of the high aspiration that one associates with religion, and it seems to me easier to get the religious feeling in Gothic than in a style embodying strong horizontals. At the same time, I think that in most Gothic cathedrals the emphasis on the verticals is unduly stressed,

and thereby a great deal of calm and serenity is sacrificed, and a feeling of restlessness imported to the building which tends to destroy the repose and peace that in these strenuous days seem doubly necessary in a building devoted to prayer.

It comes to a question of balance, like everything in nature, and at Liverpool I have endeavoured to combine the uplifting character imparted by vertical expression with the restful calm undoubtedly given by judicious use of horizontals.[57]

It must remain one of the great sadnesses of the cathedral that neither architect nor the first Dean lived to see the completed building though the plans for the nave were completed during the war years. Both men would have been aware of the fresh opportunities which the new space would provide.

One word which would be used by every commentator on the building is space. Scott is reported to have said, "Don't look at my arches, look at my spaces". Canon C. B. Naylor, a distinguished Canon Chancellor of the Cathedral at the time of its completion declared, "Scott was an architect of space".[58] In a B.B.C. broadcast in 1944 Scott said, "… it has always possessed certain characteristics, one of which was aptly described recently by an American officer, who called it 'space Gothic.' What he meant can be understood by anyone standing inside the building and looking around, when he will see only wall surfaces, with no rows of detached columns and arches forming the open arcades usually found in cathedrals and churches."[59]

After the cramped conditions of the pro-cathedral, the space, even in the chancel and eastern transept, the first portions of the main building to be completed, was vast. The completed area was way beyond any other English cathedral: York Minster is 60,952 square feet and even St. Paul's is only 84,024. Such space was going to make considerable demands on all who were to have responsibility for the performance of the liturgy. The way the separate spaces making up the whole relate to each other is an important feature in any cathedral but particularly so in this massive one. Johnson was conscious of Scott's "interlocking spaces": "One moves from one space to another, barely conscious, at first, of the vast columns and curves which provide the demarcations, aware only of changes in light and chiaroscuro, or a different ring in footsteps."[60] Human movement of an individual or a procession was going to be a crucial aspect of effective worship in this place. Effective choreography is an essential part of cathedral worship.

Interior space is defined by the stone of wall, pier and vault and the pink colour of the local sandstone at Liverpool is very important in establishing the atmosphere of the great space. The cut stones vary in size, colour and texture and the overall effect is rich, warm and welcoming: a feature remarked on by thousands of visitors. The vaulting throughout almost the whole of the building is of stone and this leads towards a great sense of unity and almost the feeling that the building has been excavated from the solid rock. The moulding of which Scott increased his confidence as the building grew is particularly important. Scott did not delegate detailing work to junior members of his team but retained personal responsibility for all the drawings with the result that everything from a great under-tower arch to a small piece of door furniture retains a unity and there are no jarring features. "The length of time spent upon the erection of the Cathedral has enabled me to draw with my own hand every detail of the building."[61] Fine detail was important to the architect; fine detail will also have to be important to all who plan and conduct worship in the building: colour, ceremonial robes, service papers, spacing, posture, pace.

The windows are massive: the east window so large that the Lady Chapel could be posted through it. But the windows are so deployed that at no point is the worshipper distracted by a range of windows which are framed by the internal buttressing. These vast side windows transmit columns of light through to illuminate space, floor, moulding, wall, robes and processions. The effect of strong afternoon sunlight through richly coloured windows produces an ever-changing rainbow of light across the stonework and has a strikingly dramatic effect on processions moving through the building.

There is a danger that such a massive building could impress a sense of formality and lack of flexibility on the way the building is used. Apart from official stalls for chapter, choir, bishop and presbytery, all the furnishings are free-standing and can be deployed according to the needs of the particular event. Naylor had practical experience of devising services in the cathedral and was appreciative of the flexibility the building provided.

> A Cathedral, because it is the mother church of the whole diocese of parishes and institutions, most of all needs to be adaptable to meet … changes, and Liverpool Cathedral has this adaptability in spite of its mediaeval appearance. The architect had the vision, the art and the skill to create in a traditionally shaped building a vast space where sight and movement can be unimpeded. Within that space worship can be composed and furniture arranged or removed to suit whatever form each act of worship is designed to take.[62]

Long before even the first part of the building was completed, the design of a five manual pipe organ by the firm of Henry Willis was under way. The vast volume of the cathedral demanded one of the great pipe organs of the world, currently with 10,268 separate pipes. The organ cases were designed by Scott as part of his total architectural design. This is one of the great musical instruments of the world and its provision from the early days of the planning would provide an extremely significant resource for effective worship. What would be needed was an organist of the highest calibre, a fine choir and a priest who had the imagination and the skill to harness music and give it its due place within worship.

In his 1944 broadcast, it is not upon the technical demands made on the architect that Scott concentrated but on something more nebulous. He narrated the story of what happened when the Dean was talking to an American sailor in the cathedral and asked him what he thought about it.

> 'Sir, with a building like this, you don't think – you feel.' This quality of atmosphere is essential for a cathedral, and indeed for any church, for it forms a background for prayer and religious services, without which a cathedral would not function properly, and in this respect a cathedral presents a problem differing from most that an architect has to solve. The practical requirements are few and simple, but appeal, both aesthetic and emotional, in the best sense of that much abused word, is an essential requirement, dominating all others.[63]

As the builders were working on transept and chancel in preparation for the consecration, Scott addressed a meeting of the General Committee in Church House in the summer of 1921 and stressed the unique nature of the cathedral and the centre of his concern.

"A visible witness for God in the midst of the great city." The tower is 331 feet high.

In this Cathedral, we shall have something – I will not say better than, but certainly different from any Cathedral that I know of, certainly in this country, and if I can make people in a reverend mood when they go in, and make them feel they want to pray – if I can produce that impression, that is all that I am aiming at. Beauty of detail and beauty of line are only means to an end.

Long before the walls of this new cathedral began to rise on St. James's Mount, people were trying to come to terms with the unique nature of the venture. It is interesting to consider how a theologian of some stature considered the venture thirty years later. A short but important publication came from Charles Raven in 1933, shortly after his leaving the post of Chancellor of the Cathedral to move to Cambridge as Regius Professor of Divinity: *Liverpool Cathedral, An Impression of its Early Years*.

For it is obvious that the building and consecration of a church on so great a scale and in a modern city created an opportunity unique in our day for the development of an appropriate type of religious activity. The Bishop and his Chapter could not fail to recognize their responsibility; nor as they faced it, could they avoid considering afresh the function of a cathedral in relation to the world of the twentieth century.[64]

Raven acknowledged the massive changes which have taken place at such speed during the previous century and the dangers in religion that "traditional equipment may become out of touch with present realities and incapable of dealing with present requirements." Raven was aware of how difficult it must have been for the ancient foundations to adapt to a new world.

The cathedrals of ancient status seemed to be so dominated by established custom, so weighted with statutory obligations, as to be hardly capable of a fresh start: they had come to occupy a fixed position and are not easily moved from their routine. Those of the new diocese are almost all parish churches with a long history behind them. In neither case could their officers face the situation with freedom to meet it *de novo*: they must emend an ancient script rather than begin to write on a clean sheet.[65]

Raven was appreciative of Scott's design for the building, for "fresh and creative vision". The new cathedral

could not be used for a slavish imitation of past methods. The artistry of the fabric called for similar artistry in its presentation of religion.
Moreover, a great modern city, cosmopolitan, industrial, adventurous,

had built a cathedral. That cathedral must develop a life worthy of the community and of the age that had produced it. The eternal revelation in Christ must be presented in terms that can be understood by the people of today. Its theology must be a real interpretation of God to minds thinking along lines of modern knowledge: its ceremonial, its music, its services must enable modern folk to experience worship: its organization must display the aspiration after fellowship and the ability of the Church to rise above legal and mechanical relationships. To reproduce ancient formularies, to imitate earlier artistic modes, to adopt a traditional constitution, unless they were demonstrably appropriate, would be to betray the hopes of the community.[66]

This statement by Raven, one of the foremost theologians of his day, lies at the very heart of this study and later chapters will attempt to record and analyse the way in which the cathedral, under the direction of its first Dean, rose to the challenge and the opportunity it offered. As the vast new cathedral, unique in size, and unencumbered by outdated and inappropriate statutes it became the centre of lively, imaginative and relevant services of worship.

In 1923, Chavasse resigned as bishop. He was concerned about his wife's health, he himself was seventy-seven and with typical Chavasse humility he felt that a new and younger bishop should oversee the consecration of the new cathedral. In the same month, Prime Minister, Stanley Baldwin, offered the post to Albert Augustus David, the Bishop of St. Edmundsbury. He had a distinguished career in education particularly as Headmaster of Clifton and then for eleven years at Rugby. He was known to have turned down preferment in the church before accepting St. Edmundsbury in 1921. Both there and later in Liverpool he was deeply involved in administration and the establishment of new diocesan structures. His biography by John Peart-Binns remains unpublished but his assessment in 'Albert Augustus David Liberal Autocrat' is balanced and astute. "There was probably no bishop on the Bench who combined David's ability, fearlessness, dignity and personal charm" but in the opinion of Binns he lacked "sound judgment".[67]

When Binns wrote, "Ability can imitate and reproduce, but only genius can create and originate,"[68] he was referring to Giles Gilbert Scott, creator of the building but the statement might be aptly applied to Frederick William Dwelly who was to be central to the establishment of worship in the building. The examination of liturgical genius will be the focus of later chapters.

By the early 1920s, the partially built cathedral was making a huge impact on the city skyline as revealed in the archive photographs of Stewart Bale. In traditional manner, building commenced at the east end so that chancel and high altar might be consecrated and used for worship – this had been the medieval pattern. At Liverpool, the eastern transept and crossing was also completed; a temporary wall filled the under-tower arch and the first third of the building was ready for use. But the bishop did not see himself as a liturgical expert, St. Edmundsbury was modest in size, though he acknowledged the need for a service of real distinction to mark the consecration in the summer of 1924. The last consecration of a cathedral on a newly consecrated site had been at Salisbury in 1225.

The bishop shared his concern with Charles Raven, his recently appointed Canon Chancellor and Raven commented on the nature of the task:

> It was evident that to mark such an occasion no repetition of a traditional form would suffice; that it would not be enough to collect together a variety of ancient ceremonies and formulae and to combine them into an Office. What was needed was a service which, while fulfilling all that past experience could suggest, should possess a coherence, a rhythm, an appropriateness of its own for the circumstances of today. Such a service might be the work not of a liturgies expert (if this means a student of past precedents) but a creative artist who perceived what the ceremony signified, knew how to interpret its significance in apposite technique, and could enable the congregation to experience and share the dramatic movement of the whole.[69]

That man was to be Frederick William Dwelly.

The opening section of this chapter, a very brief historical survey of English cathedrals, claims no originality, but the whole chapter dealing with ideas surrounding the establishment of Liverpool Cathedral is an original statement. Much published work on cathedrals has focused mainly upon architectural features rather than a consideration of the role of a cathedral within its diocese or the character of worship within its walls. Lehmberg's *English Cathedrals*[70] devotes only ninety one words to Liverpool Cathedral. He did not have access to the cathedral's archives. Central to this chapter are Bishop Chavasse's ideas about the nature and function of a new cathedral in Liverpool and Giles Gilbert Scott's thoughts about his designs for a place of worship. The words of both men are essential preliminary considerations before any examination of the worshipping life of the new cathedral under the direction of its first Dean. My book *The Building of Liverpool Cathedral*[71] was the first comprehensive history of Liverpool Cathedral, but the first chapter in this study goes way beyond the earlier publication in the way in which it prepares to address issues concerning worship in the new building.

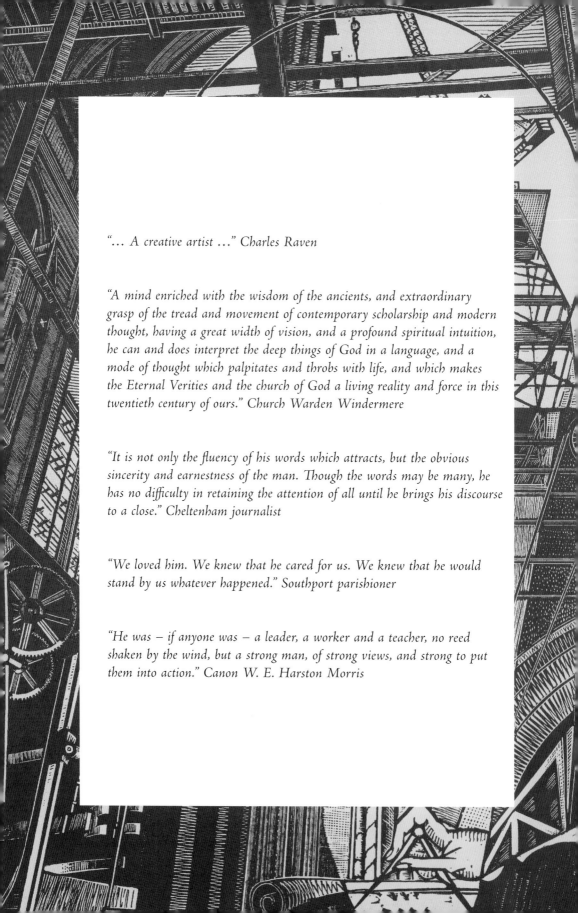

"… A creative artist …" Charles Raven

"A mind enriched with the wisdom of the ancients, and extraordinary grasp of the tread and movement of contemporary scholarship and modern thought, having a great width of vision, and a profound spiritual intuition, he can and does interpret the deep things of God in a language, and a mode of thought which palpitates and throbs with life, and which makes the Eternal Verities and the church of God a living reality and force in this twentieth century of ours." Church Warden Windermere

"It is not only the fluency of his words which attracts, but the obvious sincerity and earnestness of the man. Though the words may be many, he has no difficulty in retaining the attention of all until he brings his discourse to a close." Cheltenham journalist

"We loved him. We knew that he cared for us. We knew that he would stand by us whatever happened." Southport parishioner

"He was — if anyone was — a leader, a worker and a teacher, no reed shaken by the wind, but a strong man, of strong views, and strong to put them into action." Canon W. E. Harston Morris

The development of a priest

J UST AS IT has been necessary to survey the context of the establishment of a new cathedral, so it is important to consider the little that is known about the life and early ministry of its first Dean before focusing upon his work in the cathedral. He was fifty before he was appointed as Dean and it is essential to try to understand the nature of the man and the priest and to discern the reasons for which he was chosen for high office. Unlike many eminent clergymen, he was not a child of the vicarage but the youngest child of a carriage builder in a small town in Somerset.

His parents, Robert Dwelly and Caroline Cooper, were married in the parish church of Illminster on 26 December 1865. By his own admission, Robert Dwelly's education was limited: "I was sent to 2 Dame schools but I fear made little progress so was afterwards sent to Barrington under a master … he was a very old man."[1] At some point after their marriage, Robert and Caroline moved to Chard. *Kelly's Directory for Somerset* for 1886 makes reference to one Thomas Cooper, coach builder in Fore Street. By 1883 the firm and family house had moved to East Street. By 1897 the firm is listed simply as Dwelly and Co. Robert served several terms as one of the twelve town councillors and one period as one of the four aldermen. His name was commemorated in the town by the building of Dwelly Close in the 1960s. Frederick William, Fred to the family, was the tenth and final child and like all the others was baptised in the ancient parish church of St. Mary. In 1993 there were still some memories of the family in the town. In a letter to me in 1993 Mrs Evelynn Hounsell, aged 84, wrote, "The Dwelly family were greatly respected in the town. I can remember well Miss Dwelly, who always seemed to wear a long flowing coat. She was a very staunch church woman who used to help a great deal with the Sunday schools and the Girls Friendly Society. My husband who is 90 said the coaches Mr. Dwelly turned out were really perfect specimens, he was very thorough and proud of his work."[2]

Both parents were devout evangelical Christians and their deaths were marked with epitaphs in church magazines. Robert died in 1927 and his life was remembered by his vicar in *Chard Parish Magazine*. "He was probably the best known, and certainly one of the most respected men in Chard, and will be long remembered ... In season and out, he stood stiffly for what he thought to be right. He was no reed shaken by the wind. His life was governed by rule ... We could always count on his place in church being filled on Sundays and Wednesdays. Others might be kept away by weather or caprice, but he was there, a witness and an example to us all."[3] Frederick William was also to grow to be no reed shaken by the wind and this same image was used in a sermon in Emmanuel Church Southport delivered by Canon W. E. Harston Morris on 19 May 1957: "He was – if anyone was – a leader, a worker and a teacher, no reed shaken by the wind, but a strong man, of strong views, and strong to put them into action ..."[4]

Caroline Dwelly died less than a year later in March 1928 and is remembered in The *Good Shepherd Parish Magazine* This, a daughter church of St. Mary's, was situated just across the road from the Dwelly home.

> Mrs. Dwelly was one of the oldest and most faithful members of this church; she had an intense love for the Master, always trying to follow his steps and do His Holy Will in all things. She was a most regular and devout Communicant, and never missed the daily Evensong ... Her later years were made specially happy by the intense love and affection shown to her by all her many friends and especially by the wonderful devotion of her children of whom she was so rightly proud.[5]

Too little is known about Dwelly's early life in Chard. His old friend Charles Raven was to say in a sermon in 1960, "He was born and brought up in the West, in Somerset, without any special advantages of birth or prestige or privilege. Schooled for business ..."[6]

The ancient church of St. Mary has undergone some internal reordering but it was and is a spacious, light church and Dwelly was involved there from early childhood. When he left to go to London a local newspaper reported his remarks to the Sunday School teachers with whom he worked when they presented him with a travelling clock: "… in the past 34 years scarcely a Sunday had passed without one of the Dwellys having attended the Sunday School".[7] Prebendary G. H. W. Mallett's comments were reported in *The Chard and Illminster News*, 12 July 1941, when he recalled what Dwelly said on a recent visit to the church. "He [Dwelly] remembered on one Fifth of November, when he was a choir boy, putting a large cracker under the organ stool during choir practice."[8]

From cards and letters and fragments from a number of points in his career Dwelly's devotion to family and community was very strong and he seemed able to engender a powerful sense of community within all of his churches – an ability of great relevance in the establishment of a new cathedral community in later years.

Diary of my Holiday in London with 87 illustrations is the earliest extant piece of Dwelly's writing. He went to London between 21 June and 2 July 1897 to stay with elder brother Bert who was living and teaching in Harlesdon. The holiday coincided with the celebration of Queen Victoria's Diamond Jubilee on 22 June. It was a remarkable production from a sixteen year old boy. The report of Jubilee Day itself is well researched and full of detail about regiments and uniforms. He included some line drawings from an anonymous newspaper which suggest his fascination with grand ceremonial. He seemed not to waste a single moment of his stay and with tremendous energy, and very little sleep, he took in so many London landmarks. He attended the 10.30 am service in St. Paul's Cathedral on 27 June: "We arrived at St. Paul's just as the service was commencing, we had a good seat in front of the pulpit under the Dome. The whole service was fully choral, the sermon was preached by the Bishop of Chester. I stayed to Communion. The Bishop of Chester, Dean and two residentiary canons officiated. On the whole I enjoyed the service very much especially the singing."[9] He had been to St. Paul's for a service on 24 June: "… we heard some excellent music including Kyrie Eleison, the Sevenfold and the Dresden Amen's"[10]. He went to Westminster Abbey on the same day: "Turle's Service in D and the anthem 'How lovely are the messengers' were exquisitely rendered by the choir, after which an excellent sermon was preached by the Dean from St. Mark VI, 20". That day concluded with a concert at the Albert Hall. On the final page he thanks those who looked after him so well and "… far from least my parents for letting me go to London".[11]

As an adult, he never lived in Chard but there is written evidence of his closeness to his family and awareness of his roots. A card written on 14 July 1917 is a good example.

> On the hill where Father played as a boy – overlooking Barrington Church and village. Here 60 years ago my Father played and worked

St. Mary's Church, Chard, the church of Dwelly's childhood and early life.

below, only a few yards he lived, his father died – the baby's coffin was discovered – and now, we wander together over these parts and he is a boy again as he walks and talks of his walnut tree and the old flail shed – whilst I, his baby boy, baby of 10, feel old, mightily old because tomorrow by the will of God I am to preach in my old Parish Church, the church of my christening and confirmation – church of my choir boy's devotion – dear old church – and today I feel very old as I sit here looking at my father's old home parish church – by the grace of God he has surpassed his wildest dreams – by the same grace, cause my feeling of age, I am to fulfil the last point of my parents ideals – to be ordained – to have a parish of my own – to preach in the old church at Chard – it seems too easy to have one's wishes granted and yet so like the Heavenly Father – all my life he has enriched me – to Him here and now I would – I do – dedicate my life.

Frederick W. Dwelly[12]

Almost nothing is known about his school life apart from the fact that he attended Chard Endowed School in Fore Street, very close to the family home. There is no evidence to suggest that he had any thoughts of proceeding to university though we know that elder brother Bert had trained as a teacher in London. An anonymous obituary notice in 1957 stated: "The lad, at a late stage in his education at Chard Grammar School, was a frequent truant, with the excuse of listening to music. Though the headmaster was indulgent, the facts eventually came to his father's knowledge, whereupon the admonitions were so severe that (it appears with his mother's connivance) the young Dwelly left home for London."[13] F. W. Dillstone's account deserves more attention because of the time he spent as Canon Chancellor during Dwelly's final years as Dean.

> he moved to London after leaving school to work as a salesman in one of the great stores near Oxford Circus. He became associated with All Souls Langham Place whose incumbent at the time was a noted Evangelical leader, Prebendary F. S. Webster. Evidently realizing the potentialities of the young man who has passed through a crisis of religious experience, Webster encouraged him to go up to Cambridge and prepare for ordination."[14]

Family memory has it that he worked in Marshall and Snellgrove though on at least one occasion he was unemployed.

An important archive piece is held by Mr. Christopher Turner, great-nephew to the Dean. It is a handsomely bound handwritten journal entitled *Summer Holidays 1903*. It is an extensive account of a tour of Switzerland made by Fred and Brother Bert, the summer before Fred went up to Cambridge. "These jottings have been written primarily to brighten some of the winter evenings of dear Dad and Mater, to whom I am indebted for implanting in my soul a thirst for God's beauty, and an appreciative heart, and hence I make no apology for the use of so much "Ego" knowing their great interest in one's personal pleasures."[15] The journal indicated that he had been living in West Didsbury and returned

The spacious interior of St. Mary's, reordered since Dwelly's day.

there before leaving for Cambridge. "I returned to West Didsbury to stay a few weeks and do a little more of the ever enjoyable church work made more congenial than ever by a real and good and kind Rector."[16]

The journal is a painstaking and exuberant account of the holiday, a more mature and developed form of the London holiday account six years previous. Though handwritten, he has taken great pains over the whole volume which is quarter-bound in dark green leather. This is the product of the same man who twenty five years later was responsible for prestigious commemorative service booklets.

There are flashes of Dwelly humour throughout, sometimes at the expense of other members of the "Poly" tour party as he commented on "… the vastly differing natures of our travelling companions – one from Oxford assumed the airs and knowledge of a Don but asserted the selfishness of a pig – one woman from London suburbs demonstrated Proverbs 21.19 "Tis better to live in the wilderness than with a contentious woman'."[17] He was meticulous in recounting details of journeys by train, horse-drawn carriage or boat but the very essence of the piece is his young man's response to staggering scenery. He was a romantic in the Wordsworthian sense and indeed he quoted Wordsworth, Shakespeare and the Bible. Quotation seems to bed naturally into the text. "Now one can understand why the Hebrew poet said, 'I will lift up mine eyes unto the hills', and again, 'Thy righteousness standeth like the great mountains and Thy faithfulness reached unto the clouds'."[18]

His spirituality and mysticism were nurtured particularly by the silence and solitude of a beautiful spot. His first night staying on the shores of Lake Lucerne provided a powerful sense:

> No experience has ever been of such value to my spirit as those first few moments of thoughtfulness spent in silence alone down by the edge of Lake Lucerne – for if ever I was impressed with the conviction of God's presence 'twas that night when not only the body but the soul also was elevated, the views of the mind were expanded, narrow ideas and moral codes were surmounted, a purer atmosphere breathed, and one felt immediately healthier and stronger.[19]

On another occasion he was out in a small boat in the evening and his experience is almost a Wordsworthian parallel to an incident in *The Prelude*.

> There is so much to subdue one in that silent and solemn and awful presence; one seemed to meet the inimitable, the indestructible, the eternal; as someone has said, One had the sense of being under the brooding contemplation of a Spirit, not an inert mass of rocks and ice

– What an influence that silence had, a strange, deep, nameless influence which I can never forget, an influence which has left behind it a restless longing to feel it again, a haunting and yearning which is only satisfied when resting in THE greatest of all the Creator's works – the redemption in Christ – Resting in Christ.[20]

One might consider thoughts like these alongside Charles Raven's sermon in 1960: "He had the most extraordinary artistic gift of sensitiveness and intuition."[21] The imaginative, dramatic, mystical, inspired Dwelly of later years is here.

Several obituary notices in 1957 had spoken of young Dwelly's work among the London poor before he went to Cambridge. Almost at the end of the journal is an interesting passage. Despite not returning to London until midnight on the Saturday, he undertook a visit on the Sunday.

I paid a visit to Spitalfields Slum. What a huge contrast, no not contrast for that signifies 'agreeing to differ' – what a terrible clash. I mention this visit chiefly for my own future good, praying one may never be selfish, but remember always in one's pleasure and joys that there are brothers less fortunate and the Master said, As much as ye do it unto one of the least, ye do it unto me.[22]

Dwelly's life-long concern for people and his kindness and generosity can be observed even at this early stage in his life.

On 13 October 1903, at the age of twenty two, he left St. Luke's West Didsbury to become a freshman at Queens' College Cambridge. Unfortunately, there is no primary source archival material from his undergraduate career. The college were able to provide details about his degree: "He was awarded his B.A. in 1906 on the results of a second class pass in Part I of the Special Examination for the ordinary degree in Theology and a third class pass in Part II of the same examination."[23] He cannot be regarded as a traditional academic but there is evidence that he was very well read. From a secondary source *Yale News* there were reports of his American lecture tour and the paper reported: "Fights unreality in religion. While in College opposed artificiality in chapel services. While in college Canon Dwelly carried on a vigorous protest against unreality in college services ..."[24] During Dwelly's time in college, all students were expected to attend daily Evensong in chapel: his later career offers evidence of his desire to modify and enrich the services of the church: his friendship with Percy Dearmer, involvement with the National Mission, the Life and Liberty Movement, the *Grey Book* and the lead up to the *1928 Prayer Book*, *Acts of Devotion* and all his ground-breaking cathedral services.

The freshmen at Queens' College Cambridge in 1903. Dwelly is at the right hand side of the back row ostentatiously turning away from the camera.

For mention of the most significant experience in his student career we have to rely on a reference by Adam Fox. William Ralph Inge, later to become the famous Dean of St. Paul's,[25] had been invited to give a series of lectures between January and February 1906 later published as *Truth and Falsehood in Religion*.

They had been attended by a large audience, never less than two hundred and fifty, mostly undergraduates. One of those who heard them wrote some months later and said he could not express what he owed to the lectures; he had given up thoughts of ordination, but after hearing them he had determined to be ordained, and was ordained deacon at Trinity. This was F. W. Dwelly who afterwards did such remarkable work as Dean of Liverpool.[26]

Inge's overall Christian mysticism and modernism and many of his specific ideas reveal themselves throughout Dwelly's ministry.

> It is almost frivolous to make the whole truth or falsehood of Christianity turn upon the historical truth of a particular miracle, or the authenticity of a particular document, when among the real questions at issue are the character of the relations between the spiritual and the natural world, and the difference, if any, between revealed and natural religion ...
>
> I wish to remind you that, as a historical fact, the artistic sense has played, and still plays, an important part in the development of religion. Ideas, as we know, must be given through something. Language, if we

analyse it, consists almost entirely of metaphors, that is, of calling things something which they are not, but which they resemble. Poetry affects us more than prose, because it is more lavish in the use of symbols or metaphors; a parable often 'hits him whom a sermon flies'; a concrete image impresses us more than an abstract truth.[27]

For the whole of his ministry, what Inge said was revealed in Dwelly's work in language, poetry, symbolism and the arts generally. He referred to people who are able to express their feelings about God through the arts, including "orderly and solemn ritual".

> All religious art, whether painting or statuary or architecture or music or ceremonial, should be transparent. It should not be complete and satisfying in itself. It should suggest something behind, which it cannot fully express. The mystical quality (I use the word mystical of that which, in being what it is, suggests something beyond itself) belongs to all religious art.[28]

I believe that there is evidence in the liturgy he devised that *Christian Mysticism* and *Truth and Falsehood in Religion* 1906 remained important foundations for Dwelly throughout his life. His deep concern for the importance of the arts permeated all aspects of worship for which he had responsibility: sermons on Shakespeare or Browning, poetry within the service, the language of intercessions, response to great architecture, sensitive and imaginative use of music in worship, silence, and, maybe more important than anything else, brilliant use of human movement in meaningful ceremonial.

Having been ordained in Carlisle Cathedral in 1906, he served his title and spent the next five years as curate at St. Mary's Church, Windermere. Before the end of his time there, the Vicar, Canon Crewdson, was ill and then retired and Dwelly ran the parish as curate-in-charge with energy and enthusiasm. On 9 July 1910, James Crewdson, Parishioners' Warden, tried to sum up his ministry in writing, probably as Dwelly was searching for a second curacy. This written assessment of Dwelly's character and skills deserves to be quoted in full because it is indicative of so much which was to follow in his ministry.

> 1. He is a Parish Priest of great power and ability, he stands before the world with a standard of lofty ideals, and he demands and receives, both within and without the Church, the homage and respect which belong to his character and sacred office. He is courageous, and yet tender, he has won the hearts of the children, of the young men, and indeed of the

whole place, with the possible exception of two or three old women. He is a great comforter, and full of compassion for the sick and dying.

2. He is a born Organizer and is eminently practical, and the following are a few of the schemes he has initiated here.

(a) Boy Scouts and Young Men's Institute. These are two separate agencies and the latter is the first really successful effort in this parish to cope with lads at a difficult age.

(b) Men's Society. This activity was formed to develop a more social and corporate feeling among the older men, and during the winter months some sixty or seventy men have weekly been drawn together, and have eagerly listened, it is no exaggeration to say for hours, to his able, profound fascinating lectures on The Religious Beliefs of the East and other subjects. To see men, today, listen with sustained attention, and for so considerable a time to an avowedly religious address, and further, during the same session to see the clamour for repetition of the same addresses, is to be conscious of a supremacy over men, and of a triumph indeed which few can claim.

(c) Girl Guides. A Guild to enrich and give purpose to the lives of young girls, it has met a greatly felt want here.

(d) Sunday Schools. These have been entirely reorganized, and for the last three years the children have been taken away to the seaside for the annual treat. This effort has been quite novel here, and very successful.

(e) Choir Trip. For the last three years the trip has been extended. To plan and successfully organize a trip to London for say thirty choristers, covering as the distance does, roughly five hundred miles, and done withal with limited means is an achievement of great moment.

(f) Parochial Finances. These have been reorganized throughout, and placed on a sound working basis, every account is now clear of debt, and when one remembers that before the vestry meeting of 1908, there was an accumulated balance on the debit side of over two thousand pounds, and that it was Mr Dwelly's zeal, enthusiasm, and compelling faith which cleared the debt, one feels quite naturally proud of him.

(g) Parish Magazine. This has been placed on an entirely new basis, and for the first time ever in its history, it is self-supporting.

(h) Whitehaven Colliery Disaster 1910. During the enforced absence, through illness of the Vicar, who is also Rural Dean, Mr Dwelly, as the Rural Dean's Secretary, and entirely on his own initiative, organized a fund for this disaster …

(i) Ordination Fund. The scheme is outside the ordinary parochial machinery. Two lads are now at the moment at Cambridge University, one has recently obtained honours in the Theological Tripos there, and these lads after taking their degrees are ultimately to take Orders. This effort, this wide outlook, this regard for the church at large, and her needs, is specially noteworthy. Without Mr Dwelly's loving heart, and vigilant eye and gift for arousing the sympathy and cooperation of wealthy members of the Parish, these lads would have found it impossible to realize their vocation, through lack of means. Turning to the Schools, one Pupil teacher has already been provided with the means to qualify at a Training College, and in now able to take a much better position.

(j) Charity Organization. This valuable attempt to solve the difficulty of overlapping and indiscriminate charity, has already proved of great benefit, and the care and trouble taken by Mr Dwelly to investigate individual cases is known to all the parish.

(k) London Slums. He has an extraordinary love for this work, and he has succeeded in evoking a large amount of genuine and practical sympathy, which has been productive of much and lasting good, both to the slums, and to this parish.

To summarize. Does one overstate the case? Is he not a born organizer? 3. He is a preacher, at once able and eloquent in the pulpit having a mind enriched with the wisdom of the ancients, and extraordinary grasp of the tread and movement of contemporary scholarship and modern thought, having a great width of vision, and a profound spiritual intuition, he can and does interpret the deep things of God in a language, and by a mode of thought which palpitates and throbs with life, and which makes the Eternal Verities and the Church of God a living reality, and force in this twentieth century of ours …[29]

These sentiments are very much in line with Inge's thoughts: "Religion must come down to earth, and mix with men. It must speak in their own language to men that sit on the wall."[30]

Much that was said about him at the time of his leaving was reported in *The Westmorland Gazette*[31] and the Rector of Windermere, Rev. E. J. Nurse, predicted that their young curate might well become a bishop. He certainly departed from Windermere after a very successful first ministry in which his dynamism, adventurousness, leadership and administrative skills, and genius for friendship with old and young were all displayed.

Dwelly was appointed senior curate at St. Mary's Church in Cheltenham; it is the only medieval building in Cheltenham but its significance was overshadowed by the building in 1879 of St. Matthew's Church, only a stone's throw away. The Rector looked after the larger church and entrusted to Dwelly "the spiritual revival of the old Parish Church". Under the heading "Looker On" in a Cheltenham journal 22 January 1916, the anonymous writer applauded Dwelly's success and pointed out that "... the late Rector ... gave his colleague a free hand in the arrangement and carrying on of his work. This was the way to secure the very best results, and the success which has attended".[32] Energy, preaching skills and powers of organization were all remarked upon. He filled the ancient Church of St. Mary with those who came to hear him preach: "It is not only the fluency of his words which attracts, but the obvious sincerity and earnestness of the man. Though the words may be many, he has no difficulty in retaining the attention of all until he brings his discourse to a close". As late as 1955, a contributor to the *Cheltenham Echo* remembered that "... at whatever church he preached there was never a vacant place. During a series of sermons given on some Victorian poets at the Parish Church many had to be turned away".[33] Edna Banks wrote to him on 24 June 1955, "Your name always brings back such happy childhood memories of Cheltenham. How adept you were at writing your name in treacle on bread and butter! I still have my school girl

St. Mary's Church, Windermere.

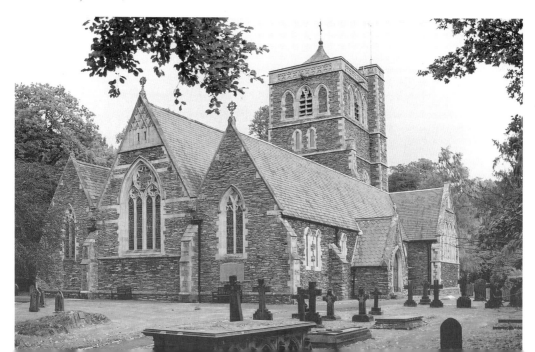

St. Mary's Church, Cheltenham, the only surviving medieval building in the town.

autograph book in which you wrote a quotation from Robert Browning. The date is February 1916."[34]

The Gloucester Echo for 30 December 1915 is reminiscent of words written about Dwelly earlier in the *Westmorland Gazette*: "It does not often fall to the lot of a young clergyman in his curacy to leave so large a mark of his connection with an important parish as has been the case with Mr. Dwelly."[35] His eventual departure from the parish was extraordinary and reported at length in the *Cheltenham Chronicle and Gloucester Graphic*[36] for 12 February 1916. His final sermon was to be delivered in the large St. Matthew's Church: a queue had formed by 4.30 pm. 2,000 people were eventually seated and many more had to stand. So many people had to be turned away that an overflow service was arranged later in the evening at St. Mary's, and Dwelly preached again. All this was achieved while he was still an assistant curate, though, as at Windermere, the illness of the Rector had left the young curate in charge. His achievements up to this point in his career have, quite rightly, been parochial; he spoke of himself as "an apprentice" as he ministered as an assistant curate. His appointment to the incumbency of Emmanuel Church Southport marked the next stage in his development and was to give him opportunity to become far more involved in the wider church nationally as well as being a long-remembered parish priest.

There is a gulf between the popular and successful senior curate in a Gloucestershire spa town and a nationally known figure. Several movements and events in his early days at Southport began to make the change. They cannot, within the limits of this study, be given adequate attention but they must be noted. The publishing of a pastoral letter from Bishop Chavasse in June 1916 drew attention to a movement called the National Mission of Repentance and Hope, an organization initiated by Archbishop Randall Davidson. Dwelly was appointed Bishop's Messenger for the dioceses of Bath and Wells, Gloucester, Manchester and Liverpool and delivered 147 addresses while carrying out the work. The church was left in some confusion and discontent when the mission ended as F. A. Iremonger commented in his biography of *William Temple*: "The National Mission had left the church in a state of chastened discontent with itself, combined with a sense of frustration that baulked and halted all efforts towards a full recovery …"[37]

There was a sense of frustration in that no changes could be made to the workings of the Church of England without the approval of Parliament and interminable delay: "it had taken as many as nine sessions to settle the salary of the Archdeacon of Cornwall".[38] Some degree of autonomy from Parliament was going to be essential before reform became possible. Rev. H. R. L. "Dick" Sheppard of St. Martin-in-the-Fields and Rev. William Temple of St. James's Piccadilly were central in what was to become known as "The Life and Liberty Movement". The movement is examined by Iremonger in Temple's biography and in Carolyn Scott's biography *Dick Sheppard*.[39] Rev. Dr. A. A. David, Headmaster of Rugby and future Bishop of Liverpool became another strong force. Dwelly was drawn into the organization and became a life-long friend of Sheppard.

Under the heading "Movement for Reform", an official statement from the organization appeared in *The Times* on 20 June 1917.

> But as soon as we consider the changes that are needed to make the church a living force in the nation, we find ourselves hampered at every turn by an antiquated machinery which we are powerless to change except by a series of Acts of Parliament. Everyone knows that the House of Commons is a highly unsuitable place for the settlement of questions affecting the church's life and work; and even if it were suitable in its composition it has no time …

> If the church is to have new life, even if it is to maintain the life which it has, it must have liberty. Those who are promoting this movement are

convinced that we must win for the church full power to control its own life, even at the cost, if necessary, of disestablishment and of whatever consequences that may possibly involve.[40]

Some years later, Dwelly entitled one of his big Cathedral services "Liberty to Grow". Freedom, flexibility, freshness are qualities discernible throughout Dwelly's ministry and come to fruition during his work as Dean of a new Cathedral, unencumbered by ancient statutes which bore no relevance to a twentieth-century community.

On 4 October 1923, Albert Augustus David, by that time Bishop of St. Edmundsbury, wrote to Dwelly, "I know that the Life and Liberty executive were going to ask you to do half-time work for them, and I have already told them that if arrangements could be made to secure that your parish will not seriously suffer I should encourage you to accept the work."[41] We know from Nan Dearmer's biography *Percy Dearmer*[42] that it was Dwelly who persuaded Dearmer to become part of the movement. Through the movement, Dwelly was to come into close working contact with some of the foremost names within the Church of England.

Although *Prayer Book* revision was an important objective of Life and Liberty, the movement towards revision was already strong in the nineteenth century. The salient events are recorded succinctly by Donald Gray,[43] and traced from the early days of the Tractarian Movement and the establishment of the Camden Society in Cambridge. Revision was also being pushed by a very different group – The Prayer Book Revision Society Association for Promoting Revision of the Book of Common Prayer, and such other reforms in the Church of England as will strengthen its Protestant and Scriptural Character. Ritualism became a small but significant element of disagreement and led to the establishment of a Royal Commission. The Public Worship Regulating Act of 1874 solved nothing, aroused intense feelings and led to the imprisonment of four priests on charges of ritualism – one of them Rev. J. Bell-Cox from the Liverpool diocese. Before the end of the century, the ritualism problem was even more to the fore through the vehemently Protestant John Kensit.

A Royal Commission on Ecclesiastical Discipline was announced in 1904. The findings of this commission revealed in Donald Grey's words "wide divergence of ways of worship within the Church of England".[44] All this was the background against which Dwelly began his ministry. He was himself firmly part of the Evangelical tradition and there is little current evidence of his attitude towards Anglo Catholic practices apart from one piece in the parish magazine which reveals a most scornful and uncharitable attitude. "I was taught that Anglo means English, but all this is anti-English in character ... it is not even Italian.

The Roman Catholics would be bilious with it." *Emmanuel Messenger.*[45]

Prayer Book revision was a prominent issue at the 1908 Lambeth conference. The Encyclical Letter at the end of the Conference reported strongly on the need for revision.

> The growing experience of the Catholic Communion in different parts of the world and among many different races has pointed to the necessity for the adaptation and enrichment of forms of service which have come down to us from other times. Such adaptation and enrichment are advisable, and indeed essential, if our Church is to meet the real needs of men and women today.[46]

Adaptation and enrichment are both words which can be applied later to Dwelly's work and can be examined in orders of service he devised.

More detailed instructions as to those areas needing attention were included in Resolution 27.

1. The adaptation of rubrics to customs which are generally accepted.

2. The eliminating of unnecessary repetitions and redundancies.

3. The enrichment of existing services.

4. The fuller provision of alternatives in forms of worship.

5. Greater elasticity in public worship.

6. The elimination of language which was obscure or misunderstood.

7. A revision of Calendar and Tables.

Dwelly was still in his first curacy at the time of this pronouncement and there is no way of knowing of his awareness of the statements. However, later in his career, certainly from Southport onwards, there is clear evidence that much of his liturgical thought was in line with these official recommendations.

W. H. Frere recommended that there should be a period of time for official experiment. It was going to be the 1920s before ideas came to fruition in the publication of the *Green, Orange* and *Grey Books*. An Advisory Committee on Liturgical Questions was established on the recommendation of Archbishop Randall Davidson in 1911 but Convocation took little account of the advice of the liturgical experts on the committee which did not meet after 1918.

After the public services and events of the National Mission, five Committees of Enquiry were established and their second report on The Worship of the Church concentrated on liturgical revision. They had been asked "to consider a report upon ways in which the public worship of the church can be more directly related to the felt needs of actual life at the present time" and they submitted their report in 1918 and were adversely critical of the *Prayer Book* and the public worship in the church. A significant influence upon and within the report came as a result of the experiences of army chaplains working with the troops on the front line. H. K. Southwell, F. B. Macnutt and Neville Talbot served on the committee and submitted an appendix to the main report. Macnutt[47] had been largely responsible for collecting the essays published in 1917 as *The Church in the Furnace*. Their experiences in France had clarified their vision that the public needed services "Simple, real and short".With improvements, the Communion Service needed to become more central to Sunday worship; the Lectionary needed major modification to provide more relevant and meaningful readings; changes were needed to Morning and Evening Prayer.

Milner-White was clear in his assessment of the situation regarding the *Prayer Book*: "Fitness for place and use has become in these days the standard by which men and things are judged; and even the *Prayer Book*, august and beloved ever, stands for judgment … It has been at best semi-used and semi-usable, and we have come to look upon it from the unfamiliar distance."[48] Milner-White, Conran and Woodward all advocated "Short, simple acts of devotion". It may not be coincidental that Dwelly's very popular collection of prayers published during his time at Emmanuel was called *Acts of Devotion*.[49] The slender volume of sixty pages was published by S.P.C.K. in three different bindings and two formats at prices ranging from seven pence to four and sixpence. In comparison with much *Prayer Book* material in long and complex sentences these devotions are "simple, real and short".[50] Stylistic change over more than eighty years makes it difficult to assess the impact of the book's use. The devotions are litanies with frequent congregational response. They have dignity without pomposity, well balanced sentences and some poetic and memorable phrases. Each devotion is limited to two pages in length; they have titles which indicate their content and an index of subjects. "On the Grace of Childhood" can stand as typical of quality and character.

> Let us give thanks for Christ's revelation to us of God's love of children and of their infinite value in his sight.
>> *Alleluia. Blessed be God, Eternal Friend of children.*
>
> For his tender compassion towards them; for His burning indignation against those who do them wrong; for His deep and overflowing love, drawing them with irresistible attraction to Himself; for His message of their nearness to the Father of all.

Emmanuel Church, Southport, where Dwelly was Vicar from 1916 to 1925.

Alleluia. Blessed be God, Eternal Friend of children.

For the beauty of children and their joy in all beautiful things, for their mirth and laughter, and for the joy and light they bring into the world.
Alleluia. Blessed be God, Eternal Friend of children.

For their enthusiasm, their abounding energy, and their love of the heroic and adventurous; for their candid, generous trust in those around them, and for their quick response to calls of love and service.
Alleluia. Blessed be God, Eternal Friend of children.

For the childhood of Jesus our Lord, for his birth and helpless babyhood; for His Mother's gentle care and nurture, and for all unknown souls who nursed and tended him.
Alleluia. Blessed be God, Eternal Friend of children ..."[51]

From "A Litany of Remembrance":

O Lord, open Thou our minds to see ourselves as Thou seest us, and save us from all unwillingness to know our infirmities, for the sake of Jesus Christ our Lord and Saviour. Amen

From weakness of purpose; from want of earnest care; from indolence and indifference and from all spiritual deadness of heart.
Save us and help us, we humbly beseech Thee, O Lord.

From weariness in continuing struggles; from despondency in failure and disappointment; from self-conceit; from delight in supposed superiority; and from all the harms and hindrances of offensive manners;
Save us and help us, we humbly beseech Thee, O Lord.

From all hasty utterances of impatience; from the retort of irritation and the taunt of sarcasm; from all infirmity of temper in provoking or being provoked; from love of unkind gossip and from all idle words that may do hurt;

Save us and help us, we humbly beseech Thee, O Lord ...[52]

Though Dwelly was becoming more active and more widely known nationally, the very centre of his work was his ministry as Vicar of Emmanuel. On his arrival he was only the third incumbent and the church was less than twenty years old. There was considerable social diversity within the parish boundaries; finances could easily have been a problem but it was an imposing, spacious church far larger than Windermere or Cheltenham. Some older members of the parish who had known Dwelly as their Vicar like to think of Emmanuel as the mother church of the diocese because it was there that the future Dean of Liverpool was able to use his imaginative skills in the liturgy and worship of his church.

Powers of organisation discernible during both his curacies were further developed. His Peace Day celebrations on 19 July 1919 were planned with confidence and flair, the confidence and flair which were such a feature of his later and greater work at the cathedral in, for example, the weekend visit of all the Lambeth Bishops, the Scout service and the Affirmations service.

> The Mayor is caring for the old folk and part of the children; but what about all the others – and especially do I think of the gentlemen who have won Peace for us, the returned soldier and sailor? I feel we must do ourselves the honour as a parish of entertaining them. It will be expensive. No one wants to do catering that day, but I have secured the Prince of Wales Hotel for this, and though the cost is great, I do not fear but you will be proud that I have done it in your name. We must entertain those who have returned in a royal manner. You will be so good as to send me a cheque for the purpose; also I would like the men in the congregation to buy a ticket and come along to swell the welcome, for without a number of hosts we cannot raise a cheer for the returned.[53]

Not content with arranging an expensive lunch, he proposed a massive celebratory procession for all the rest of the parish.

> Then I want your help for a jolly procession. Will you decorate bicycles or cars or carriages and meet at Bradstock Lockett Home at 4.25 (prompt) to make a triumphant Peace procession, and if you cannot have any decoration, will you and your friends hire a trap or landau or motor and

join in the procession, for there will be many there that are only decorated with a flag. There are already a large number of entries – it is now a secured success (if fine) – but I feel you and your friends can make it an unprecedented success worthy of the mighty occasion.[54]

Over fifty of his parishioners had been killed in the war and Dwelly embarked on an audacious memorial scheme within the church. He planned to furnish and establish an elaborate war memorial chapel in the south transept at a cost of over £4,000 pounds to be raised entirely from donations from the congregation.

His organisational skills were employed beyond the bounds of the church and two events remained memorable in the town for years: a great Dickens festival in which he had large numbers dressed as characters from Dickens's novels, and the dedication of the town's impressive war memorial in Lord Street.

From his very first year, the parish *organisations* were established and were soon flourishing: the Mothers' Union, the Church Workers' Guild, the Communicants' Guild, a Scout troup, the Galahads – a rather socially divisive middle-class Sunday School, Girl Guides. "Gifts were pouring into the church – bookmarks and service books, hymnbooks, Advent hangings for the Sanctuary, pulpit hangings, and the oxidized silver cross which still stands behind the altar".[55]

Big, special services became regular features at Emmanuel. In preparation for the National Mission services a special choir of one hundred and fifty voices was enrolled and trained to add to the resources of the regular robed choir.[56] Lee also reported the existence of congregational choir, Mission choir and robed choir, all of which were flourishing. His Christmas Wreathing Service took place in a packed church and was reported in a local newspaper (unidentified):

> Very reverently, and in a quaint, old-world way, the members of the schools, the Galahads, and Bible Classes moved to their several little bits of wreathing to the singing of the carol, Noel, Noel. Only four of the verses of Once in Royal David's city were required to accomplish the entire wreathing of the church, not a single portion of the church being left unwreathed, the pillars included, which accomplished, the whole congregational choir grouped around the Star of Bethlehem, and burst forth into singing Halleluia Chorus. The effect was wonderfully inspiring. The choir seemed to number about 180.[57]

Though not a trained musician, music was important to him and within the services he devised. We know that he played the piano as a boy and that his wife was an accomplished organist.

Dwelly liked the use of banners, some of which still survive in the church, and he made effective use of processions as part of his big services. One former parishioner remembers, as part of a procession, Dwelly scooped up a baby from its mother's arms, and processed it round the church before returning it. Although a large parish church, Emmanuel because of narrow aisles and modest chancel did not give full scope to Dwelly's choreographic skills and flair and imagination in the use of space and human movement: the cathedral years lay ahead.

Even during his Cambridge days, Dwelly had been critical of the total inflexibility of the *Book Of Common Prayer*. That dissatisfaction was strong among members of the Life and Liberty Movement and among the First War army chaplains and the 1920s became a period of serious liturgical discontent and Dwelly, together with some eminent figures in the church, was deeply involved in the creation of new experimental liturgy. The 1922 meeting of the new Church Assembly accepted an important proposal concerning *Prayer Book* reform that "any revised forms of service should not be incorporated into the *Prayer Book*, but should be in a separate volume and sanctioned for use for a specific period."[58] The three most significant experimental publications became known as the Green, Orange and Grey books – the only significance of the titles rested in the colour of the covers. The most recent publication about that period of *Prayer Book* revision is by Donald Gray in 2006. No thorough consideration of this territory is relevant in this context but it is important to take notice that Dwelly was involved together with some of the most significant Anglican clergy of the day during his first incumbency.

The Green Book emerged from the Catholic end of the Church and was published by the English Church Union in 1922. *The Orange Book*, largely the work of Frere, contained the Alcuin Club's proposals. *The Grey Book*, with the overall title *A New Prayer Book* with a foreword by the Bishop of Manchester, William Temple, was published in three parts between April and June 1923, along with introductory pamphlets. *The Grey Book* had its official roots in the Life and Liberty Movement and the proposed services were the work of Percy Dearmer, R. G. Evans, later a Bishop of Southwark, F. R. Barry, later a Bishop of Southwell, Leslie Hunter, later Bishop of Sheffield, Mervyn Haigh Bishop of Winchester, and Frederick Dwelly. The actual wording of the services remains anonymous but, with only slight modifications, some of Dwelly's prayers in Acts of Devotion appear in the third volume, *Short Services for Occasional Use*.

The preface to the third volume states the intentions of the writers and compilers succinctly:

> The services which follow are intended for use at Morning and Evening Prayer, and at other times as occasion requires. The compilers of this

book believe that there is a need for more experiment and freedom in worship in the church. This means not only more elasticity in the regular services, but also a greater variety in the services provided: special services for those who do not come to the usual offices, services of preparation for communicants, services for guilds and fellowships and for special occasions.[59]

The importance for Dwelly of the implications of this final sentence will be seen throughout his ministry at Liverpool Cathedral both before and after he was appointed as the first Dean. It is interesting to compare these ideas with Dwelly's ideas about the formulation of special services set down by Stanley Morison in *English Prayer Books*,[60] and with some of the actual services devised for use in Liverpool Cathedral in the thirties and forties.

The writers of the preface acknowledge that many of their published devotions:

approximate to the type of devotion generally known as extempore (a type which should have a larger place in public worship) and they do not even claim that limited permanence which belongs to more formal acts of worship ... we are ... convinced that the church will be wise to reserve within her ordered garden of prayer a corner where the more simple natural thoughts and emotions in the hearts of our people, which are at present rather repressed in the worship of the church, may find some kind of expression.[61]

The preface to the second volume comments first on Matins and Evensong and makes practical suggestions

Ways of shortening both services have been suggested ... We have also felt that it was desirable to break away from the present uniform introduction, which is apt to be unreal ... We have ventured ... by way of experiment to provide a different set of versicles and responses for Mattins, and a different arrangement of collects. In the revision of the Occasional Offices, the aim has been to shorten and simplify and to introduce a more human note where we felt it was needed. It has to be remembered that many hear the Baptismal, Marriage, and Burial Offices, who are not in the habit of attending other services and are not familiar with the teaching of the Church. It is very necessary, therefore, that these services be made as intelligible to such people as is possible.[62]

At the start of the suggestions for Matins, three alternatives are suggested by way of introduction in place of Exhortation, General Confession, Absolution and Lord's Prayer. The General confession is maintained for festivals but the shorter less linguistically complex confessions are offered as alternatives.

> Almighty God, the Father of our Lord Jesus Christ, of whom the whole family in heaven and earth is named, deliver us now from the vain things that have power over us, and enable us to rest our souls in thee and yield them to the guidance of thy loving Spirit. Make us ready to offer thee the joy that is thy gift, and worship thee with glad and thankful hearts. In the light of thy perfection help us to see our shortcomings and be sorry for our faults; and grant, we beseech thee, that, strengthened by our worship together, we may serve thee and our fellow men more faithfully in our daily life, and come at last to thy eternal kingdom; through the same Jesus Christ our Lord. Amen.[63]

The compilers even went so far as to provide an alternative Confession of Faith though the Apostles' Creed was to remain mandatory "at least for Great Festivals".

> We believe that God is Spirit: and they that worship him must worship him in spirit and in truth.

> We believe that God is Light: and if we walk in the light as he is in the light we have fellowship one with another.

> We believe that God is Love: and that everyone that loveth is born of God and knoweth God.

> We believe that Jesus is the Son of God: and that God has given to us eternal life, and this life is in his Son.

> We believe that we are children of God: and that he hath given us his Spirit.

> We believe that if we confess our sins: he is faithful and just to forgive us our sins.

> We believe that he who doeth the will of God: shall abide for ever. Amen.[64]

Writing of this character is going to be discernible in many of Dwelly's Cathedral services over the next three decades. The statement is short; sentences are balanced and dignified and use is made of the conflation of biblical material.

Dwelly could not be called a "theoretical liturgist": there is evidence from material in the parish magazine that he kept his congregation up to date with liturgical developments and that Emmanuel had been used as testing ground for material for the *Grey Book*: "A fateful time for the Revision of the Communion Service. Very hard and intricate lobby work; many private conferences; and at last a marvellous persuading of the Assembly by what seemed to be not less than an outpouring of the Holy Spirit. The Green Book has had its bitter tendency taken away. The revision which has been used as a reverent experiment at Emmanuel has passed."[65]

Dwelly was working at a time before a parish or choral Eucharist became the main service on Sundays in church or cathedral and he was not noted for celebrations of the Eucharist during his days as Dean but one aspect of his concern is interesting in the light of the publication of *Common Worship* in 2000. That publication provides a range of options for the Eucharistic Prayer. Dwelly was part of a group which 80 years before was advocating a range of alternatives. His words again in his parish magazine:

> Hitherto it has not proved possible to devise one single alternative Canon which all who desire revision would agree to accept. This being so the only honest and charitable course would appear to be the authorization of alternative Canons in one and the same liturgy, provided always that these Canons contain nothing that can be considered contrary to Holy Scripture, or incapable of defence and explanation by those definitely prefer some other form ... The old idea of rigid uniformity has led in the past to disruption. Its failure is made manifest in the present disorders which we all alike deplore. Is not diversity itself an essential element in the Christian ideal of Fellowship? And if it is, may we not well hope that an ordered variety in worship will lead us to a truer and stronger unity than uniformity is ever likely to achieve.[66]

Another area in which Dwelly and others were ahead of their time is that of the ministry of women in the church. The matter was considered at a Church Council Meeting in June 1921 and in a subsequent article in the magazine Dwelly's attitude is clear.

> The bedrock question is: Has the Ministry of Women the sanction of Holy Scripture? For myself I answer that question in the affirmatives ... In my judgment it will be the part of wisdom for the Church people in this parish and throughout the rural deanery and diocese simply to revive the order of Deaconesses as recommended by 252 Bishops at Lambeth. When this is accomplished, the future will take care of further developments. It is pure folly to hustle the matter. The Holy Catholic church has been an exclusively man administered institution for nearly 2,000 years. When one looks out today upon the deplorable

The church in which Dwelly tested his fresh ideas. An interior capable of being used dramatically and able to seat a congregation of over 1,000.

state of Christianity in this and every other country, one is driven to the conclusion that what the church needs today is the active ministrations of God-fearing earnest women. They may reach and hold people men have failed to reach and hold.[67]

Despite the absence of much personal archive material, it is possible to give a reasonably accurate account of Dwelly's interests and ecclesiastical achievements up to 1924 but harder to make an authoritative statement about his personality, though some attempt must be made. In the Preface to my biography *Frederick William Dwelly: First Dean of Liverpool*, I wrote: "In his life there was tragedy, and yet there is exuberance, delight, sparkling humour, joyful creativity, dynamic leadership. He was tender, caring, devoted, faithful, magnetic, whilst at the same time being obtuse, autocratic, unbending, stubborn, harsh."[68]

Even before his move to Liverpool Cathedral, I believe it is possible to pronounce him to be dynamic, determined, untiring, enthusiastic, ebullient, confident, a brilliant communicator, an organiser of people, services and events, a pioneer, a faithful trusted friend, an individualist, sensitive to people and places, an artist with words and human movement, musically aware, widely read, spiritually alert, faithful priest, a magnetic leader. He was beginning to be known more widely within the Church of England but it was going to take an event in the summer of 1924 to highlight his abilities and make his name known throughout the country and beyond.

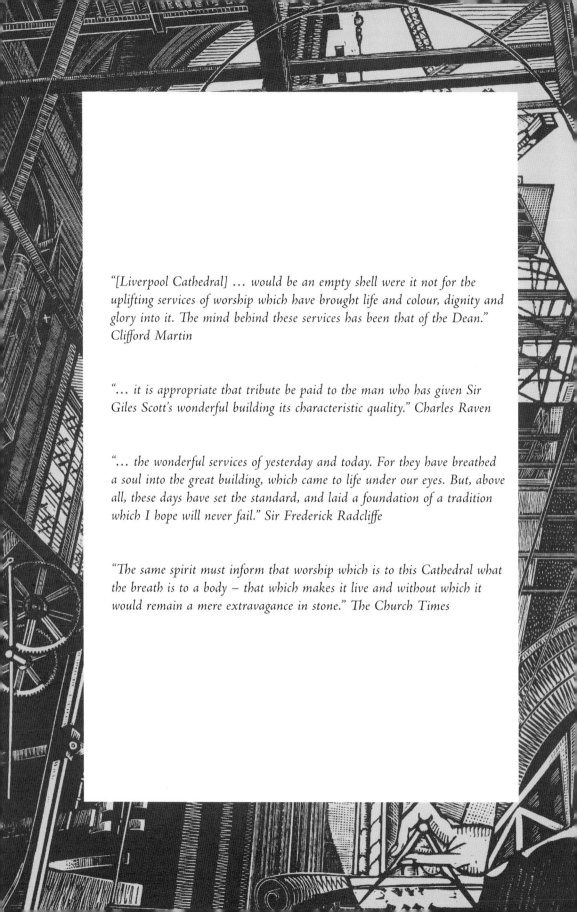

"[Liverpool Cathedral] ... would be an empty shell were it not for the uplifting services of worship which have brought life and colour, dignity and glory into it. The mind behind these services has been that of the Dean." *Clifford Martin*

"... it is appropriate that tribute be paid to the man who has given Sir Giles Scott's wonderful building its characteristic quality." *Charles Raven*

"... the wonderful services of yesterday and today. For they have breathed a soul into the great building, which came to life under our eyes. But, above all, these days have set the standard, and laid a foundation of a tradition which I hope will never fail." *Sir Frederick Radcliffe*

"The same spirit must inform that worship which is to this Cathedral what the breath is to a body – that which makes it live and without which it would remain a mere extravagance in stone." *The Church Times*

Consecration

T HE DAY of the Consecration of the Cathedral Church of Christ in Liverpool, 19 July 1924, was pivotal to the whole future life of the Cathedral just as it is pivotal to this study. On that day the architectural genius of Giles Gilbert Scott and the liturgical genius of Frederick William Dwelly coincided. In one sense the service on that day was the culmination of the life's work of a forty three year old priest: in another sense it marked the very start of his true ministry. "If any person at all is to be entitled to take credit for the events of this week in Liverpool Cathedral, that person, above all others, is Mr. Dwelly."[1] Before the event, many more people than the reporter for the *Catholic Times* of 19 July 1904 must have feared that the great empty, partly finished shell might have been an irrelevant anachronism. "Will Liverpool's new Cathedral be like York Minster, a cold and dead memorial of the past robed in the lifeless splendour of the centuries that have gone but always void of contact with the life of today?" He saw it as "entirely unsuited to the needs of protestant worship ... a matter chiefly of prayer and preaching".[2] After two hours and twenty minutes on 19 July 1904 the answer was a universal negative.

It was almost by accident that Dwelly was involved in any way with the Consecration Service: he was simply a priest in the diocese with no particular connection with the Cathedral project. The fullest account by Charles Raven of the way in which he became involved appeared in 1955 in the *Liverpool Diocesan Leaflet* at the time of his retirement. The way in which he became involved is so typical of the man that the statement must be quoted in full.

At the time when the great adventure of the building of Liverpool Cathedral is entering upon its last phase it is appropriate that tribute should be paid to the man who has given to Sir Giles Scott's wonderful building its characteristic spiritual quality. Ever since its consecration in 1924 Liverpool Cathedral has stood for an imaginative, vital and appropriate presentation of Christian faith and worship, for a worthy commemoration of national and local events, for a generous and scholarly treatment of theological and moral issues, and for magnificent music and deeply impressive ritual. It has thus become a unique centre of relevant, intelligent and aesthetic worship. In all these elements of its life the Dean, F. W. Dwelly, has been the principal inspiration and the executive officer.

His first achievement, the great service of consecration, was typical of his whole career. He came to it almost unknown; and the circumstances of his coming deserve to be put on record. Bishop David had confided to me, his newly-appointed Canon, that having himself no expert knowledge of liturgies or ceremonial, he did not know how to get a service worthy of the occasion. I had spent the first four days of Holy Week at Emmanuel, Southport; and on my last evening there had sat up till after midnight with the Vicar, planning his Easter service. When I went to bed, the script was almost illegible – a mass of corrections and turkey tracks. With my morning tea, appeared the same script in print and ready for distribution. When I asked Dwelly whether he had a printing press or a tame magician on the premises, he replied, 'You took a lot of interest in the service and I thought you'd like to see it before you left: the local paper is printed on Wednesday night: the foreman printer is a pal of mine: I took down the service on my bike and asked him to send up the printed form with the milk.' Naturally I told this history to the Bishop, and said, 'You've got this man in your own diocese: he knows all about liturgies and church music: he has imagination and a sense of dignity: he will construct your service, produce it, and plan all the details from the processions to the ceremonial.'

So I was not surprised that the Service itself was superbly designed and executed, and that when the arrival of the King and Queen twenty minutes too early, in a programme synchronised to an exact precision, threatened to destroy the sequence of the very many processions, Dwelly rose at once to the occasion, set chairs for the royal visitors in the King's Porch and carried through the whole programme without a sign of anxiety.

From that day onwards it has been the same. He has lived in and for

A view through the Chancel towards the Sanctuary, Reredos and East window.

the Cathedral, exercising all his thought and ingenuity in discovering fresh opportunities for it: collecting a vast wealth of precedents, forms of service, music and local knowledge; and gathering round him a great company of artists and craftsmen, musicians and singers, men and women of all kinds devoted to the welfare of the Cathedral and ready to sacrifice time and care without stint in its service.

To have been associated with Dr. Dwelly as I was in the closest partnership for the first eight years of his work, to have watched the expansion of that work in the many years since, to have rejoiced in the triumphal survival and constant renewal of the adventure through the tragedy and problems of war, and to see it now still going on from strength to strength – these are privileges which any man would reckon among the most precious of his life-time. And through all these events and the memories which they have inspired it is the figure of Fred Dwelly, his friendship, his genius, his magnificence, his selflessness, his love of God and man that stands out as at once the symbol and the instrument of the Cathedral's life.[3]

Charles Raven would not have had an opportunity to recommend Dwelly to the Bishop as a priest capable of devising a consecration service before Easter Sunday – 20 April that year and the consecration was scheduled for 19 July. To have devised and written one great service in that time would have been remarkable: Dwelly devised twenty five services to be held within the octave. It is known that he had the support of Canon Morley Stevenson and Rev. J. W. Tyrer but impossible to assess the nature of their involvement. The Special Correspondent of the *Church Times*, 25 July 1924 is clear as to where praise should go.

> The form and order of the services was an inspiration. I know something of the immense amount of care, thought and study which have been devoted to its compilation ... To provide a form which should adequately combine ancient and modern, East and West, was no light task. From Egbert downwards through the centuries the ancient forms of East and West have been studied with care and discrimination, and this form and Order of the Cathedral Church of Liverpool may for all completeness challenge comparison with any in the past.[4]

The Church of England Newspaper of the same date is clear in its praise:

> At the outset I must bear testimony to the superb way the ceremonies were organized and carried out without a single hitch. It may be invidious to single out any individual for special praise, but again and again the name of the Rev. F. W. Dwelly, the Ceremoniarius, was mentioned. It was mainly due to his unwearying patience and attention to detail that the processions were so splendidly marshalled. The services, too, both on Saturday and Sunday, were in large measure the fruit of Mr. Dwelly's knowledge and careful search in the ancient treasure store of Consecration Service forms. Writing last month, the Bishop of Liverpool said: 'We have received more help in our task than we can easily acknowledge. But there is no difficulty is singling out one who deserves the chief share of our gratitude, namely, the Rev. F. W. Dwelly, of Southport. He was

assisted by Canon Morley Stevenson and the Rev. J. W. Tyrer. What they did not know about liturgical details and precedents (which is not a great deal) Mr. Dwelly knew where to find, and he spared neither time nor labour seeking it. His well-known gift of devotional expression was invaluable in the composition of all the Consecration Services, and we have indeed been happy to find in the diocese itself a contribution of so much sympathy and skill'.[5]

The much depleted Dwelly archive has almost no papers from the period covering the actual writing of the service but two pieces are significant. There was a single folded sheet from the Bishop, 11 June 1924: "*The Consecration of Liverpool Cathedral* Concerning the ordering of the ceremonies July 19 1924." The range of Dwelly's research is apparent in the list of organizations who helped:

> Through the bureau of the Life and Liberty Movement the following have given generous assistance in the compilation of the Service Books, and the precedents involved in the same:
>
> > The Dean of Canterbury
> > The Secretary and Consulting Members of the Alcuin Club
> > The Librarian of Corpus Christi, Cambridge
> > The Librarian of Lambeth
> > The Librarian of the London Registry
> > The Chairman of the 'Grey Book' Group
> > The Chancellor of Salisbury Cathedral
> > The Chancellor of Worcester Cathedral
> > The Chancellor of Lincoln Cathedral
> > The Controller of Oxford University Press
> > Dr. Percy Dearmer
>
> His Majesty the King has graciously approved the following arrangements for the due performance of the ceremonies of the Consecration of Liverpool Cathedral according to precedents set at:
>
> (1) Canterbury May 4th, 1130 in the presence of Henry King of England and David King of Scotland.
>
> (2) Salisbury, June 7th, 1225, in the presence of Henry, King of England."[6]

The Bishop understood the importance of the right atmosphere at the service and recognised the danger that people might be overwhelmed by the spectacular aspects of the service. All the diocesan clergy were asked to explain the

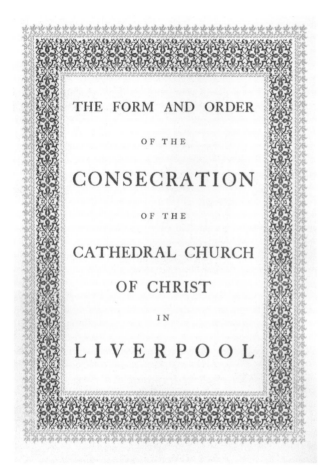

The first of Dwelly's famous Cathedral service papers, sixty four pages long.

THE FORM AND ORDER

OF THE

CONSECRATION

OF THE

CATHEDRAL CHURCH

OF CHRIST

IN

LIVERPOOL

symbolism from their pulpits on the Sunday before Consecration. Dwelly was so concerned that those attending the service should have real understanding of the words and movements that he built explanation into the service book. Dwelly and his Cathedral service sheets became famous throughout the country and beyond. The service Book for 19 July 1924 led the way and was sixty two pages long, printed in black and red on cream paper – the Cathedral hallmark for the next thirty years. Four sheets roughly typed and duplicated were produced by the Rev. J. W. Tyrer and headed Liverpool Diocesan Service Book Commission, The Sources of the Liverpool Cathedral Consecration Service. There had not been a cathedral consecration on an unconsecrated site since the that of Salisbury Cathedral in 1225. For legal reasons it was important that precedents be followed but vitally important that the service be made real and

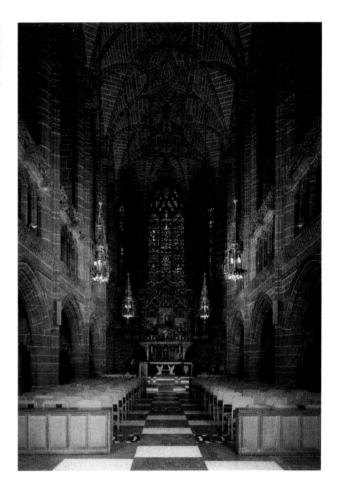

The Lady Chapel had been consecrated in 1910 and functioned as Liverpool Cathedral until the consecration in 1924. The original windows were destroyed by bomb blast.

relevant to the twentieth-century worshipper. Dwelly's task was to weave an imaginative, meaningful and relevant service from disparate elements.

The consecration in Liverpool in 1924 was of a church which was to become one of the great Cathedrals of Christendom, a vast and glorious space and Dwelly realised that his service must attempt to match the quality of the building and so mark the co-incidence of a great architect and a great liturgist. "It is this service that undoubtedly set the scene for all that was to come for Dwelly and for Liverpool Cathedral."[7].

Tyrer drew attention to twenty actions or words and identified their origins in liturgical history:

The procession around the outside of the church.
The knocking at the church door and the singing of psalm 24.

The arrival of Bishop Albert Augustus David before the service.

Petition for Consecration and the Bishop's consent.
Delivery of the keys to the Bishop.
The prayer beginning, "We beseech thee O Lord graciously enter ..."
"Peace be to this house."
Psalm 122, "I was glad when they said unto me ..."
Singing of Veni Creator.
Alpha and omega and the sign of the cross.
Placing the keys on the Holy Table.
Prayer "O Eternal God, mighty in power ..."
The passages of Scripture.
The prayer "O God, the Sanctifier of all things ..."
Sursum corda, The Preface
"It is very meet, right ..."
The Consecration Mark.
The reading and signing of the Sentence of Consecration.
The prayer "Blessed be thy name, O Lord ..."
The blessings of the Bishop and the Archbishop.
The hymn "Only-begotten, Word of God eternal."

Vigil services, "Watch of Prayer and Meditation", in the Lady Chapel were held throughout the night with each rural deanery being allotted one hour between 6 pm and 6 am and the Bishop urged that as many people as possible attend a Communion Service in their own churches at 8 am on 19 July. Five thousand people attended the Lady Chapel services. Despite all his responsibilities, Dwelly could not but accept an invitation from Lord Derby to go to Knowsley to be presented to the King and Queen the night before the event. Dwelly's thoughts and feelings after this meeting were recorded in a hurried letter to his parents. At a time of such pressure, his exuberance is typical of him.

> Dear all of you
> It is long past midnight – I am just in – but I cannot go to sleep without a word to you – when I was announced in the Presence Chamber Lord Derby said – Your Majesty – the creator of the service which you take part in tomorrow. I bowed low to the King and he said I am deeply interested in it. It must have been very hard work – to which I replied

Ceremoniarius Frederick William Dwelly leads a section of the procession around the outside of the Cathedral.

'No great fun' and he laughed loud and repeated the same to Lord Derby and to the queen – what happened after that I cannot tell you only that we talked some time in a laughing fashion and then I talked to the queen but its all a dream to me – then the bishop came and claimed me and took me to York and we had no end of a go – he was exceedingly gracious. Cantuar was as he always is wonderful.

I am full of sadness – I'd so like you to share this. Tomorrow – no today – its all done – the crowd at the Cathedral tonight is wonderful. Bert is most helpful –

[The final greeting is completely illegible.][8]

In a study of this limited length, it is not possible to present a full examination of the service. The service is simply commented on under eight headings which can be applied to further Cathedral services throughout his future ministry: preparation, organisation, structure, choreography, text, music, symbolism, service papers.

The preparation and research for the service and Rev. J. W. Tyrer's brief note on the sources drawn upon has already been mentioned. Although it is

The Bishop having made a consecration mark on the north wall of the building.

CONSECRATION OF LIVERPOOL CATHEDRAL 19TH JULY 1924 TEAR

Queen Mary signing the Deed of Consecration.

only a brief resume of extensive research it sheds light on how Dwelly began to formulate the service.

a. Knocking at Church door with Ps. 24 seq.

Found in Pontifical of Egbert (10th century, not 8th) and in Sarum. Ps. 24 (without knocking) is found here at Consecration of chapel of Wyle-Champflour (A.D. 1624 – Bath and Wells) and St. Catherine Cree (London – A.D. 1631); but these stand pretty much alone. But whole of Ps. 24 as bishop enters Church or immediately after, used in Bishop Andrews' Form (A.D. 1680) and frequently since.

b. Petition for Consecration and Bishop's Consent.

Usual in English 17th Century Consecrations. Bishop's consent usually expressed in words 'In the name of God let us begin.'

c. Delivery of Keys to Bishop.
Occasionally found in English 17th Century Consecrations, e.g., that of Peterhouse Chapel (A.D. 1633).

d. The Prayer, ' We beseech thee O Lord, graciously enter', etc.
Translated from Latin Collect, 'Domum Tuum, quaesumus'. Found in Egbert and in Gregorian Sacramentary (8th Century), but not in Gelasian.

e. 'Peace be to this house', etc
First two clauses in Egbert; third new. 'Peace be to this house' (without addition used in Sarum and at Wyke-Champflour, but not usual in 17th century Consecrations in England.

f. 'I was glad', etc. (Anthem used at Coronation of George V.)
Ps. 122 does not occur in Egbert, but (tho' later on in service) in Sarum Ps. 122 (with one or more of the other verses) commonly used at beginning of English 17th century Consecrations.

g. Veni Creator.
New (it occurs in Modern Roman Rite).

h. Sign of Cross with A. and O.
Taken from alphabet ceremony used in medieval Western rites of Consecration from 9th Century downwards including Egbert and Sarum and of Gallican origin – not used in England in 17th century.

i. Placing Keys on Holy Table.
New. (So far as I am aware).

j. Prayer, 'O Eternal God, mighty in power', etc.
Used, probably for the first time, by Bishop Barlow (of Rochester and afterwards of Lincoln) at Consecration of Langley chapel (A.D. 1607), and ever since, though with considerable alterations.

k. The Passages of Scripture.
New. In medieval rites there are no lections of Scripture at consecration of churches except at the Mass, and in the English 17th Century ones, none except for the Mattins and Holy Communion (which usually formed part of the Consecration).

l. The Prayer, 'O God, the Sanctifier of all things'.

Adapted in a shortened form from the Prayer 'Deus sanctificationum', found in Egbert, Sarum and the Gelasian (7th Century).

m. Sursum Corda
Egbert, Sarum, etc.

n. The Preface 'It is very meet, right"
Translated (with a certain amount of adaptation) from the first half of the Preface 'Vere digrum … adesto precibus …'. (Sarum, Egbert, etc.)

o. The Mark of Consecration
In the medieval rites (e.g., Sarum, Egbert) the Bishop made several consecration marks with his thumb on the walls of the church.

p. Reading and Signing of the Sentence of consecration.
Used in English 17th Century Forms of Consecration.

q. The Prayer 'Blessed be thy name, O Lord'.
Common in 17th Century Forms of consecrating Churches in England. First appears in Bishop Andrews' Form (A.D. 1620) from which it is only slightly altered.

r. The Blessings of the Bishop and Archbishop.
In spirit and form these resemble the English medieval Episcopal Blessings; but I have not found any exact equivalent for them.

s. The Hymn 'Only-begotten, Word of God eternal;'.
This looks like a translation of some Latin Hymn, but which I do not know. The 17th Century French Breviary hymn 'Patris aeternae Sobles coaeva'. (by Charles Guiet) has some thoughts like it and in in the same metre.

t. The Procession round the Church outside at the beginning is medieval (Sarum and Egbert).

In the above the word 'new' merely means there are no 17th Century or medieval precedents.[9]

The Bishop and Raven had both realised that no slavish following of precedents would produce a memorable, imaginative, meaningful and relevant Consecration service. What was needed was the flair, vision and artistry which Dwelly could bring to the results of academic research. Though not himself a musician, he understood the effectiveness of music in worship. He understood the effectiveness of human movement and the importance of the colour of robes within the muted shades of the cathedral. His sensitivity to language and the ability to combine ancient formulae with his own words showed throughout. Dwelly the creative artist and Dwelly the spiritual mystic shone through the whole service. The ceremonies on 19 July 1924 might well be his greatest achievement but there is ample evidence of the way in which he researched and prepared for less significant occasions.[10] *The Sunday Times* for 20 July stressed how much Dwelly had brought to the service:

> There was pageantry and pomp, as befits all Royal Ceremonies; but the atmosphere in the Cathedral was one of mysticism, something spiritual and inexplicable, a kind of service which inspired religious worshippers in medieval ages, and yet so adapted that the churchmen and churchwomen of today found in it comfort and inspiration.[11]

The *Church Times* on 25 July declared: "… The form and order of the service was an inspiration. I know something of the immense amount of care, thought and study which have been devoted to its compilation."[12] Nearly all the newspaper and journal articles commented on the excellence of the organisation which had ordered the whole event. Nothing was left to chance and Dwelly rehearsed meticulously. The Vicar of Mossley Hill Church wrote to him immediately after the final rehearsal: "Well done, old man, it was great! The service is very wonderful, and considering the number of parsons who each knew the job better than you do, there were very few boss shots!! I always think they are more difficult to manage than laymen at a ceremonial."[13] Frederick Dillistone[14] in his biography of Raven reports on the precision of Dwelly's organisation and rehearsals. The processions were so numerous and extensive that they began their entry at 2.10 pm, fifty minutes before the formal start of the service. All this had been organised by Dwelly so successfully that the *Manchester Guardian* described the consecration Ceremony as "an affair of ecclesiastical pomp such as this realm has not seen for many centuries nor for many years in likely to again."[15] The bound copies of The Services of the Octave contain copies of twenty-four other major services. The organisational clarity brought by Dwelly to the whole sequence is quite remarkable. Between the 19 and 26 July sermons were preached by two Archbishops, fifteen Bishops, three Deans, one Archdeacon, and one Canon. Clarity of organisation as revealed in the rubrics of the service paper will be considered later in this chapter. Dwelly's organisational skills had been commented on favourably during his first curacy in Windermere and his time as senior curate in Cheltenham. His civic and ecclesiastical organisation at Southport are fully reported and he always showed himself to be completely unworried by vast numbers. His excellence in managing the larger organisational canvas was balanced by care over precise detail. In conversation with the writer, the late Canon John Winstanley reported his experience on the day of his ordination when he was to read the Gospel. At the rehearsal he said, "I shall be standing about here." Dwelly replied, "No you won't, you will be standing exactly here."

An effective structure is one of the most important features of any successful service, especially one which is inevitably long. On 19 July the ticket holders had to be in their places not later than 2 pm and they were not able to begin to leave the Cathedral until 4.15 pm. I have not discovered any reports of the service which criticised it for being too long. Dwelly managed to order the various elements of the service in such a way that variety and careful continuity produced a satisfying whole. Every piece of the service has its own character and focus. Many historical precedents had to be included but Dwelly structured them in such a way that they appeared natural and relevant.

The service paper itself, as will be examined later, helps to reveal the structure to all the participants and it is broken down into twelve sections. I, The Preparation, was very simple, quiet and lacking any pomp.

> At the second hour after noon the Bishop, supported by two of his chaplains, attended by a clerk in Holy Orders who shall act as his Proctor, and conducted by the clerk in Holy Orders whom he has commissioned to order the ceremonies in his name in such wise that nothing be left undone that should be done for a complete outward and visible sign of the inward and spiritual meaning of the service of Consecration, shall enter the church in plain attire and, assuring himself that all is in order for the ceremony, shall kneel in the Presbytery and say: The Lord's Prayer. The Bishop shall then proceed to certain points in the Cathedral, and shall bid the people prepare themselves for the solemn ceremony of Consecration. This done, he shall withdraw to prepare his own heart and mind, and to be vested by his Chaplains.
>
> Then shall the Cathedral organist, H. Goss Custard, make music.[16]

Both the Bishop and the Congregation were able to prepare themselves and the stillness and quietness were in marked contrast to the brilliant sound, as yet unheard publicly, of the organ, and the splendour of the sequence of processions. In 1955 in the *Diocesan Review*, Bishop Clifford Martin was to write "You have to go to Liverpool Cathedral if you want to see how to walk to the glory of God."[17] There were all the Liverpool diocesan clergy, at least nineteen Deans and over forty five Bishops, the choristers and lay vicars of the Cathedral Churches of the Northern Province, six Metropolitans of the Anglican Communion, eight local

Albert Augustus David installed on the Bishop's Throne.

Mayors, the Lord Mayor of London, and the Lord Mayor of Liverpool with his Civic Procession, the Royal Procession, the Cathedral Procession and finally the Archbishop of York's Procession.

The Bishop of Liverpool waited outside the west doors and knocked at the door but was denied admission. He walked around the outside of the building while the Litany was chanted. He knocked unsuccessfully a second time and waited until after the entry of the Royal Procession. Only at the third knocking was he successful as the service moved into (II): The Delivery of the Keys to the Right Reverend the Lord Bishop of the Diocese and the formal request that he consecrate the Cathedral and (III) his entrance into the Cathedral. After simple dialogue and prayer at the start of the third section, the singing of the anthem by Parry, *I was glad when they said unto me, we will go into the house of the Lord* must have sounded particularly dramatic and prepared the congregation for the significance of what was to come. During (IV), the invocation and the sign of Alpha and Omega, the congregation knelt for the singing of *Veni Creator* before the Bishop "alone and unattended" carried the keys through the congregation and through the choir and presbytery. The focus of (V), the dedication is entirely upon the Bishop at the Holy Table. At (VI), five short passages of Scripture were read by different people from different places in the chancel. Then during the singing of the hymn *Only Begotten, Word of God eternal* the members of the Chapter were individually verged into the sanctuary where the Chancellor read two short passages concerning the sacraments. At (VII), after the Sursum Corda the whole attention was on the Bishop for the words of consecration culminating in the words, "vouchsafe to bless, hallow, and consecrate this holy table: and bless and consecrate this whole building with the everlasting fullness of thy sanctifying power; who livest and reignest, ever one God, world without end. Amen."

The Rejoicings (VIII) were led by the Bishop and sung to new music by Martin Shaw composed for the occasion. This was the first of many pieces of music which Dwelly was to commission for use in great services. The section culminated in the whole congregation singing the Doxology. During (IX), The Witness of Consecration on Stone and Parchment, there was movement down from the sanctuary towards the chancel steps after the making of the consecration mark on the pillar. The full procession moved westwards during the singing of the hymn *Christ is made the sure foundation*. The Sentence of Consecration was read by the chancellor and placed upon the table before the King and Queen and the section was concluded by the singing of the hymn, *City of God* as the Archbishop of York was led to preach the sermon (X), which focused upon the idea of the living Cathedral: "We are wont to think of the great cathedrals of the past as the creation of ages of faith which we wistfully contrast with our own. But this cathedral proves that the same faith, purified and deepened, is living and moving in the midst of this twentieth century's doubt and stress and toil." At The Time of Offering (XI), the alms of the King and Queen, Archbishops, Bishops and Deans were presented together with the ornaments and vessels, all to the singing of *O worship the King*. The Primatial Blessing, XII, was the last spoken part of the service and three hymns were sung as the processions moved from the building. The quietness of the Bishop's first entry being balanced by *Praise, my soul, the King of Heaven* "in the singing of which the congregation is requested to join heartily."

From the beginning, Dwelly's skills as a choreographer were outstanding: "When Cosmo Gordon Lang, the Archbishop of Canterbury, visited the Southport Church Congress in 1926 he declared that it was Dwelly who 'had taught the Church of England how to process.' And this was done in no ostentatious or pretentious way."[18] In 1955 in the Liverpool Diocesan Leaflet Bishop Clifford Martin wrote, "Every procession is an act of worship."[19] 1924 was before the days of the Cross Guild and their unique contribution to Liverpool choreography but from the start Dwelly appreciated the vast spaces provided by the architect and understood the potency of human movement: the Bishop in prayer at a faldstool as the procession moves round and past him, the Bishop's walking the length of the Cathedral "alone and unattended". Dean Dillistone wrote an unpublished article to mark the centenary of Dwelly's birth and in it he underlines the significance of Dwelly's concern for movement in worship:

> It was, however, in the first realm, 'the cosmic language of movement', that he made his outstanding contribution to worship in the Church of England. To some degree processions had been introduced into Anglican liturgical worship as a consequence of the Oxford Movement but generally speaking these followed medieval patterns, with a focusing of attention on what was being carried or on the dignitary whom the procession was designed to honour. In Dwelly's vision, all the participants had a part to play in the dramatic framework which, like that of the great cosmic recurring cycle, encircled the words and actions of the service itself.[20]

The opportunities for movement at the Consecration Service were limited because of the need to pack in as many people as possible into the partly completed Cathedral but even so the processions were dramatic and meaningful. As the space available increased, so did Dwelly's choreographic exploits, which will be examined more closely in later chapters.

Language dates more noticeably than movement and it is necessary to remember that Dwelly has been dead for over sixty years. He had the great skill of producing dignified, memorable prose though to modern ears some of it may sound florid. Dwelly had no easy task at the Consecration in that precedent demanded certain forms of words but did not provide a total script: Dwelly had to weave existing and new text into a seamless whole and succeeded brilliantly in that few of the congregation would have recognised what was Dwelly and what was not. At the entrance of the Bishop, the first prayer is a translation from the Latin in the Pontifical of Egbert:

> We beseech thee, O Lord, graciously enter thy house, and within the hearts of thy faithful people establish for thyself an everlasting habitation that they may be glorified by the indwelling of him by whose building they live, through Jesus Christ our Lord. Amen

The next two greetings are also in Egbert, but the third is not:

> Peace be unto this house and all that worship in it.

> Peace be to those that enter and to those that go out from it.

> Peace be to those that love it and that love the name of Jesus Christ our Lord.[21]

In the pre-Reformation period a relic would have been placed within the altar, a symbolism unacceptable in Protestant twentieth century Liverpool. The ceremony of the placing of the keys on the altar was new and an appropriate new prayer had to be provided:

> O Lord Jesu Christ, who hast the key of David, who openest and no man shutteth, give thy power, we pray thee, to us thy servants, and grant that this house, now opened for thy service, may always be filled with thy presence, and may ever remain a refuge for thy faithful people. Who with the Father and the Holy Ghost livest and reignest, one God, for ever and ever. Amen.[22]

The medieval consecration rites did not make provision for lections of Scripture. Dwelly's provision is new and imaginative, and typical of him. There are five very short readings, none more than two sentences in length, and read at different and appropriate places within the Cathedral.

The consecration mark drawn on the floor by the Bishop in 1924 is marked with water annually by a young chorister.

Tyrer had not found precedent for the exact words of the Bishop's or the Archbishop's blessings though they contain elements from known sources. We can only assume that they are of Dwelly's composition.

May the Lord Jesus Christ fill you who have come to this Consecration with spiritual joy.

May his spirit make you strong and tranquil in the truths of his promises.

And may the blessing of the Lord come upon you abundantly. Amen

May God, the Fountain of all blessing, fill you, who have gathered in this house on the festival of its Consecration, with the understanding of sacred knowledge.

May he keep you sound in faith, steadfast in hope, and persevering in patient charity, and

May the blessing of the Father, the Son, and the Holy Spirit, and the peace of the Lord be with you always. Amen.[23]

"In Quires and Places where they sing" and where the choral resources are highly developed, there is a danger that music becomes almost detached from the general flow of the service. At Consecration and later great services Dwelly seemed aware of the danger and did not upset the balance. From his 1897 holiday journal we know that he played the piano and his years at Southport provided evidence for his interest in well-presented choral music in the service but he made no claims to be a trained musician. Ralph Dawson's obituary to Dwelly in *Emmanuel Messenger* in June 1957 quotes a pertinent remark from Edgar Robinson, for many years the Cathedral Choral Conductor.

One of his friends, the Cathedral sculptor, Mr. Carter Preston, said to me last week, 'He had a gift of true imagination which is very rare, very rare indeed. If you struck the match, for him the flame of it soared to the sky.' I remember also how another friend, the late Mr. Edgar Robinson, choral conductor of the Cathedral choir, said the same kind of thing in other words: 'It is a constant source of wonder to me that I, who am a trained musician (whose life's work is music) yet cannot see the possibilities of interpretation of a piece of music half as clearly as does the Dean.'[24]

The Consecration Service with its augmented choir might have been a temptation to try to use too much special music. He resisted the temptation: the music is well-chosen and appropriately placed and woven comfortably into the whole service. The organ music to accompany the entrance of the many processions would have had an exhilarating effect on the congregation. This was the first time that the organ had been heard in public.

The arrival of the King and Queen provided the opportunity for the singing of one verse of the *National Anthem*. The single choir anthem of the service was reserved for the formal entrance of the Bishop into his Cathedral, and Parry's *I was glad when they said unto me, we will go into the house of the Lord*. The words are wholly appropriate for that moment and the music, which had been composed for the Coronation of King George V, is dramatic and exhilarating. Within minutes there was the musical contrast of the singing of *Veni Creator Spiritus* to the plainsong tune as the congregation knelt in prayer and the Bishop traced the Cross and the alpha and omega marks on the floor. The music for the *Rejoicings*, immediately after the consecration itself, had been specially composed by Martin Shaw, and led perfectly into the congregational singing of the Doxology. Only two verses of *Christ is made the sure foundation* were used as part of The Witness of Consecration on Stone and Parchment. Later in his ministry, Dwelly occasionally used even a single verse of a hymn because he felt it appropriate. The main hymn singing came towards the end of the service and as processions began to leave: *O worship the King* had descant by Martin Shaw, *Jerusalem*, *The King, O God, His Heart to Thee Upraiseth*, and finally *Praise, My Soul, the King of Heaven*.

A great deal of special choral music was used in many of the Dwelly later services, but that music was performed because the service required it and not because there was a big choir who wanted to perform "concert" items.

As part of Dwelly's imaginative temperament, the use of symbolism in word, posture, gesture, movement, dress was natural. Symbolism needs to work by suggestion rather than through explanation and, although some explanation was included in the rubrics, within the service symbolism spoke for itself. There were fixed symbolic actions, traditionally part of consecration, that Dwelly was obliged to use but his genius lay in the way he was able to stage particular sequences so making the symbolism potent for the worshippers, both the leaders and the congregation. Page 30 of the Consecration servicesheet provides a helpful example:

"Then the Bishop shall bid the congregation keep silence, kneeling for a space in prayer, on behalf of the Cathedral to be hallowed."[25] At this moment, the Bishop was very much part of the congregation as he knelt on a faldstool several yards in front of the steps up into the chancel.

"Then shall follow the hymn *Veni Creator Spiritus*; the congregation kneeling. As this invocation of the Holy Spirit is being sung the Bishop with his crosier shall make upon the pavement the sign of The Alpha and the Omega."[26] The marking of alpha and omega had been part of consecration from the ninth century. Dwelly had much reduced the size of the marking and by combining the action with *Veni Creator Spiritus* from the Roman Rite and by having the congregation kneeling Dwelly has intensified the significance and made the whole congregation feel their own calling upon the Holy Spirit. The re-marking of the inscription annually continues to this day and is a powerful link from past to present and to future.

"The Book of the Gospels and the Book of the Ordinal shall be carried to the Holy Table before the Bishop.

Then taking the keys in his right hand, and the crosier in his left hand, the Bishop, alone and unattended, and bearing in mind the flock committed to his charge, shall measure the length of the fold of the Temple of God, passing through the Choir to the Holy Table."[27] At the following Dedication he placed the keys on the Holy Table. In pre-Reformation days, relics would have been placed within the altar, a practice which would not have been meaningful or acceptable in Protestant twentieth-century Liverpool. At Dwelly's hand, the whole sequence was strong and culminated in an original prayer.

> O Lord Jesu Christ, who hast the key of David, who openest and no man shutteth, give thy power, we pray thee, to us thy servants, and grant that this house, now opened for thy service, may always be filled with thy presence, and may ever remain a refuge for thy faithful people. Who with the Father and the Holy Ghost livest and reignest, one God, for ever and ever. Amen.[28]

There was no ancient precedent for Bible readings and the five short passages were of Dwelly's choice and instead of all being read from the one spot, they are read from a spot appropriate to the reading: At the place where prayers are said. At the lectern. At the place for the laying on of hands in confirmation. At the Solemnization of Holy Matrimony. At the place of Divine Commission.

In one sense, the most powerful piece of symbolism of the consecration took place at a much smaller, quieter and less spectacular service at 8 am on the Sunday morning, "At the Administration of Holy Communion which is the consummation of the Rite of Consecration of Liverpool Cathedral." To have had the first celebration of Holy Communion at the Saturday service would have made it far too long and presented serious organizational problems. The final act in the presence of about five hundred people early on the Sunday was right.

The actual service book was a remarkable Dwelly achievement and, in that

Opposite Bishop, Archbishop, King and Queen depicted in the window in the North West Transept.

form, possibly without precedent. The service paper went way beyond simply providing the words for the service. The organisational skills show in the way that the service was divided into its various sections. The way the rubrics were written gave congregational guidance as to the symbolic significance of all that was happening. The high quality of the service book was in direct parallel with the high quality of the service and the way that all was performed. "House style" might seem an inappropriate phrase in the context of church services but the Liverpool service papers from the Consecration onwards have a recognizable style. The paper used is always cream of high quality and the printing in black and red. Text is placed generously on the page, well-spaced and with wide margins. Font size varies and there is careful use of short sections in capital letters rather than lower case.

There were twenty-four further services within the Octave: some of special significance like the Dedication of the North Transept in the presence of the King and Queen on the Sunday morning to the Enthronement of the Bishop on the Friday. Apart from some years during the war when there was paper shortage, almost all the Dwelly services up to his retirement in 1955 are stored in the Cathedral archives and their examination will be undertaken in later chapters. Of course, Dwelly's reputation does not depend on one service on 19 July 1924, but the success of this service brought this comparatively unknown Southport clergyman to the forefront of Anglican liturgy as he stamped his style and quality on the worship, just as Giles Gilbert Scott is stamped upon the fabric of the building. What became known as "special services", services arranged for different groups in the community, were to become an important feature of the Cathedral's ministry in the future but even within the Octave can be seen the seeds of this later development in the way in which services were created with particular groups in mind: Parochial Church Councillors, Young People, Freemasons, Mothers' Union and Girls' Friendly Society, Sunday School Scholars, Social Workers, Missionary Workers, The Mersey Mission shipping and Sailors, Free Churchmen, Friendly Societies. It might be interesting to think back to the service for Free Churchmen at the time of the Unitarian controversy to be considered in a later chapter.

The newspaper reports of the day are universally adulatory and far too long to be quoted in full.

> To me ... the austere simplicity of the service seemed exactly adapted to the rugged stateliness of those great red sand-stone pillars and arches. Everything seemed to harmonize and blend ... I must bear testimony to the superb way the ceremonies were organized and carried out without a single hitch. It may be invidious to single any individual for special

praise, but again and again the name of the Rev. F. W. Dwelly, The Ceremoniarius, was mentioned. It was mainly due to his unwearying patience and attention to detail that the processions were so splendidly marshalled. The services, too, on both Saturday and Sunday, were in a large measure the fruit of Mr. Dwelly's knowledge and careful search for ancient treasure store of Consecration service forms. Writing last month, the Bishop of Liverpool said: 'We have received more help in our task than we can easily acknowledge. But there is no difficulty in singling out one who deserves the chief share of our gratitude, namely, the Rev. F. W. Dwelly of Southport.

Church of England Newspaper.[29]

There was pageantry and pomp, as befits all Royal ceremonies; but the atmosphere in the Cathedral was one of mysticism, something spiritual and inexplainable, a kind of service which inspired religious worshippers in medieval ages, and yet so adapted that the Churchmen and Churchwomen of today found in it comfort and inspiration.[30]

The Sunday Times.

An interesting *Church Times* article in September 1924 reported that the interest in the new Cathedral did not diminish after the great services of the Octave.

… there has, so far, been no falling off in the attendance at the services. The Cathedral each time is crowded to the doors – so crowded indeed that it has not yet been found possible to take a collection in the ordinary manner, and the worshippers have been left to make a voluntary offering of money as they pass out of the building … Before the Consecration the attendance at Mattins was almost negligible, and the attendance at Choral Evensong was but scanty – an average of some thirty persons would, I think, be a generous estimate. Today the average attendance at Mattins is about fifty, and at Evensong, the Lady Chapel is usually quite full. This result was, I think, as unexpected as it is welcome. That the Cathedral services on Sundays would continue, for some time at least, to attract very large numbers was anticipated, but no one looked for quite so substantial an improvement in the daily services at the Lady Chapel. Perhaps, equally remarkable, is the congregation which gathers in the Cathedral every Sunday evening at 8.30 for an informal service. This service, as I previously stated, was not even contemplated forty eight hours before it actually took place, and its success was so instant and has been so continuous that it has become quite clear that such a service, at this hour and of this character, has met a popular demand.[31]

It was Dwelly and Raven between them who led these popular services until Raven's departure for Cambridge and Ely. It was only the Second World War and blackout restrictions which brought this service to an end.

Dwelly received an instant crop of letters and gratitude and congratulation from some very significant names in the church.

> Bishopthorpe,
> York,
> July 22nd 1924.
>
> Dear Canon Dwelly, [he was not a canon of course]
> You must allow me to put on record as Archbishop of the Province my congratulations to you for your great share in the conception, and carrying out of the Consecration Service on Saturday. I have already told you what I have felt about it, and how deeply it impressed the King and Queen, and I am sure everyone who was present. I have just been writing to the Bishop, and I have said to him that the service was one full of spiritual movement. The mind and soul were carried along by the processions and ceremonies from point to point, and I saw no hitch in the orderliness and silence and dignity with which all the various processions fulfilled their place. It must have been a great joy to you to see your contribution to what I may call true spiritual art embodied in the service, as it must have been in an even greater degree to the Architect to see his vision embodied in the building. I write hurriedly and most imperfectly, but I am just leaving for Bradford and London, and I am reluctant to do so without sending you a word however inadequate of congratulation and gratitude.
> Yours sincerely, Cosmo Ebor[32]

It is interesting to note that Cosmo Lang has been aware of the joint, almost parallel contributions of Liturgist and Architect, Dwelly and Scott.

Randall Davidson, Archbishop of Canterbury sent his appreciation through his Chaplain, Mervyn Haigh

> What a wonderful triumph for you personally among others the last few days have been! The forms for the Consecration and Dedication represent a sort of *GreyBook* in excelsis, and were a joy to all who were fortunate enough to use them And what an immense amount of thought and work must have lain behind them and all the arrangements and ordering of the whole thing. The Archbishop has already written to the Bishop and the chairman of the Cathedral Committee expressing something of his

great joy and gratitude at all these wonderful happenings, and has there mentioned appreciatively what he knows to be your part in making them possible, and he has asked me just to let you know personally how warmly he appreciates what you did …[33]

On 27 July a grateful Albert Augustus wrote expressing his friendship, admiration and thanks:

My Dear F. W. D.
After the praises of Kings, and the preference of Queens for your company, to that of any other, the unstinted admiration of both Archbishops … I shall not attempt to be one who 'also ran' to quote the Earl of Derby.

I overheard your speaking of your mother and father to their Royal Majesties and I resolved forthwith that one of the Royal copies of the Service must be given to them … make it so, my boy.

Bless you for all you have been to me this week of modern Pentecost.

Tell your mother that the King said no service had ever before in his life made him realize that he had a religious heart.

I expect they will think, as I did that day, of Isaiah LX.

    Yours ever!
        Albert Augustus[34]

Giles Gilbert Scott's involvement with Liverpool Cathedral had begun over twenty years before and on the eve of the Consecration his achievement was marked with a knighthood. From 19 July 1924 onwards, the achievements of two men were inextricably linked because the newspapers on 1 December announced Dwelly's appointment as a Canon and the next day a letter arrived from the Archbishop of Canterbury.

I rejoice to see that you are to have a fitting status in the Cathedral of Liverpool. We all owe you gratitude for your notable efforts in connection with the Cathedral and the ministry therein from its start onwards. May you go from strength to strength.[35]

He did.

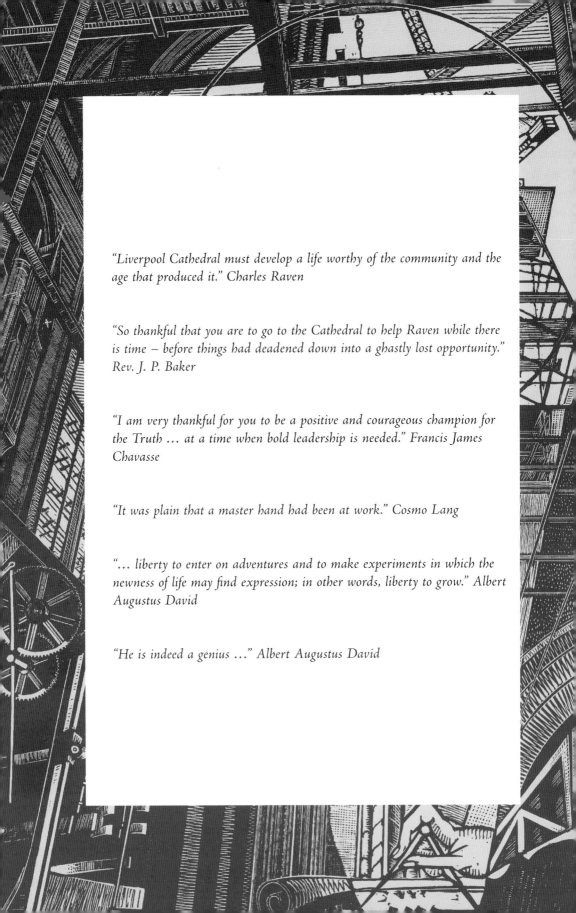

"Liverpool Cathedral must develop a life worthy of the community and the age that produced it." Charles Raven

"So thankful that you are to go to the Cathedral to help Raven while there is time – before things had deadened down into a ghastly lost opportunity." Rev. J. P. Baker

"I am very thankful for you to be a positive and courageous champion for the Truth … at a time when bold leadership is needed." Francis James Chavasse

"It was plain that a master hand had been at work." Cosmo Lang

"… liberty to enter on adventures and to make experiments in which the newness of life may find expression; in other words, liberty to grow." Albert Augustus David

"He is indeed a genius …" Albert Augustus David

F O U R

Canon Dwelly

I N J U L Y 1 9 2 4, though Ceremoniarius for the consecration services, Dwelly was simply the Vicar of Emmanuel, Southport and it was to be seven years before the formal foundation of the Dean and Chapter with Dwelly as the first Dean of Liverpool with the immense responsibility of leading the Cathedral through its formative years. This chapter must examine his performance between 1924 and 1931 in an attempt to decide why he was offered the Deanery. The years were crucially important both for the Cathedral and for Dwelly. All the excitement and freshness of consecration was over and the building had to accommodate the daily and weekly services in a meaningful manner and, from 1925 onwards, building had to move forward on the construction of the tower and the central space. This was the time when the Cathedral clergy had to be able to rise to the challenge of Radcliffe's words in 1924. "The laymen of Liverpool are giving you this great gift: I sometimes ask myself if you will be able to use it."[1]

This was also the time when Dwelly might have returned to spend the remainder of his ministry as a very imaginative, popular and successful parish priest in an appreciative and rewarding parish. This was not to be and the newspaper of 1 December 1924 carried the news that Dwelly was to be appointed to a new canonry.

The responses to the news from some of the national leaders of the church gave evidence of Dwelly's standing in their eyes. Randall Davidson, Archbishop of Canterbury wrote immediately:

I see that you are to have a fitting status in the Cathedral of Liverpool. We all owe you gratitude for your notable efforts in connection with the Cathedral and the ministry therein from its start onwards. May you go from strength to strength.[2]

Chavasse, his former Bishop, wrote from his retirement in Oxford:

I am delighted to see in this morning's *Times* the announcement of your appointment to a residentiary canonry in Liverpool Cathedral. It is a fitting crown of the great services you have rendered to the Church in the Diocese, and will, I am sure, prove highly acceptable to Clergy and Laity alike. I am very thankful for you will be a positive and courageous champion for Truth … at a time when bold leadership is needed.[3]

The Church Times reported that the news "has been spontaneously welcomed throughout the Diocese … He will be a great acquisition to our already first-rate Chapter, and all schools of churchmanship in the diocese are equally delighted by the Bishop's action."[4] His clergy colleague, Rev. J. P. Baker, Vicar of Mossley Hill who had written so enthusiastically at the time of the consecration wrote again immediately:

My dear Man,
I am simply delighted. With all my big people dying off here and my best friends amongst the clergy going further afield I was beginning to despair. I am so thankful that you are to go the Cathedral to help Raven whilst there is time – before things had deadened down into a ghastly lost opportunity. Now I am happy about things. You and Raven will be brothers, and others will come to your aid in the course of nature.[5]

Possibly the most significant letter was written by Charles Raven and marked the start of eight years of the closest active cooperation and a friendship which remained strong, despite geographical separation, until Dwelly's death in 1957.

My very dear future colleague,
I am delighted that the decision has come so quickly and that we are to have you here in May. It is not only a tremendous joy that we shall be in closer touch, but a vast encouragement and relief. The past three months have pretty well worn me out. I've done 92 addresses etc on all sorts of unusual subjects since Oct 1st, and I have months more of the same sort ahead. You know, I think, how lacking in initiative are all the staff except the Bishop: they are dear delightful folks but very ordinary, and Liverpool at present demands more than the ordinary. So I've just had

to go all out – and after last spring and Copec I'm running on a rather rackety engine. I hope I haven't trodden on the old men's toes or seemed to take on too much myself; but the risk had to be run. Now with you coming I can sing a sort of Nunc Dimittis. You will bring exactly what we want – vision and executive power – and in directions that I can't touch. This means hope and security – just when I was beginning to feel a bit depressed.

You will be terribly missed in Southport: but will after all be in close touch with that part of the diocese. Liverpool will give you scope, and you will know the conditions – that one can't handle the Cathedral as if it was a parish church.

Coop rang me up last night to say that he had just heard and to assure me that the diocese would be unanimous in welcoming you. My

Canon Dwelly

goodness, dear man, what dreams we may, please God, be able to realize. Anyway we have our opportunities. I am proud to feel that I had a small share in creating it.

Ever yours

  Charles[6]

Before his installation as Canon, he undertook a six week lecture tour in America at the suggestion of Rev. G. A. Studdert-Kennedy who had recently returned from a similar tour. The plan was that he should visit thirty dioceses and speak in sixty four different places. The letters remaining in the archive give evidence of his great popularity and his ability to work under extreme pressure. The text of only one of his deliveries has been retained. He preached in the partly-completed Cathedral of St. John the Divine in New York and some of the newspapers carried the text. He spoke on "the sacramental meaning of a Cathedral". The final paragraph is a great challenge to any group responsible for the establishment and running of any cathedral and is clear indication of Dwelly's awareness of the significance of the cathedral experience.

> But the man who has passed beyond individualism, the man who has discovered the fulcrum of his personality, will build for future generations a place large enough to be a place of unity sufficiently lofty that there is no sense of limitation for the growing soul. When there is nothing that is not of the best and where everything suggests the compelling power of that intimate revealing other one who loves to redeem man so that all may be free to reach up to the highest in the lovely and the true as well as the good.[7]

There are thirty-eight letters in the Dwelly archive relating to the American visit and from these alone it is clear what an impact he made and how many people wanted his comment or assistance in the devising of services. There was a suggestion for an American edition of *Acts of Devotion* and the offer to publish his lectures if he so wished. Individuals asked for help on the devising of services, for suggested books on prayer and for additional material for use at the Eucharist and the Choral Offices. He made at least one radio broadcast but there is nothing of the text preserved in the archive. Dwelly always seemed to be able to make immediate and powerful impact on individuals and groups and this was certainly the case on the American tour: "Even though you have not been long in this neighbourhood, the good that you have done has been of such stimulating effect that we are all getting the advantage of it."[8]

Fortunately, Dwelly had never lacked unbounding energy and his early years at the Cathedral provide ample evidence. One of the most important parts of

Cathedral worship was "the 8.30". This was not a service invented at Liverpool but it was introduced by Raven in the summer of 1924 at very short notice and Dwelly shared the responsibility for these services with him after his installation. In character, nothing could have been further from the magnificence and pageantry of the Cathedral's famous special services but the 8.30 drew people from across the diocese. It was timed as a late Sunday evening service so as not to draw worshippers away from Evensong in their own parishes. The congregation, many of them teachers and young professionals, filled the Cathedral. As people gathered, there was half an hour of organ music from Cathedral Organist, Harry Goss Custard, but it was not a choral service. A couple of congregational hymns, prayers and a central address was the regular shape of the service. Some distinguished speakers, lay and ordained, accepted invitations to preach though Dwelly and Raven were the most regular speakers. Frederick Dillistone, who knew both Raven and Dwelly, commented on the importance of the service and these contrasting priests in his biography of Raven.

> … what held the congregation together was undoubtedly the double influence of two strangely disparate personalities. Dwelly would lie flat on one of the great oak tables in a darkened vestry before going in to preach; Raven would pace up and down, almost physically sick, rehearsing his words and gestures like an actor. Dwelly captured the audience by his sheer informality of approach, talking to them as his friends for whom he really cared, about important matters which they had not sufficiently taken into account. Raven captivated them by his looks, his gestures, his command of his subject, perhaps most of all by his ability to relate the great themes of the New Testament to personal needs and duties.[9]

Another cooperative venture mainly in the hands of Raven and Dwelly was the Bishop's experiment in post ordination training. Liverpool was the first diocese to set up formal continuing education for the young clergy. They attended Tuesday morning sessions in the Cathedral led by Raven and Dwelly. Owen Chadwick (1990) was to describe Raven as "the most powerful preacher in all England"[10]. He could be devastatingly scornful of youthful pretensions in his students but was greatly appreciated by a future Archbishop, Michael Ramsey, when he was a curate at Liverpool Parish Church and attended the Tuesday session.

As the regular weekly round of Cathedral services and events was being established on St. James's Mount, Dwelly's reputation across the whole country was extending and at least some of the demands on his time and expertise are reported on in the archive materials. There is an intriguing letter from the Old

During the twenties and thirties, Choir, Presbytery and Sanctuary were the central stage for the performance of the liturgy. The eastern crossing and the transepts had to seat the congregation.

Palace, Canterbury, November 2 but without a year. From what was to follow shortly in Canterbury, the year might well have been 1928.

> My beloved Dwelly,
> Ever so many thanks for that, your latest and most brilliant effort – I set it down in front of the A at his desk and made him go right through, to the accompaniment of my commentary of praise in the best Grey Book style! He was really impressed and added 'It's such splendid language too' …
>
> So does the light radiate – and Liverpool lead the way in interpreting the Gospel and revising all Revised Prayer books and claiming for religion like another Hildebrand – compared to which even such cathedral building is bagatelle.
> Love and power to you.
> MH [Mervyn Haigh, Chaplain to Randall Davidson, the retiring Archbishop of Canterbury][11]

The Dean of Canterbury at that time was George Bell who was a friend of Dwelly over many years and shared in the imaginative invention which was such a feature of Dwelly's best work. As Dean of Canterbury he was responsible for planning the installation service for Cosmo Lang as the new Archbishop. Bell had consulted the Bishop of Truro and the Dean of Wells over some fundamental modifications to the service: Augustine's chair was moved from the Corona onto a platform at the east end of the nave and the enthronement was to be at the hands of the Dean and Chapter of Canterbury rather than the Archdeacon. From correspondence it is evident that Dwelly had played a central role in the writing of and the rehearsal of the service itself. Lang was delighted with the results:

> The Dean … had taken infinite pains about all the arrangements. He had given full play to his vivid imagination in order to make the ceremony symbolic not only in ecclesiastical life, but of the national life, including the Arts. Hence the series of independent representative processions, admirably marshalled. Never certainly had any previous Archbishop been enthroned on a scale of such colourful and symbolic significance.[12]

In Lang's biography, recognition for the success of the service is given to the Bishop of Truro, the Dean of Wells, Percy Dearmer and Fred Dwelly, although the letters to Dwelly after the event would suggest that Dwelly's role had been of paramount importance, not only in devising and writing the service, but also in the rehearsal and running of the great national event.

> The Deanery
> Canterbury.
> 5 December 1928
>
> My dear Dwelly,
> I hardly know how to thank you – I could not thank you sufficiently for all you did to make yesterday's service so marvellous. It would have been very different, and very much less impressive in all sorts of ways without you and your brain and your art and imagination, and your outstanding executive and organizing capacity. Indeed you made the whole difference both in composition of the service, and its most thrilling moments, and in the arrangement of all the details of the ceremony – plan, marshalling, processions, robing, bringing the greater chapter in and so much class that I cannot fault it! Thank you a thousand times. And you were so magnificent to work with – for everyone else. The whole church owes you a great debt: I rejoice that you and I were so brought together, and worked

so radiantly for so noble an occasion. The opportunity was a wonderful one – and thanks to you wonderfully used. It was a work of the whole church of Christ …

Let's work together before long.

    Yours ever gratefully,

      G. K. A. Bell[13]

The letter is handwritten and difficult to decipher but the spirit of it so resembles the letters Dwelly received after the Liverpool Consecration service four years before. Lang had written to Dwelly immediately after the 1924 Liverpool service and he wrote to him again on 5 December, the day after his enthronement, a letter very similar in content and tone.

> I must send you a word of special thanks for the invaluable help which you gave to the Dean and Chapter in the arrangements for the memorable Service yesterday. I heard from many quarters that the movement of the various Processions went without the slightest hitch and with great dramatic silence and solemnity. It was plain that a master hand had been at work. That this great drama should have been presented with such moving solemnity and without any kind of interruption is, I am sure, greatly due to you, and I have my own debt of gratitude because the smoothness of the whole great proceeding contributed much to my own peace and quietness of mind. With much gratitude.
>
>   Yours sincerely,
>
>   Cosmo Cantuar.[14]

Albert Augustus David seems not to have been able to attend the service but his wife did and there is an important letter to Bell on 6 December showing clearly the Bishop of Liverpool's acknowledgement of the genius of Liverpool's first Dean.

> My dear Bell,
>
> You and Canterbury are very welcome indeed as far as Liverpool is concerned for our contribution to your great day, and I am sure that Dwelly enjoyed bringing it. He is indeed a genius and you can now measure our good fortune here. To whom much is given – We never grudge his services elsewhere. It is only that he is one of the few people I know who can make persons walk straight, and that he has a sense of fitness in liturgical form, and nearly always in language; but he is full of the spirit of worship and never allows me to forget that highest significance of what we are doing.[15]

Albert Augustus fully understood that in Dwelly Liverpool had genius to match that of the architect of the Cathedral. Though later the relations between Bishop and Dean were to break down completely, at this period they were great friends and appreciated just what the other brought to their new Cathedral and there were significant liturgical achievements even before the formal establishment of the Dean and Chapter and they were important growing years for Dwelly as he came to understand the great architectural instrument he was called upon to use. He was learning about his Cathedral but he was in working contact with others: there was no danger that Liverpool became isolated in its newness. The influence of Dwelly upon the worship in other cathedrals has so far been totally neglected and demands exploration before there can be any comprehensive assessment of Dwelly's influence and achievement.

Dwelly's short written comment to Bell was so typical of him: "Oh but it was fun playing with all the spirits of the past and bringing out of the treasures things new and old." "Fun", that same word he used when talking to the King about the Liverpool Consecration service. Dwelly's very human delight in what he was called upon to do shows itself in the freshness and humanity of his liturgy to be examined more closely in later chapters.

Archbishop Cosmo Lang in the Chapter House at Canterbury Cathedral, part of his installation as Archbishop of Canterbury in December 1928.

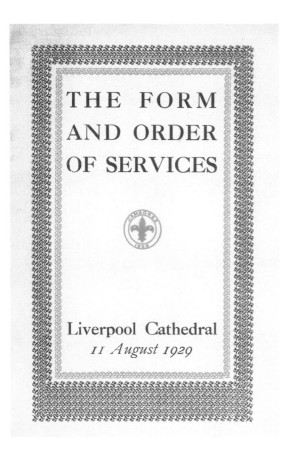

Early example of large format, and frequently elaborate, service papers.

THE FORM
AND ORDER
OF SERVICES

Liverpool Cathedral
11 August 1929

The archive contains the text of at least part of a lecture delivered by Dwelly in March 1928 on the subject of Art and Worship. It is type-written with hand-written amendments. Raven had deep respect for Dwelly's skills as the creator of fine services but admitted that Dwelly could not always adequately explain the thinking which lay behind some of his best work. The text is an intriguing mix of the practical and specific with the intangible and the less clear though there are patches of poetic insight. He was clear in his belief that worship "is not a thing you can make" but "you may take part in it – enter into it … Then you glow."[16] Art and worship were closely associated in his mind: "Art must be that expression which will enable me to reflect as St. Paul would put it, the glory of the Lord from glory to glory."[17] We know of the importance of the art of the musician to Dwelly and he considered the fundamental question which must be central to the musician: "What will connect that perfect connection of thought and emotion which will enable the whole body of people to be caught up in the stream of worship?"[18] Surrounded by the great art in the Cathedral building he was determined that worship should not be fettered by past association: "The Cathedral is not to be tied down to the traditions of old, but must make traditions of new worshipful material."[19] The implications of this statement are to be observed at every stage of his Cathedral ministry and the high quality of everything offered had to be beyond question: "Expression must be of the highest and the Cathedral must make a tradition of the highest."[20]

For Dwelly the Cathedral building was of the highest quality and he was clearly influenced by this as for him the very building exuded worship

> We shall not at the Cathedral, as indeed no one ought to, we shall not submit art to mere association, or we shall fail in linking art to worship in the Cathedral, which of all modern buildings that I have seen, is essentially in stone and metal and needle-work a combination of the subtle expressive joys and the many arts with that great spirit which we call worship."[21]

Dwelly was sensitive to the involvement, or otherwise, of the members of the Cathedral congregations and he saw any coldness and lack of involvement as behaviour unworthy of the building:

> And if 300 people stand and have no motive and no sense of expression of that which is the highest within them – utterly cold – then there will be on that occasion nothing that is worthy of the building and the service will not really achieve anything with God. It is that achieving unity with God which is the purpose of worship.[22]

This is an important statement in the light of the hundreds of special services arranged for a wide range of professional bodies in the city, or children's groups or musterings of members of the armed forces. He was always keenly aware that the relevance of the service must be recognized by all attending and aware of the demands which his services were making: "You must bring a great big open heart and mind that desires to be caught up into the stream of worship, and then you will know something of the divine expression."[23]

The final section of the lecture focused upon what he called "the line of thought that governs us when we are planning services"[24] and the first ingredient he highlighted was good manners. This is maybe not a phrase one would have expected but it lies behind so much of the elaborate processional ceremonial in the Cathedral. Directness was also highlighted: a quality which despite elaborate ceremonial demands a simple relevance in the service: "There is always a directness which must come in: you cannot allow individual mysticism in corporate worship. You must keep, as it were, your feet on the earth, that is, always keeping in close touch with life as it is."[25] Directness was linked in his mind with a basic simplicity which exists at the heart of his services and never swamped by elaborate ceremonial. Again reference was made to the building itself: "Simplicity, and a sane outlook then follows quite easily, and you will find that with this ordered simplicity and sanity – just as the arches of the building leads up to the roof of our Cathedral, leads up to simplicity and peace – so in the order of worship everything moves with that same strength."[26]

The security and discipline he felt within Cathedral worship gave him the confidence to break new ground: "you can make all sorts of adventures. Liverpool Cathedral is a place where adventure surplants you in the stone and metal and needlework."[27] He was appreciative of Scott's adventurousness in his design and details and believed the worship should have the same spirit: "In the same way the spirit of worship always calls for adventure." This lecture text may well be incomplete and not clearly argued but the sentiments there expressed reveal themselves constantly in his work for the next twenty-seven years.

Dwelly's name was known at the highest levels in the country. On 30 April 1929, Bell wrote telling Dwelly that he was to leave the Deanery at Canterbury to become Bishop of Chichester. From that letter it was clear that Bell would have been supportive of Dwelly's elevation to Canterbury. "I saw the PM and told him my various "ploys" – which made him say 'You want an active man there!' How happy I should be if such a one as you were to come."[28] This was not to be and "Dick" Sheppard was appointed to Canterbury to the delight of both Bell and Dwelly. It was clear that the future Bishop wanted the skills and experience of his Liverpool friend to ensure the high quality of the enthronement service: "Are you coming on June 11? It would be very nice if you would; and I hear you are most kindly looking at the Consecration Service. Have you the Chelmsford Enthronement Form? I hear that was excellent – and your handiwork. I want the Chichester to be good too."[29]

A letter came to Dwelly from Cosmo Lang[30] on 1 May 1929 headed "Confidential":

> My dear Canon Dwelly,
> I have been asked to be responsible for drawing up a Form of Service for the Special Thanksgiving in which the King will take part on some Sunday later in the Summer. You have given so much time and thought in these recent years to the drawing up of Special Services for special occasions that I would be grateful to have some hints or suggestions from you.
> It is desired that the service should be short and very simple, and it

would probably take place in Westminster Abbey. It is proposed that it should be broadcast throughout the country; also that the Form of Service should be communicated to the Dominions so that the whole Empire can take part. The idea is that there should be some hymns, whose words and tunes would be familiar to the people everywhere, at the beginning and at the end, and that there should be no specially elaborate music. It will have to be decided whether the Te Deum should be sung which naturally in view of its traditional position of worship in the Church on occasions of Thanksgiving I would personally wish. Also it is desired that there should be either a short Psalm or a selection of verses from the Psalms, and a short Lesson or a selection of verses from Holy Scripture in the same way as there is such a selection for the Easter Anthem and the Comfortable Words in the Holy Communion. And there must be some special Thanksgiving Prayer for the King's recovery.

Would you be so kind as to put your expert mind upon this most important but most difficult matter? I must try to get help from many sources and I naturally turn to you. I would be very grateful if you could give me some suggestions as soon as possible as it is desired that the matter should be well in hand by the middle of this month.

Yours very sincerely,

Cosmo Cantuar

The Cathedral Consecration service had been of great national importance but this service was going to be celebrated world-wide and needless to say Dwelly was able to send a detailed response within a fortnight. Fortunately, a carbon copy of the letter remains in the archive but not copies of "the enclosed suggestions". It is interesting to note the way Dwelly has thought about different ways in which the service might be celebrated in different places.

My Lord Archbishop,

In further reply to your Grace's letter, I have the honour to submit the enclosed suggestions. I also send copies of the background that we have for such services, with copies of the prayers then used in case you may wish to refer to them. Also a draft suggested Litany of Deliverance, which may be of use in parishes where the Service will be in the Open Air and the Choir will proceed thereto singing a Litany.

I am sorry to have been so long in forwarding these suggestions to your Grace – a love of pruning my stuff is the reason, and even now could do much more polishing with advantage.

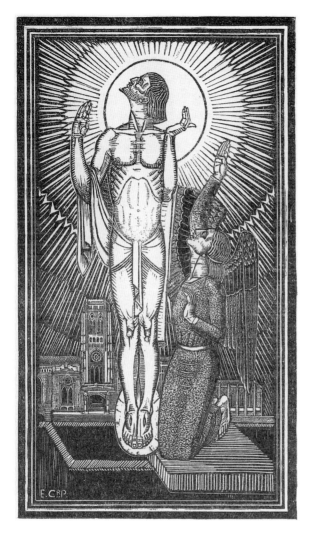

Work typical of Edward Carter Preston whose engravings frequently embellished Cathedral service papers.

Allow me to explain the ordering of the suggestions I have tried to remember:

(a) To retain a connecting link with the earlier forms of thanksgiving for a King's recovery.

(b) To develop the same along the lines of your own teaching of 'hallowing grace', thus bringing the mode of approach to God into harmony with our day.

(c) To acknowledge before God that synthesis of the ways of healing which our age is learning to appropriate and to do so in a way which will not be entirely unacceptable both to the medical profession and to our praying folk, and that without missing the glory of the transcendent.

(d) That the healing of the King is due in some measure to the martyrs of science and therefore a mention of them comes in the Prayer before the Blessing.

(e) To slightly adapt one of the ancient blessings so that Broadcast listeners may be conscious that you have not forgotten those 'scattered upon a thousand hills.' Some people will come to give thanks: others will listen to give thanks.

If I can be of any further service to your Grace,

I beg you will command,

Yours dutifully,[31]

The receipt of this letter was acknowledged the following day by the Archbishop. There are so few Dwelly services for which posterity is allowed to examine the thoughts behind the finished product that this is an important statement and certainly underlines the previously stated ideas about the importance of preparation for Dwelly's liturgy.

While Dwelly was at work on this service he received a letter from 10 Downing Street offering him a prestigious London living.

> I am desired by the First Lord of the Treasury to write to you with reference to the living of St. Edmund the King, Lombard Street. This living which is vacant by the death of the Rev. G. A. Studdert-Kennedy is in many ways of special importance and, after much careful consideration, the Prime Minister has come to the conclusion that he cannot better serve the interests of the Church as a whole than by offering to submit your Name to His Majesty for appointment to it.[32]

There is no evidence to suggest that Dwelly announced himself to be interested in the post. He had become Vice-Dean in 1928 in addition to his post of Canon Ceremoniarius but the offer does indicate the significance of Dwelly's standing within the wider Church. During the 1920s Dwelly had important contacts with many influential figures within the Church from Archbishops downwards. He had first met H. R. L. "Dick" Sheppard when he was Vicar of St. Martin-in-the-Fields and their friendship continued until Sheppard's death. The Rev. Percy Dearmer, one-time Rector of St. Mary's Primrose Hill and author of *The Parson's Handbook* was twenty years Dwelly's senior but the two became good friends. I cannot find evidence of their first encounters though we know from Nan Dearmer's biography of Percy that it was Dwelly who first encouraged Dearmer to become involved in the work of the Life and Liberty Movement.

Through that organisation came the focus on Prayer Book revision and the two men were part of the small group responsible for the publication of *The Grey Book*[33] in 1923. His name was on the list of those who were consulted over the research which led to the Consecration service in 1924 though Dearmer had not visited the Cathedral and was not present at the service.

In 1906, with Ralph Vaughan Williams as the musical editor and Dearmer as words editor, the first edition of *The English Hymnal* was published. As a result of Vaughan Williams's suggestion, Dearmer appointed Martin Shaw as Organist and Choir Master at Primrose Hill. The book set new standards in both words and music but it was regarded as being a High Church hymn book. It was the Life and Liberty Movement which helped give rise to Dearmer's next successful hymn book, *Songs of Praise*. Work began on it in 1924 by Dearmer, Rev. A. S. Duncan-Jones, Dwelly and a few others. Nan Dearmer in *The Life of Percy Dearmer* quoted Dwelly: "When the differences on 'Church before Party' happened, P. D. took the line that we can sing people into putting Church before Party even if we cannot teach it. He maintained that the religion of the people is the religion of hymns – we must have Songs of the Spirit."[34] The joint editors of the new book were Dearmer and Martin Shaw and *Songs of Praise* was published in 1925 and, thanks to the support of Albert Augustus David, was adopted as the official hymn book for the new Cathedral, even though he had ordered *Hymns Ancient and Modern*. Some of the ideas behind the publication of the first edition were expressed in the Preface, Revised Edition:

> the present generation desires to enter into the heritage of noble religious verse which is ours. That heritage is ours by right of the great poetry in which the English tongue is supreme, by right also of the magnificent prose which since Coverdale and Cranmer has formed the substance of our Christian worship, though it was never adequately matched by the hymns in common use. Our English hymns, indeed, few of which are earlier than Dr. Watts and most of which were the product of the Victorian era, have not been altogether worthy of the English Bible and English Prayer Book; and the bulk of the tunes to which they were sung illustrated a period of British music which the musicians of today are anxious to forget ...[35]

Songs of Praise was enormously popular and influential, not least because it was adopted for use in many schools and colleges. It was certainly appropriate that a new hymn book should be seen to be right for worship in a new Cathedral whose liturgy aimed at freshness and vitality where Walt Whitman's *Pioneers* became a popular hymn, regularly used at ordination services. The choice of

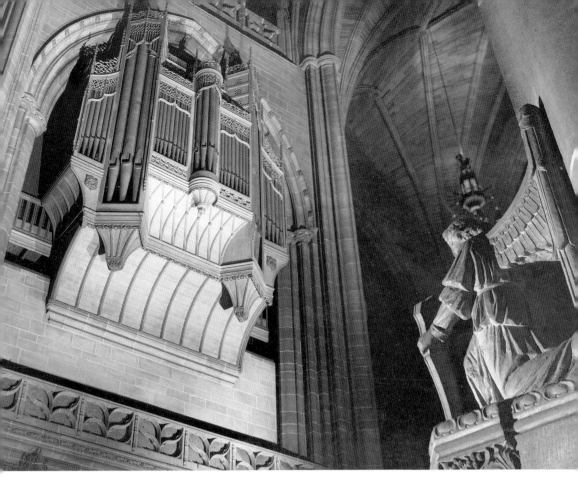

A dramatic view of one of the organ cases. The instrument from the start was designed to be an important visual feature in the building as well as producing wonderful sound.

this new hymn book was typical of Dwelly and his wide interest in, and use of, poetry within the services.

Bishop Chavasse had been clear in his idea of a large building capable of holding large congregations for "diocesan and popular services" and the new Sub-Dean was responsible for many of these before the formal establishment of the Chapter. Dwelly had an opportunity on 11 August 1929 to fill the Cathedral in celebration of the Boy Scout movement with which he had been actively involved since his days in Windermere. The Scout Movement had decided to celebrate the twenty-first year of its foundation with the first Boy Scout World Jamboree, to be held in Arrowe Park on the Wirral, in the Diocese of Chester. Liverpool Cathedral, and not Chester, was chosen as the venue for the religious celebrations on Sunday 11 August.

Dwelly prepared a twenty page service booklet to cover services at 11am, 3pm and 4.45pm. The morning service was basically choral matins The 3pm was titled "The People's Service of Thanksgiving and Prayer for the Gift of the Scout Ideal" and began with a request from Sir Arnold Rushton, President of the Liverpool Association of Boy Scouts, to the Bishop to pronounce a blessing, almost certainly composed by Dwelly.

> May the Almighty God Bless you with the courage of the Spirit of Youth.
>
> May he give you firm faith eager hope and unconquerable charity
>
> That being fortified with such defences of his grace you may be partners with the pioneer of universal peace even the Young Prince of Glory Jesus Christ.

The Bishop preached the sermon; there were four hymns, and three pieces of special music from the choir: one verse of *Jesu, joy of man's desiring* by Bach, *Hallelujah* by Beethoven, and *Expectans Expectavi* by Charles Wood – this cut by Dwelly who felt that it ought to end at the musical highest moment on "To Thy great service dedicate" – such a decision was typical of Dwelly's autocratic rule. There was a suitably short litany prayer.

The 4.45 Service of Welcome to the Scouts of the World was created for the scouts themselves drawn, as the service paper indicated, from 33 countries, 5 dominions and 27 countries and islands of the colonies. The service began with two stirring hymns, *Jerusalem* sung to Parry's tune and *Mine eyes have seen the glory of the coming of the Lord*, to the Battle Hymn of the Republic tune. A lengthy procession of the flags of all nations, and dignitaries from the city the Scout movement, and the Cathedral moved up into the Presbytery. The Bishop's sermon was flanked by two verses of *All people that on earth do dwell* and two verses of *Praise the Lord! Ye heavens adore him*. A short reading was followed by the Scout Law and Promise, the prayers and the singing of *I vow to thee, my country* sung kneeling as prayer. After the blessing, the *Song of the Pioneers* and *Praise, my soul, the King of heaven* brought the service to a close. The service had a simple grandeur which was wholly appropriate to the young people for whom the service was created. Statutory Evening Prayer was said in the Lady chapel at 6pm and the 8.30 took the form of a Service for Parents and Friends of Scouts, preacher the Chaplain to the First Windermere Scouts, F. W. Dwelly.

The Cathedral Builders' Quarterly Bulletin for September 1929 commented briefly but enthusiastically on the event.

> It would be difficult to exaggerate the impression made by this service on those fortunate enough to be present. The dignity of the ceremonial, the imaginative simplicity of the Order of Service, and the beauty of the music, combined to strike a chord to which every individual in the vast

congregation responded as one man, and the sense of spiritual unity bridging all barriers of creed and language, race and colour, was so moving as to be almost overpowering. As long as the Cathedral is put to such noble use as this, there is no need to be despondent for the future.[36]

In 1930 the Cathedral celebrated the Jubilee of the establishment of the diocese and that year happened to coincide with one of the ten-yearly Lambeth Conferences at which the bishops from across the world-wide Anglican Communion gathered in Canterbury. There is no evidence within the Cathedral to indicate why these two important events should have come together, but between 12 and 14 July, over two hundred bishops travelled to Liverpool. All the arrangements were meticulously handled and the clarity of the organization was typical of Dwelly. There is a beautifully produced limited edition booklet carrying a welcome from Bishop and Lord Mayor and the full time-table details of the week-end. Nothing was left to chance:

> Afternoon tea will be served during the journey. Guests will please leave their baggage on the train on arrival. They will find it in their hosts' houses on their return from the Banquet. The Cathedral guests masters travelling on the train will assist in labelling the baggage, and will complete any arrangements necessary to relieve guests of care during their visit.[37]

After a visit to the Cathedral and dinner at the Town Hall, over one hundred and ninety, carefully numbered cars, drove the guests to the respective vicarages in which they were to spend the night. The address at the dinner was given by the Bishop who made an interesting comment on jubilee and liberty; a comment highly relevant to Dwelly and his work within the new Cathedral.

> You will join us in the Cathedral tomorrow in giving thanks for the fifty years' work, and to answer the call of the jubilee for the proclaiming of liberty, not to do what we like, not liberty to try things because they are new, but liberty to enter on adventures and to make experiments in which newness of life may find expression; in other words, liberty to grow.[38]

The forty-six page service book provides a good record on the character and quality of the whole which can be viewed under the same headings as the Consecration service: preparation, organization, structure, choreography, text, music, symbolism, service paper.

There is deep preparatory thought about the whole nature of the service which was a unique bringing together of two celebrations, the fiftieth year of the foundation of the diocese and the gathering of the Lambeth Conference

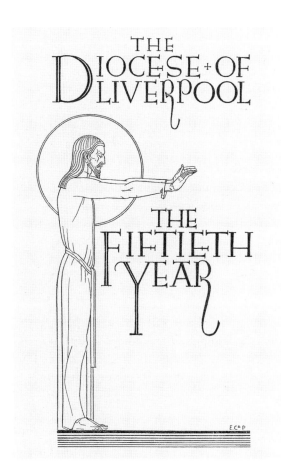

THE
DIOCESE + OF
LIVERPOOL

THE
FIFTIETH
YEAR

E.C.ᴬ.P.

Carter Preston design for an important service paper. The figure is reminiscent of his stone figures both inside and outside the Cathedral.

Opposite Plaster models of two Carter Preston carved figures.

Bishops. His central idea was the Jewish tradition of Jubilee: "In the fiftieth year ye shall observe Jubilee ... ye shall proclaim liberty." Before the start of the service an ancient form of synagogue service was used.

The organization both before and during the service was immaculately carried through, from the moment their Lordships boarded their train at Euston, to the dignified and orderly processions and the use of Bishops from different parts of the world to lead sections of the service. *The Church Times* was to comment: "... an ungrudging tribute must be paid to the way every detail was thought out. Each person knew his place and duty. There was not a hitch from beginning to end. The 'stage management' was perfect."[39]

The varied service was clearly structured with organ music from 2 to 2.30, the short piece of Jewish synagogue worship leading up to The Preparation and the short anthem, *This joyous day*. The words of The Hallowings were drawn

One of a whole series of Carter Preston prints featuring phases of the building programme and used extensively in service papers.

from several sources, almost certainly by Dwelly, and set to music by Edgar Robinson. The service was constructed from seven sections: The Welcoming, The Testimonies, The Magnifying of the Name of God from Age to Age, The Celebration of the Fiftieth Year, The Memorial, The Sermon, and Intercessions and Blessings. Choreographically the service by its nature was simpler than the Consecration but it involved huge processions, and appropriate movement of The Archbishop of York, the Bishop of Liverpool, and other Archbishops into the Sanctuary. The only lengthy prayer was the Bishop's Solemn Prayer of Hallowing. Much of the rest of the text is of a responsory nature, with good use being made of a range of speakers from around the church and the world. *The Church Times* declared the service to be "the most memorable service held in Liverpool."[40]

The music used was listed on the service paper and had the wide range typical of Dwelly choice.

This Joyous Day	Henry Lawes
The Hallowings	Set by E. C. Robinson
Anthem Amen	J. S. Bach
Welcoming Amen	Orlando Gibbons
City of God	Faux Bourdon by Martin Shaw
Te Deum Laudamus	Vaughan Williams
The Invocation	G. P. da Palestrina
Let Saints on earth	Ravenscroft's Psalter
The Old Hundredth	Arranged for trumpets and Drums, E. C. Bairstow
The Enablings	Gustav Holst
Pioneers	Martin Shaw
Ewing	Descant H. Goss Custard

As was typical of Dwelly services, the music was woven into the whole fabric and never sounded like a musical interlude. The symbolism underlying the whole service is highlighted in part of the text of the Hallowings sung before the formal commencement of the service:

Sound the trumpet.
Ye shall hallow the fiftieth year.
Thou shalt cause the trumpet of the Jubilee to sound about the tenth day
Of the seventh month.
Ye shall proclaim liberty.
Stand fast therefore in the liberty wherewith Christ has made you free.

The service was a balanced reflection of the world wide nature of the Anglican Communion expressed through the presence of its Bishops and Archbishops and also the localised Liverpool celebration of the first fifty years of the diocese.

The service book needs to be viewed alongside the smaller format *The Diocese of Liverpool. The Fiftieth Year*. In essence this was simply details of timetable arrangements for the whole visit of the Bishops together with short notes of greeting from Albert Augustus David, Bishop, and Lawrence Holt, Lord Mayor. The booklet is embellished with three wood cuts by Edward Carter Preston who clearly designed the whole thing. The Service book was forty six pages long: carefully divided by means of headings into sections and printed so that the text had space on the page and led the worshipper comfortably into the movement of the service. It was more than a form of words to be used just for the service: it was a memorable souvenir document to be taken away and pondered upon. Legacies to the Cathedral by the end of the twentieth century gave evidence to the fact that Cathedral service sheets were collected and carefully stored. Dwelly's performance as a highly organised and imaginative liturgist was observed by most of the leaders of the Anglican Communion world-wide. To many of them it would have come as no surprise that in 1931 Dwelly became the first Dean of Liverpool.

A clutch of papers, largely undated, in the archives is evidence of Dwelly's working contacts with a number artists – in particular Vaughan Williams, Gustav Holst, Martin Shaw, John Masefield, and Edward Carter Preston, and, of course, Cathedral Organist, Harry Goss Custard. Important musico-logical research relating to Holst and Vaughan Williams manuscripts has been undertaken by Judith Blezzard.[41] The organ had been incomplete at the time of the Consecration and it was 1926 before the whole instrument was dedicated at a service in the afternoon of 18 October. A unique Willis organ and a highly talented organist were to become vital elements throughout Dwelly's ministry. The first piece played at the service was Bach's Fugue in E-Flat Major and the event was recorded by the instrument's chronicler J. Meyrick-Roberts.

> It was now that the organ was heard for the first time, the organist giving a dignified rendering of the great master's music, building up the tonal qualities of his instrument to a superb fortissimo. This was followed by the choir singing *Praise of all created things* [Gustav Holst] a highly effective work, and well sung. The organist now made more music, playing in brilliant manner Basil Harwood's *Paean*. In this work many tonal combinations were displayed; contrasts of one department with another; and a gradual working up of tone towards the exciting finale, until the cathedral was ringing with joyful sound; when, suddenly, the ear was arrested by a new tone. The mighty tuba magna, with its colossal and glorious voice, was heard for the first time.[42]

At 7.30 that evening was the first of six recitals to be given during the week by Harry Goss Custard, Charles Macpherson, St Paul's Cathedral, W. G. Alcock, Salisbury Cathedral, and G. D. Cunningham, City Organist, Birmingham. The first recital and the Dwelly service which proceeded it is commemorated every year on the Saturday closest in date to 18 October. It is not unusual to have a thousand people present from all parts of the country. The cooperation between Dwelly and his Cathedral musicians can be traced throughout the period of his ministry. Having a great musical instrument at his disposal Dwelly used it with imagination and flair, occasionally added to with tubular bells, trumpets and drums.

Through the work he did with Percy Dearmer over the compilation of *Songs of Praise*, Dwelly had working contact with a number of writers and composers, and, from letters in the archives, particularly with Ralph Vaughan Williams, Martin Shaw and John Masefield – twenty five letters in all, many infuriatingly undated. What was clear was that Dwelly was not simply content to use existing material as part of the Cathedral services. Martin Shaw prepared a setting of the Easter Anthems and dedicated it "To the inspirer, F. W. D".

My dear Freddy,
Here's the Easter Anthem – I hope it's something near what you want. All the choir responses at the beginning should go briskly. Of course it ends really with 'even so in Christ shall all be made alive' and any attempt to make the Gloria a big thing would be anticlimax so I have just given it simply. I would very much like to come to the last rehearsal

Edgar Robinson and the choristers in the Ambulatory in the 1930s.

and performance. I'll pay my fare if you can get me put up I'm too hard up for hotels.

You will see I have done two trumpet foreshadowing fanfares before the great words each time – first 'Christ is risen from the dead' and last 'In Christ shall all be made alive'.[43]

A service on 9 February 1930 brought together the work of Poet Laureate, John Masefield, and Martin Shaw. It was at first envisaged by Dwelly as a masque for performance in a service immediately after the sermon. The eventual service was called *Kinship with the Sea* and was celebrated in another very fine service paper containing the following explanation.

The purpose of this service to offer to Almighty God our thankful remembrance of the life and work of all who follow the calling of the sea, and the spirit in which their work is done.

To that spirit of disciplined adventure we owe the existence of this Port. Our prosperity depends on it. As we cherish the best in it, so we shall best serve our country. As we share it, so shall nation be brought nearer to nation in mutual understanding and the common service of mankind.

And it is the gift of God.

Today we ask that He may preserve and strengthen it in all seafarers, make it manifest in the whole life of our city, and use it for the welfare of this country and the peace of all the world.[44]

In a biographical book, *Up to Now*, Martin Shaw revealed his responses to Dwelly.

The most wonderful experience of this sort that I have ever had was at Liverpool recently. That arch-designer, Canon Dwelly, dropped in at my house casually one afternoon and asked me to compose a wedding anthem for the first wedding that would ever take place in Liverpool Cathedral, and named a date a few days ahead. Such is his way. He also suggested that I should pay a visit to Liverpool and preach in the cathedral, for the consecration of which I had composed all the special music. Though, as I have said, I feel in a pulpit like a fish out of water, such is Dwelly's hypnotic persuasiveness that I feebly consented ...

There is no one who can 'bring it off' like Dwelly ...

On the Sunday morning Dwelly took me all round the Cathedral from on high and I had the unique experience of hearing my own anthem, splendidly sung by Goss Custard and his fine choir, float up to me. They also sang my *Pioneers*, which Dwelly told me was always now chosen for ordinations. Who but Dwelly would have thought of Walt Whitman's being sung at an ordination.[45]

In 1928, Vaughan Williams composed his *Te Deum in G* and inscribed it, "Composed for Liverpool Cathedral and dedicated to Albert, Bishop of Liverpool". Though until 1931, Albert Augustus was Bishop and Dean, it was Sub-Dean Dwelly who was devising the services: there was never a Canon Precentor in his time. It was clear to everyone that this new Cathedral was not slavishly following what all other Cathedrals were and had been doing. As Scott had not slavishly followed medieval Gothic models, though working with the Gothic forms, so Dwelly was not being held to any straight performance of Prayer Book services, though he was not abandoning all that was excellent in Cranmer's work.

Through the influence of Dwelly, Edward Carter Preston, a multi-skilled artist, became involved in the establishment of the Cathedral, responsible for much of the design of special service papers and as the main Cathedral sculptor between 1931 and 1955. He and Dwelly became close friends and he was certainly drawn towards the work of the Cathedral through what Dwelly was doing. The Bishop wrote to Sir Frederick Radcliffe on 8 January 1931:

> You will have heard of our discovery of Carter Preston, the sculptor here. Scott was much impressed by a piece of his work which Dwelly showed him, and has given Carter Preston a commission for Stations of the Cross in a church in a building somewhere. I rather hope you will get designs for him for your 4 figures. Carter Preston who is the finest kind of agnostic wandered into the Cathedral on Christmas Day and said to Dwelly afterwards 'You came very near to the ineffable'. He is a kind of prophet like Blake and lives very high.[46]

A letter from Dwelly to Radcliffe on 17 April 1931 would seem to indicate that Dwelly had been influential in Carter Preston's appointment as Cathedral sculptor.

> So that is why Carter Preston wanted critical books on the early church – he is a reticent man and never breathed a word of this to me, but I loaned him the latest critical books as well as Lightfoot and Chase. I am glad you are considering him for some figures, though I do not know that his style fits in with Phillips, indeed I should doubt it. All the work of Carter Preston that I have seen in sculpture is far more severe and

Carter Preston depicted himself as one of the figures in Liverpool's War Memorial in front of St. George's Hall.

restrained but it may be that you are looking for this, if so, then you have found him.[47]

Carter Preston's Art Deco figures fit perfectly into Scott's timeless Gothic building in the same manner as did Dwelly's fresh and imaginative services.

It is known from Julia Carter Preston, one of Edward's daughters, how frequently Dwelly visited their house and studio at 88 Bedford Street South and how close was the friendship of the two men. Scott regarded Carter Preston highly as a "collaborative artist" in the whole Cathedral project. In a letter to the sculptor on 25 March 1942, Scott wrote "I think the Dean, you and I are the happiest of men in our work."[48] In the same piece Sharples quoted another letter of 7 May 1937, p. 29, "I think you can take it that there are only four people need to seriously considered in regard to aesthetic matters, viz.: Sir Frederick

Radcliffe, the Dean, yourself and myself."[49] Dwelly, Scott and Carter Preston recognised the freshness of approach which was essential to all their work as liturgist, architect and sculptor. Sharples quotes a fragment of an undated letter to Radcliffe, in which Carter Preston stressed the importance of not being fettered by tradition but able "to live in one's own age as Sir Giles has done in his treatment of the Gothic elements and as all artists have done who were worthy of the name."[50] There is no evidence that Dwelly felt himself to be liturgically fettered by tradition either. The working friendship of these three men has left an indelible mark on the Cathedral – in the fabric and in the worship.

Alex Bruce wrote, "Cathedrals, and their role, were news in the 1920s, interest being in part generated by the establishment of Liverpool Cathedral, as well as Bennett's work at Chester."[51] Dean Darby of Chester died in office a fortnight before being 89 in November 1919 and his successor was announced on 31 March 1920: he was Frank Bennett, Rector of Hawarden. Bruce's book does not make a single reference to Dwelly. He does, however, stress the great importance nationally of Bennett's determination that cathedrals should be open and free and always open between services on Sundays. Trevor Beeson declared, "During the next seventeen years he transformed the life of Chester Cathedral and, by demonstrating what a cathedral might become, exerted an enormous influence on cathedral life throughout the country."[52] Before his coming to the cathedral he admitted his own lack of understanding of a cathedral and its staff. "I do not think it ever struck me that I had anything particular to do with the cathedral or the cathedral with me. I regarded it, probably quite wrongly, as a place where leisured people received largish salaries and I looked upon deans as the fortunate occupants of an office in the Church of England that could easily be dispensed with altogether."[53] This seems to be an extraordinary misjudgement from one who was to become one of the most significant deans of the twentieth century. *The Nature of a Cathedral*[54] was one of the most important statements about the nature and function of a cathedral. Bennett was strongly critical about what he observed in operation in many of the cathedrals he visited and by 1925 he had visited all but three.

"… what began as a Family House of Prayer for all, has come to be regarded as something very like the special property of a small corporation." We have lost sight of what cathedrals were meant to be."[55] The problem of outdated statutes was noted in the first chapter of this study and they concerned Bennett: "Obsolete statutes are a very awkward basis to work on and in many particulars they should be brought up to date."[56] What he had to say about a dean and his cathedral was prophetic as far as Dwelly was concerned: "If the Bishop ought frequently to be in his cathedral, the dean ought to live in it … He must be more than the Bishop's 'senior curate' in the cathedral."[57]

Dwelly's skill in devising meaningful ceremonial must surely have been appreciated by Bennett for whom "ceremonial is doctrine in action" "… cathedral ceremony … tended to pomposity, to honouring unduly individuals, to emphasizing meaninglessly inappropriate items in the service. Had a tenth part of the labour and skill that has been put into cathedral music been put into cathedral ceremonial, had that ceremonial maintained our English Use, of which we have no need to be ashamed, the Church of England would have been saved for half or more than half of its present confusion."[58] While not commenting on the Liverpool ceremonial, Bennett declared his admiration for Liverpool Cathedral: "How spaciously and splendidly we can build a cathedral church, Liverpool stands as a monument today. Given the necessary vision, our children will build as never was builded before."[59]

Bennett must have known of Dwelly's artistry and skills in the devising of ceremonial. From the Order of Service we know that he was present at the Consecration service in 1924. Also from the 1931 service paper we know that Bennett was not a "Guest from the Northern Province" at the service to mark the foundation of the Dean and Chapter. The Dean of Manchester was, even though Manchester is further away from Liverpool than is Chester. I can produce no evidence to suggest why two such forward-looking Deans so close geographically should not have shown their affinity. The only possible suggestion I can offer arises from Giles Scott's animosity towards Bennett. Scott had undertaken all the architectural restoration work at Chester from 1907 until the arrival of Bennett who dispensed with Scott's services on rather flimsy grounds. Scott and Dwelly became great friends and Dwelly was famously supportive of his friends.

Both Deans were appreciative of good music in the services of the church and Bennett[60] was particularly appreciative of Choral Evensong. "If the music is well chosen, it affords refreshment and uplift to often large congregations, and provides a great and proper field for the rendering of church music both old and new."[61] Both deans placed great value on their musicians and especially of the boys of the choir: "The children of our choirs are perhaps the greatest of our responsibilities."[62] From the way his choristers spoke and wrote of Dwelly and from the way he tried to keep in touch with them for years after, particularly when they were serving in the forces during the war, there is no doubt that Dwelly felt the same sense of responsibility. Bennett expressed his concern for his former boys after their voices had broken. "Something can be done by an Old Choristers' Association, especially for older ex-choristers. The boys of 15–20 something like a Guild of Servers seems to me to be absolutely essential, if those who are responsible for them are to have alert but quiet consciences."[63]

He clearly had in mind "some official position to carry them through their adolescence."[64] By 1931, Dwelly had done something about this through the foundation of the Cross Guild, the team of former choristers who still play a key role at all choral services.

Dwelly was made a Provisional Canon in 1925 and four years later he became Vice-Dean. His great services both within the cathedral and nationally received high praise and it must have been in many people's minds that he would eventually be offered the Deanery. He was a popular personality, brilliant with children. Nan Dearmer remembered the popularity of his conjuring tricks with the Dearmer children in their holiday house in the Cotswolds. Patrick David, son of the Bishop wrote to me, "... as children we adored him – like a favourite uncle. With his interest in youth work and adventure training he had a way with young people."[65] And Mary Raven daughter of Charles, wrote, "... he arrived on our doorstep our first Christmas with a sack (literally) full of presents for myself and my three siblings ... he loved children and knew we were strangers in the city."[66] Mrs Diana Luck, daughter of the Bishop, wrote to me of him as "that very colourful character who played such a prominent part in all our lives. When I was about nine I invited him to be my Godfather – my own having died – and he carried out his duties with tremendous flare – he was always full of ideas and fun and used to take my brothers and myself to so many interesting expeditions."[67]

The early years of any community, particularly a church or a cathedral, are always going to be of crucial importance for sound growth, and the development of trust and confidence of the wider community. Though Albert August David acted as both Bishop and Dean from 1924 to 1931, all the archival evidence indicates the central importance of Dwelly in helping to establish the worshipping life of the new community. So many of the qualities listed in the Apologia are discernible in his work. His powers of friendship, kindness and generosity revealed within the whole community. Dynamism, adventurousness, dedication, strength, originality, powers of leadership and administration were all being developed and revealed during this period of apprenticeship for high office. From the start his artistry underpinned all the great services and he was building his working relationships with a number of artists and the end products were services which were dignified, memorable and relevant. Dwelly and Raven, the theologian, forged a strong working partnership. During the early years of the 1930s, Dwelly's theological stance became more clearly discernible with the establishment of the Deanery and some of the unfortunate public controversy which was to arise.

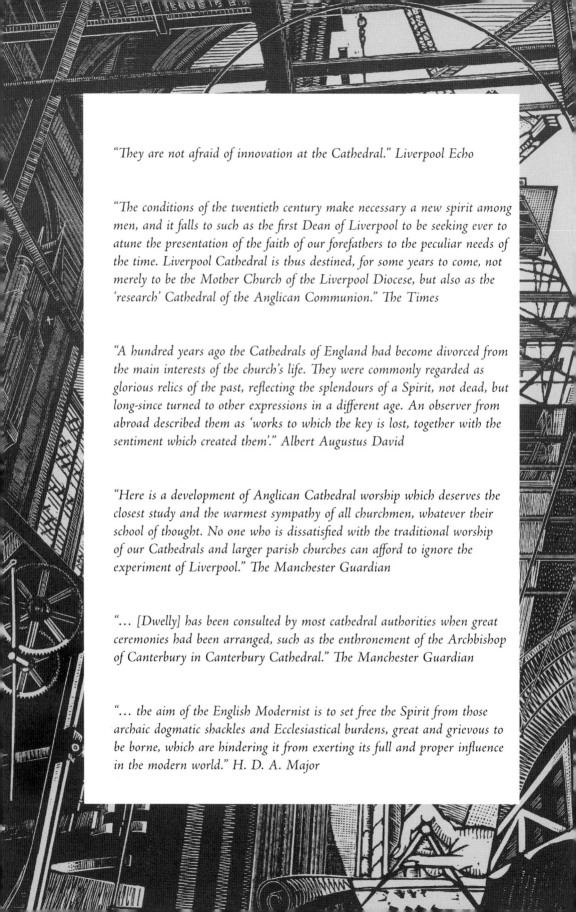

"They are not afraid of innovation at the Cathedral." *Liverpool Echo*

"The conditions of the twentieth century make necessary a new spirit among men, and it falls to such as the first Dean of Liverpool to be seeking ever to atune the presentation of the faith of our forefathers to the peculiar needs of the time. Liverpool Cathedral is thus destined, for some years to come, not merely to be the Mother Church of the Liverpool Diocese, but also as the 'research' Cathedral of the Anglican Communion." *The Times*

"A hundred years ago the Cathedrals of England had become divorced from the main interests of the church's life. They were commonly regarded as glorious relics of the past, reflecting the splendours of a Spirit, not dead, but long-since turned to other expressions in a different age. An observer from abroad described them as 'works to which the key is lost, together with the sentiment which created them'." *Albert Augustus David*

"Here is a development of Anglican Cathedral worship which deserves the closest study and the warmest sympathy of all churchmen, whatever their school of thought. No one who is dissatisfied with the traditional worship of our Cathedrals and larger parish churches can afford to ignore the experiment of Liverpool." *The Manchester Guardian*

"… [Dwelly] has been consulted by most cathedral authorities when great ceremonies had been arranged, such as the enthronement of the Archbishop of Canterbury in Canterbury Cathedral." *The Manchester Guardian*

"… the aim of the English Modernist is to set free the Spirit from those archaic dogmatic shackles and Ecclesiastical burdens, great and grievous to be borne, which are hindering it from exerting its full and proper influence in the modern world." *H. D. A. Major*

The establishment of the deanery

O N 29 June 1931 the Dean and Chapter of Liverpool Cathedral were incorporated by Order of Council – making history once again, because such an event had not taken place since the Reformation. Peart-Binns[1] in Michael Smout, *Four Bishops of Liverpool* reported that three names were before the Crown as nominations for the Deanery: Charles Raven, 'Dick' Sheppard, and Fred Dwelly. On 2 July in a scribbled note Dwelly recorded how he received the news of his preferment:

> At about 11.30 – a telegram came and Chris read it to me from the bishop saying Ramsey Mac has set his mind at rest – this means I am to be Dean of Liverpool – so the desire of a life came true – I know I am not big enough for it but I am grateful to God and my first wish is that Mother and Father should know for it is to them I owe my desire to please God my love for Church and nature and they would be so proud. Few men get the whole desire of their life and so great a privilege – none could be more grateful. Now for morning prayer and prayer habit in the freedom of the gift which God has given to the world through love – it is that I must develop for it is his gift.
>
> The words that come to me as I kneel down and pray shall be my resolve.
> This shall be my rest for ever
> Here will I dwell for I have a delight therein
> He shall be my son and I will be to them a father.[2]

In the light of some things which were to happen within a short time, Peart-Binns's judgment on the part the Bishop must have played in the appointment is pertinent: "In the appointment of the Dean, David allowed affection to override intellect where intellect should have won."[3]

Dozens of letters of congratulation on the appointment remain in the archive from a wide range of people from Liverpool, Southport, Cheltenham, Chard and right across the country. "Dearest Dwelly, Of course we all knew you were to be Dean, and the only possible first Dean; but, oh, I am so glad it has all gone through. Thank God for Liverpool. We never meet but I love you just as ever. I am such an asthmatic crock now that I can hardly move or talk. Your loving, Dick" [H. R. L. Sheppard][4] "Very many congratulations on this opportunity to make your genial self of even greater value than ever. Bernard Chavasse."[5] "Chard is very proud of you, and how delighted your dear little mother would have been. Grace Chaffey."[6] "Liverpool … looms largely in the *Church Times* and the references to yourself always arouse my interest, and, inasmuch as you are one of the few persons connected with the Cathedral of whom nothing is said in disparagement, invariably give me pleasure. It seems a very long way back to the old days at Queens' and so few of my contemporaries has risen in fame. A. F. S. Harding."[7] "Cathedrals should be centres of enthusiasm and not ecclesiastical almshouses and I know your influence will radiate out from Liverpool into those Cathedrals which at present only cumber the ground. I dropped into Westminster in the middle of Evensong some time ago, about 6 people, a vast choir and a man with a loud bass voice proclaiming 'even Aaron's beard' that was all I could hear, the repetition was monotonous and the spiritual uplift small. Bishop of Fulham."[8] "I congratulate you on the office and I am only so glad that the Church will have a real live wire to electrify some of our old Deans! Rev. Arthur Thornhill.[9] "Now at last the world shall see what a Dean should be – and do. Haveloch Davidson."[10] "… your friends among Free Churchmen desire very warmly to congratulate you on what is no less a joy to your friends because they have seen it coming for a long time … You belong to a wider community than your own branch of the church. We all claim you, and esteem you very highly for your worth and your work's sake. Nichol Grieve."[11]

Dwelly's appointment was positively received in the papers; *The Post and Mercury* for 21 July summed up his achievements in a paragraph:

> Canon Dwelly is the author of *Acts of Devotion*, a book which had run into five or six editions before the name of the writer became generally known. This work is accepted in practically all the dioceses as standard and guide. He has been entirely happy in his work at the Cathedral – indeed he radiates kindly geniality. He is a great reader, exceptionally

well informed on church history, and closely in touch, too, with the theological and social thought of the day. His sermons impress by their frank and helpful handling of the difficulties of everyday life, and by their unfailing note of high idealism. As a speaker to children, Canon Dwelly has few equals.[12]

It goes without saying that the services associated with the establishment of the Dean and Chapter would be well-researched, imaginative and splendid. Despite all the time needed for planning and preparations, the Cathedral services continued throughout the summer with a number of special events, including such diverse services as South Division of Liverpool Brownies, the Anniversary of the Consecration, the Dedication of the Chavasse Memorial, Celebration for the Royal Lancashire Agricultural Society, a Special Musical Service and Celebrations of the Centenary of the British Association for the Advancement of Science, with sermons by Rt. Hon. J. C. Smuts, Sir Oliver Lodge, and the Bishop of Birmingham.

The central service for the Foundation of the Dean and Chapter, while containing elements of a formal legal nature, also provided ample opportunity for Dwelly's inspirational and dramatic qualities. The Preparation, the true start of the main service, was held in the Chapter House where the Chapter Clerk read a greeting from the Archbishop of York, William Temple, a greeting which made reference to the special qualities of worship associated with Liverpool Cathedral.

> Liverpool Cathedral has won a distinctive place in the life of our church, not only by its splendid beauty, but by the varied expression which it has already given to Christian aspiration and worship. I have no doubt that it will, under the new conditions, continue to lead the way in freshness of devotional expression and in helping the new world of our time and the times that are to come to offer its best in the service of Almighty God.[13]

The judgement of the Archbishop, to my mind, reinforces the central focus of this whole study – the complementary qualities of the Cathedral building and the worship within its walls.

Dwelly welded this short legal prelude effectively to the main service out in the Cathedral largely through his use of the choir and the processions. Having led the Bishop to the Chapter House the choir, while standing outside, sang two verses of the hymn, *The Church of God a kingdom is*. After reference to Bishop Chavasse, the choir sang a single verse of *Let saints on earth in concert sing*. The decision to use brief references to well-known hymns was a common Dwelly device, a device which resembled the use of an image in poetry. This distant music would have been audible to the whole congregation, so making them feel a part of the Preparation ceremony, and the choir's procession from Chapter House to stalls was accompanied by their chanting of biblical verses, one of Dwelly's conflations. The words themselves were wholly appropriate and the chanting of the words as part of an entry procession would have created a strong atmosphere of expectation and devotion.

The choir singing of the hymn *Come down O Love Divine* to Vaughan Williams's. *Down Ampney* preceded the main procession of ecclesiastics. It is interesting to note that the Dean's Own Sea Scouts were part of his entourage – young men from the First Windermere Troop which he had founded over twenty years before. In the light of problems which arose later, the presence of "a representative of the non-anglican ministers", the Rev. F. Heming Vaughan, Minister of the old Toxteth Chapel (and a Unitarian) was significant in revealing publicly Dwelly's and David's inclusiveness and ecumenical spirit. Lawrence Holt, prominent Liverpool Unitarian, was also part of the processions. The Bishop's words relating to the non-anglican cathedral supporters were reported in *The Times*, 5 October, 1931 "Many who professed no allegiance to the Church of England were eager with us that Liverpool, the home of great enterprises, should provide as nobly for witness of God and for his worship as any of its civic and commercial purposes. There you have a blending of Christianity and citizenship strong enough among us, then and now, to transcend from time to time most of the barriers that divide us, and to reflect a blessing alike upon the city and the Church."[14] Liverpool Cathedral had been built, not by a religious order, but by the people of the Liverpool Diocese and there has always been a strong sense of "civitas" in many of the great special services.

Canon Thompson Elliott, Vicar of Leeds, and former Vice-Dean of Liverpool was reported in *The Daily Post*, 10 October, 1931. He summed up admirably the qualities which Dwelly always achieved in his great cathedral services.

> It is, of course, in accordance with expectation that the ordering of the service should be beautiful and impressive, and that in its use of ancient precedent it should be intimately in touch with the modern life and thought, with touches of originality which made the old new. In this inspired use of ancient words in close relation to modern needs, combining dignity and beauty with a certain homeliness, if one may so phrase it, Liverpool Cathedral is setting a standard which is already having a deep influence throughout the Church of England. Ceremonial there is, stately and even at times elaborate, but every detail in it has a meaning, and that meaning is not obscure to any sympathetic member of the congregation.[15]

The sentiments expressed about this service in 1931 are in line with many of the reports of Consecration in 1924 and numerous other examples of Dwelly's work throughout his ministry in the cathedral.

The main part of the service began with the choir singing the anthem *They buried him, and then the soldiers slept*, specially composed for the occasion by Martin Shaw. Quite typically, the music played a prominent part in the service but its appropriateness to the moment militated against any feeling that the service was a splendid concert. There were two further anthems to the music of Bach, the Supplication was to the music of Palestrina, and three versicles in the versicle and response were sung by a single treble voice. The service made effective reference back to the dedication of the Lady Chapel and then to the Consecration itself by surprisingly but appropriately singing verses from *O Come, all ye faithful* and *Jesus Christ is risen today. And did those feet in ancient times* and *O worship the King* gave ample opportunity for congregational participation, while back at the Chapter House the choir singing of *O for a faith that will not shrink* must have been a most prayerful, quiet ending to the whole service and mirrored the singing of *The Church of God a kingdom is* at the start of the service.

The whole event exemplified Dwelly's strong structural sense which enabled him to design an effective service. His skill with words enabled him to write a meaningful and memorable text. His choreographic sense handled the processions and general movement which the service demanded. His musical sensitivity greatly enhanced the whole and the worshippers at that famous service must have left the Cathedral with the sense that the Dean had once again revealed his imagination, his flair, his sense of drama, his unerring ability to conceive of a service which would match the building and relate powerfully to the worshippers.

The subject headings used for the examination of the Consecration Service can be applied to this service also. In a pastoral letter to all the clergy in the diocese, the Bishop gave some explanation of the preparation and research which had gone into the service.

> By careful selection of material from manuscripts we have been enabled to follow a true line of development from the day when King Edward-the-Confessor attended the foundation ceremony of the Cathedral at Exeter. We have drawn particularly from manuscripts that give a reference to what was done at Canterbury, Lincoln, Exeter, Salisbury, Worcester, Evesham, and Hereford. But there are points where precedent cannot help us because the procedure for installing the Dean and Chapter of Liverpool is a new one.[16]

Dean Dwelly.

F. W. Dwelly. Dean.

Careful selection had to be made from past precedent so as to be appropriate for the time.

Thus at Exeter after the signing of the parchment, the Principal Chapter will be led to the occasion, our newly installed Canons will receive and wear a simple Chapter habit. It will be my part to declare to the people and present to the Dean the Cathedral Statutes, in the drafting and submission of which to the Privy Council the main responsibility was mine. I shall also deliver to the Dean *The Book of the Fellowship of the Lord Christ*, which governs my relationship with the Cathedral as its Visitor, together with the keys which were entrusted to me at the consecration. When I pass to him the 'incomplete chalice', I charge the chapter through him to 'fill up the sufferings of Christ in His Body.' This old ceremony will cover a new meaning for us in the unfinished Cathedral awaiting completion at our hands ...[17]

An article appeared in *The Guardian* on 9 October 1931 by the Dean of Chichester who had himself been a part of the whole ceremony. What he had to say is highly relevant to the influence Dwelly and his work in Liverpool Cathedral had on a wider canvas. The first part of the article goes way beyond a critique of the service and touches upon territory central to this study.

A puzzled and distracted world is looking hungrily for some embodiment of the ideals and hopes that it cherishes. There is a profound conviction abroad that vision is what the peoples need, if they are not to perish, at least as much as knowledge. Moral qualities alone can overcome the sense of helplessness that increases as man finds himself unable to cope with the mighty forces of selfishness that his amazing discoveries seem only to have made more powerful.

Some such feeling as this – unspoken but potent – is surely an element in the renewed interest of English people in the great cathedrals that has now for a number of years grown with an increasing momentum. These great fanes stand as a magnificent witness to a superb faith. Wistfully men turn to them as they tread their courts in their thousands with unuttered questions. 'Has the inspiration gone? Can it be recovered?' The great ceremony that took place in Liverpool last Sunday was a bold assertion that it can. The bishop in his sermon quoted the judgment of a foreign observer to the effect that the cathedrals were 'works to which the key is lost, together with the sentiment that created them.' Fifty years ago, he reminded his hearers, there were men in Liverpool who rejected that judgment. They believed that the key could be found again. Throughout those fifty years they had held to their conviction, and it had been justified. As the Bishop of Glasgow and Galloway said in the afternoon service, though the original founders of Liverpool Cathedral had, for the

Liverpool Cathedral entry procession depicted in a railway poster in 1937.

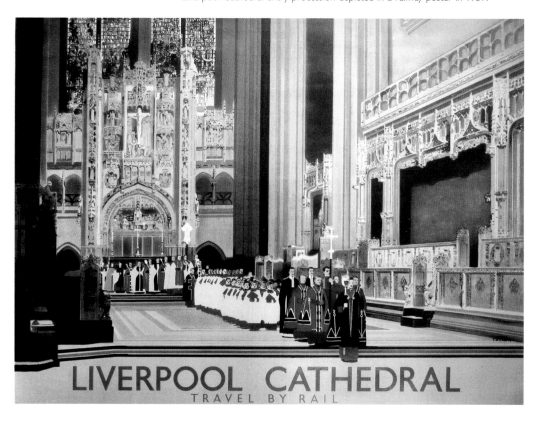

most part passed away, they had seen of the travail of their souls and been satisfied. The installation of the Dean marked an important stage in the process. Sufficient of the building to make a real church had first to be created. The next step was to establish on a permanent basis a staff strong enough to make use of the great opportunities that are open to a cathedral on Merseyside, within doors open to welcome the traveller from the East and from the West.

The rediscovery of an inspiration that had been potent in the past, and its adaptation to modern life. That is the keynote of Sir Giles Scott's great building. It is the keynote of the uses to which it has been put. It sounded throughout the week's celebrations that have clustered round the establishment of the chapter. The ideal found expression in the vesture of the ministers, in the words of the liturgies, and in the music that accompanied them. All were marked by freshness and originality. Yet in no part was there any feeling of the merely theatrical The 'stunt' impulse was absent, because those who were responsible for the worship had drawn from ancient wells, but had used their draughts of living water to fertilize the plant of sincere conviction. They had something they passionately wanted to say. They were able to say it with discretion and dignity because they knew that what they wanted to say was but part of

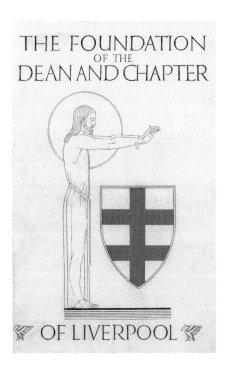

a greater thing that had always been, the onward march of a force that had shared all that was best down the ages. To achieve this is never an easy task. To have done it in Liverpool is almost a miracle. It is a city of ancient prejudices, where every diversity of religious expression finds it hard to forget old antagonisms. The prejudices, doubtless, accounted for the absence of certain visible elements that would be looked for in almost every other cathedral today. Thus the bishop wore his scarlet chimere and not a cope for the other members of the cathedral body the eye of an artist had chosen a habit that blends aptly with the red stone and light oak of the building. Canons and singing boys wear a cassock of dull red, and over it surplices of unbleached

Canon Charles Raven reading at the service to mark the establishment of the Dean and Chapter in October 1931.

Holland; the canons having, in addition, almuces of black stuff, edged with grey fur, and lined with dull red, forming a hood behind. Something was needed to break the clash between this scheme and scarlet and black and white of the bishop and his chaplains. The solution was found in the gorgeous green gowns of the vergers, for which the scarlet of the continental 'Suisse' affords a precedent, though no one has ever thought of developing the idea before.

The music had the same character of ancient inspiration and modern life. Before the imposing procession moved out from behind the altar, the distant strains of the Gradual Psalms could be heard, Plainsong alternating with faux-bourdons. As it came in sight it was greeted by crashes of sound from trumpet and drum, fanfares composed by Mr. Martin Shaw that provided a thrilling opening; Dr. Vaughan Williams's melting *Come down, O Love Divine*, completed the procession, and, when all were in their places, the Hymn of the Dedication, written for the occasion by Dr. John Masefield, was heard – *They buried him, and then the soldiers slept.*

This was sung to a setting by Mr. Martin Shaw. Composed almost at the last moment, it achieves astonishing success. Words and music alike should secure it a place among Easter anthems. The best of the well-known hymns, Parry's *Jerusalem*, the *Old Hundredth, Adeste Fideles, Hanover* and two of Bach's loveliest anthems all fitted into the picture.

The liturgy moved round certain points. First a Supplication for all who had a portion in building or serving the cathedral, instinct with the spirit of devotion that Orthodox worship retains. The foundation of the Dean and Chapter by the delivery of the Statutes was followed by a blessing from the bishop on the kneeling canons grouped in front of the altar. Dr. Dwelly's first act as dean was to confirm the creation of the College of Stewards under the Presidency of Lord Derby, and to install Lord Crawford, Dr. Masefield, and Mr. Martin Shaw as representatives of a distinguished body that includes General Smuts, the Bishop of Chichester, Sir Stanford Downing, Professor Lloyd Morgan, Professor J. L. Myers, and Mr. F. C. Eeles. The whole company then moved down to the chancel steps for the installation. The dean's stall is returned, but stands by itself with two seats for assistants on either side. The chancellor, Dr. Raven, having recited the King's mandate from a sumptuous scroll, placed Dr. Dwelly in his seat, with the customary formula, to which was added a turn of phrase characteristic of the whole service, 'May you apprehend that for which you have been apprehended by Christ Jesus'.

The climax was reached in the symbolic acts that followed. Three small boys, who through the long ceremony had patiently carried the keys, a chalice covered with a corporal, and a Gospel book, came forward with their charges. 'Take heed that the door of this fold be ever open to the sheep of his pasture,' said the bishop as he delivered to the dean the keys of the cathedral that had been entrusted to him when it was consecrated, and the Gospel book, 'and do thou see that food for their spiritual life is here prepared according to the Word of these Holy Gospels of our Lord Christ.' Then the bishop delivered into the hands of the dean the unfinished chalice, as his voice rang out in the words, 'The Cup of Blessing.' There followed a space of silence, deliberate, prolonged. It was the numinous moment, to which Christina Rossetti's words, 'God the Spirit so hold us up, that we may drink of Jesu's cup,' sung to Monk's March in a way that breathed tenderness and strength, were the exactly right response. It was not surprising that the new dean found difficulty in saying the words allotted to him. 'By this know you, O Father in God, that we of this Cathedral church, one and all, are ready to share with you the joy of life through death, and of achievement through suffering, to drink of the outpoured and partake of the broken, that the Church in this diocese of Christ's vineyard may rise to newness of life and ever have cause to rejoice in its dedication'.

There was one great act still to come. After the dean had taken his place in the seat appropriated to him on the south side of the altar, the bishop, with the Chapter grouped kneeling behind him, broke forth into the Solemn Prayer of Hallowing. Preceded by the Salutation and the Sursum Corda it was cast in Preface form, and was set to an original, but quite pleasing tone. This part of the service, and others also, gained greatly from the fact that the bishop has a resonant singing voice, which he used valiantly. A quiet and contrasting close followed when the dean 'alone and unattended' moved down the long choir and at the chancel steps led the great congregation in a simply said Lord's Prayer.[18]

The Dean of Chichester had commented on the fact that the traditional priestly vestments of the Church were not worn but he commented very favourably on the dress on the large number of what he called crucifers and vergers. Dwelly devised a system whereby the Cathedral had a large and reliable team of laymen to play a leading role in Cathedral processions. The young choristers had served their Cathedral faithfully from an early age until their voices broke. Dwelly established an organization known as the Cross Guild who became largely responsible for the processions for which the Cathedral became justly famous. Dwelly knew where to go for assistance over vestments and turned to his old friend and expert Percy Dearmer whose *The Parson's Handbook* had become the definitive guide to vestments and ceremonial. Nan Dearmer, later reported "Percy preached in the Cathedral and took part in consultations with Canon Dwelly over dress and ceremonial. The Dean tells me the distinctive vergers' gowns and many cloaks warn on processional occasions were all devised with Percy's help and advice."[19] We know from Julia Carter Preston that both her father and mother were involved in the design and making of the earliest garments.

I have not seen anything resembling the Cross Guild and its work in any other Cathedral though people declare its establishment to have been a brilliant idea. In his short unpublished article on Dwelly, Frederick Dillistone stressed the significance of Dwelly's use of movement and processions and the vital part played by the Cross Guild.

... no feature of the worship of the cathedral has been more impressive than that of the colour and orderliness of these processions. What may at first sight seem an undue proportion of the total floor space has been kept open for free movement: the absence of fixed pews has made it possible to relate movements to the particular character of whatever service is being solemnized. Far too often in English Cathedrals and churches fixtures for seating purposes have made it impossible for there to be dignified movement; and, indeed, to cover the floor with ugly pews or undistinguished chairs merely detracts from any proper appreciation of the building's architectural beauties ...

I do not know whether in designing the building Scott realised that he would make dramatic patterns of movement possible. Nor do I know whether Dwelly consciously interpreted their function in the total act of worship. It is nevertheless the case that the neo-Gothic design made movements possible in a way they never could have been in a traditional Gothic interior. The absence of pillars and a screened division between the choir and the rest of the building helped: the siting of the Lady Chapel apart from the main axis of the Cathedral also helped: in particular the provision of substantial arches on either side of the High Altar made it possible for processions from the eastern retro-choir to enter the Cathedral through the Sanctuary in full view of the assembled congregation. Simultaneously other processions could advance down the aisles on the north and south of the choir while, after the opening of the great central space, a procession could come from the west along a central aisle which was always kept some eight feet wide.[20]

Dillistone actually worked with Dwelly as the Canon Chancellor before Dwelly's retirement and so his comments on the use of the building are particularly significant. So much of the Cathedral was planned before Dwelly's time, so he had not influenced Scott's layout but he was strongly aware of the possibilities which the architect had presented to the liturgist.

An unnamed journalist, T. J. B., commented on a growing Cathedral tradition, "an acute and increasing perception of the value of music in all its services." He commented favourably on the whole musical part of the service and made a perceptive general comment:

One would say that its keynote was the balance preserved between music intended to heighten and increase the devotional aspect of the service and music intended to inspire and uplift a great congregation.

They are not afraid of innovation at the Cathedral. They are willing to install a hidden battery of drums and trumpets, and, having secured them, to pursue their use to a logical conclusion, not only with the organ, but on their own in fanfares and flourishes. Nor do they mind working up a pure 'effect', such as the tremendous crescendo, culminating in a prolonged pause, with all the available power of trumpets, organ and voices, on the end of the line 'Now above the Sky he's King.' I have heard this done before in the Cathedral, and the effect is so impressive as to justify what purists might regard as a liberty.[21]

Cathedral memories assert that Dwelly had a liking for tubular bells: some of the older sheet music has reference to their use and it is known that the Cathedral had been presented with a set of tubular bells though they no longer exist. The acoustic of the completed Cathedral has a nine and a half second resonance and the whole building is metaphorically lit up by music and Henry Goss Custard, Organist and Edgar Robinson, Choral Conductor knew how to secure the dramatic effects which were occasionally called for in Dwelly's liturgy.

In his sermon the Bishop considered the plight of cathedrals a hundred years before "glorious relics of the past, reflecting splendours of a spirit, not dead, but long since turned to other expressions in a different age." He paid tribute to all of those who from the foundation of the diocese had laboured towards the provision of the Cathedral. He was to stress the vital importance of the men who were to lead the community.

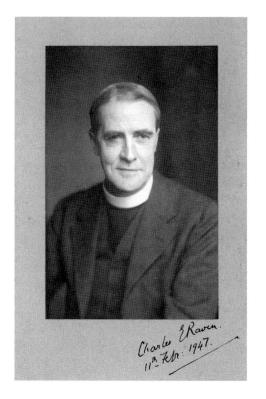

Charles E Raven.
11th Feb: 1947.

A later photograph of Charles Raven when he was Regius Professor of Divinity at Cambridge.

It was a mark of their wisdom that even before the building had begun to grow they had made provision for men who should one day give their lives to its service. For a Cathedral, however splendid to the eye, is incomplete and powerless apart from the men by whom its God-given life shall first be accepted within, and then spread abroad to do its work outside. Today we mark another

A dramatic shot of the excavation below the Central Space. The temporary brick wall cut off the building site from the worship in the part-built Cathedral.

stage towards its completion as we celebrate the establishment of our Dean and Chapter. To me that celebration will bring its climax when presently I shall give my benediction to my friend and faithful fellow-worker, who will by then have been installed at the hand of another friend of many years, as ruler of this Cathedral Church.[22]

That "other friend" was Charles Raven who in 1932 resigned his post as Chancellor to take up the post of Regius Professor of Divinity at Cambridge. In 1933 he published *Liverpool Cathedral: An Impression of its Early Years*[23] as he made clear not a standard history and in the preface he quoted Radcliffe's challenge, "The laymen of Liverpool are giving you this great gift: I sometimes ask myself if you will be able to use it"[24]. Raven's short account went on to explain the reasons lying behind the publication which was "To answer Sir Frederick's question and fulfill our obligation to the College, this brief account has been written." He declared that it could only have been written by someone who had been part of the community during the crucial years of its establishment but who had subsequently stepped back from the Cathedral and its work.

It is to Raven's writing that we must refer for any direct statements about the theological beliefs which were part of the foundation of the whole worshipping life of the Cathedral. There is no existing written account of Dwelly's theology but his handling of liturgy, the freshness that he brought to Cathedral worship, the way he attempted to open the Cathedral to the whole life of the city, his determination to gather a wide range of distinguished members into the Cathedral's College of Council, is indicative of Dwelly's personal theological stance, firmly based in modernism. Raven wrote that the basis of the Cathedral's life was not to be found under one single party label.

> ... the Chapter would claim that they are Catholic in the sense of maintaining the universality and continuity of the Christian revelation and of insisting upon the prime importance of corporate fellowship, the beloved community, and the sacramental principle; Evangelical in proclaiming the need for a radical change from self to God, the fullness

Work on the Western Transept viewed from Gambier Terrace.

of salvation and of abundant life in Christ, and the supreme duty of evangelism; Modernist in acknowledging the unity of truth, the necessity of perpetual growth and consequent restatement, and the freedom to prove all things.[25]

The early years of Liverpool Cathedral in the twenties and thirties are the years when Modernism was most influential and Raven and Dwelly were clearly aware of H. D. A. Major's seminal work, *English Modernism*. His words are clearly fundamental to Dwelly's beliefs and Dwelly's work even before his arrival at the Cathedral: "... the aim of the English Modernist is to set free the Spirit from those archaic dogmatic shackles and ecclesiastical burdens, great and grievous to be born, which are hindering it from exerting its full and proper influence in the modern world."[26]

> Modernism consists in the claim of the modern mind to determine what is true, right and beautiful in the light of its own experience, even though its conclusions be in contradiction of those of tradition ... The intellectual task of Modernism is the criticism of tradition in the light of research and enlarging experience, with the purpose of reformulating and reinterpreting it to serve the needs of the present age.[27]

The alternative creed published in the Grey Book (1923) is the creed of modernism.

> We believe that God is Spirit: and they that worship him must worship him in spirit and in truth.

> We believe that God is Light: and if we walk in the light as he is in the light we have fellowship one with another.

> We believe that God is Love: and that everyone that loveth is born of God and knoweth God.

> We believe that Jesus is the son of God: and that God has given to us eternal life, and this life is in his son.

> We believe that we are children of God: and that he hath given us of his Spirit.

> We believe that if we confess our sins: he is faithful and just to forgive us our sins.

> We believe that he who doeth the will of God: shall abide forever. Amen.[28]

This is reminiscent of Inge, the theologian who had such an influence on Dwelly's final decision to enter the priesthood and much of his writing in *Truth and Falsehood in Religion* referred to in chapter 2: "It is almost frivolous to make the whole truth or falsehood of Christianity turn upon the historical truth of a particular miracle, or the authenticity of a particular document ..."[29]

In the light of serious theological controversy resulting from the invitation to a Unitarian preacher, the importance of Modernism is crucial. "[Modernism] does not offer a set of dogmas, but it does ask for a modern interpretation of the older ones. It insists that religion is more vital than theology and must be distinguished from it."[30]

In *The Church of England in the Twentieth Century*, volume 2, Roger Lloyd indicated another feature of Modernism which is so applicable to Dwelly: "The modernist's God was emphatically a deity who was awake, alive, alert; and there has been no historic school of theology which has held a richer version of the doctrine of divine inspiration"[31] Such a statement forms a natural lead towards Christian Mysticism, a term observable throughout Dwelly's life right back to the young man on holiday in Switzerland. Raven refers to mysticism in *The Eternal Spirit* "... it is very noticeable that a large number of students approaching the quest for truth from widely different angles find in the spiritual experience, commonly known as mysticism, the culminating achievement of mankind and the element in the light of which all else is explained."[32]

Horton Davies's comment on mysticism is highly relevant to the Dean at the centre of the Unitarian controversy and the Dean who was central to the public worshipping life of his cathedral. The fruits of modernism and mysticism are observable in so much that he did.

> ... mysticism locates religion neither in the brain nor in the will – but in the heart. Religion is, for the mystic, essentially the adoration of God and worship is the corporate expression of adoration. In the second place, in an increasingly ecumenical century thoughtful Christians were less interested in the discriminatory theological labels that divide, and more in the experience that unites both catholic and protestant.[33]

The significance of this statement for Liverpool Cathedral will receive further attention in chapters 6 and 7 of this study.

Raven the liberal modernist was clear about the urgent current needs of the church.

> By common consent the supreme task of the church at this time is to interpret its inheritance of doctrine, cultus, and organization so as to satisfy the minds, meet the spiritual needs, and adjust itself to the

The view from the Dean's stall,

environment of the twentieth century. The changes in outlook, temper, and social structure characteristic of the past hundred years have been so vast and so rapid as to make it well nigh impossible for institutions to keep pace with them.

Raven had a real appreciation of Scott's achievement:

> Sir Giles Scott had given expression in architecture to the hope for a church which should stand for fresh and creative vision. His work was not 'period' design: it could not be used for a slavish imitation of past methods. The artistry of the fabric called for similar artistry in its presentation of religion.

He crystalised all that was central to the challenge of a new Cathedral.

> Its theology must be a real interpretation of God to minds thinking along lines of modern knowledge: its ceremonial, its music, its services must enable modern folk to experience worship: its organization must display the aspiration after fellowship and the ability of the Church to rise above legal and mechanical relationships. To reproduce ancient formularies, to imitate earlier artistic modes, to adopt a traditional constitution, unless these were demonstrably perfect and demonstrably appropriate, would be to betray the hopes of the community.[34]

Raven's thoughts lie at the heart of this study: he realised that Scott's undated Gothic achievement was no dead copy of an outmoded architectural form. One has only to look at Scott's use of runs of plain ashlar blocks devoid of decoration and his extensive use of Carter Preston's sculpted figures to see modernism comfortably incorporated into the Gothic frame. Raven later in the piece placed architect and Dean in parallel: "The Cathedral was endowed by its architect with the beauty which can of itself tranquilize, unify, and inspire; it also possessed on its staff an artist whose medium is public worship."[35] Dwelly incorporated modernism into the traditional language and services of the Church; his choreography had all the clean lines of modernism.

In thirty five pages of tightly written prose Raven attempted to answer four questions. What was the theological basis of the Cathedral's life? On what principles were its services, its ceremonial, its ordered activities planned? What was its duty towards the people of Merseyside, the Diocese, the church at large? How was its corporate life to be organised and the relation of its officers, one to another, to be determined? Some of the points he made are clearly observable in the life of the Cathedral over the next two decades.

Over theological issues, he avoided party labels by insisting that the Cathedral was Catholic, Evangelical and Modernist and that, in line with current theological thinking Johannine in character with strong focus on the words light, life and love. In the light of some of the unfortunate disagreements in the Cathedral and the Diocese in the Thirties, part of Raven's summing up are pertinent:

> ... theology became for them not so much an objective system of dogmas as an interpretation of the meaning of life and of its richest experiences. It must take into account not merely the formularies of the past but the best thought and energy of the present; not merely the Christ of the New Testament but the Risen Christ of the Cathedral's dedication, manifested by His Spirit 'yesterday today and for ever'. To such a theology creeds and traditions are fingerposts, not boundary fences; faith is not static but dynamic and adventurous; religion is not a compensation but a romance, not a system of duties but a way of living; and the Church is a symbol and an instrument whereby all men everywhere may be enabled to live eternally. It was freely stated that the building of the Cathedral could only be justified if by it men were helped to see that every dwelling and shop and office and factory was also a house of God, and to labour together for this end.[36]

The Chapter knew that they had to "keep theology constantly in touch with life." In this determination the character of Dwelly's services would be of great importance. Raven traced the experimental nature of Liverpool Cathedral liturgy back to the Consecration Service and his words must be quoted in full because they convey so clearly the Dwelly genius so required by the genius of the building itself.

> [T]he services of the consecration of the Cathedral may fairly be claimed as a new expression of public worship. It was evident that to mark such an occasion no repetition of a traditional form would suffice; that it would not be enough to collect together a variety of ancient ceremonies and formulae and to combine them into an Office. What was needed was a service which, while fulfilling all that past experience could suggest, would possess a coherence, a rhythm, an appropriateness of its own for the circumstances of today. Such a service must be the work not of a liturgical expert (if this means a student of past precedents) but of a creative artist who perceived what ceremony signified, knew how to interpret its significance in apposite technique, and could enable the congregation to experience and share in the dramatic movement of the whole. A study of the service will show how far this intention was fulfilled, but only those who took part in it could realize how every detail from the marshalling and movement of the processions to the massing of the groups, from the sequence of the action to the structure of the prayers and the choice and incidence of the music, was built up into a single and impressive design. If religion was life at its highest, then worship could not be the repetition of a familiar routine: it must contain discovery and freshness of inspiration, must reveal new possibilities of communion and new insight into the ways of the Spirit.
>
> So the conviction gradually became clear that every great service must be in the highest sense a work of art. As such it presupposes a threefold capacity in those responsible for it. There must be first a clear perception of the intention of the whole – what is the good news that God would reveal at Christmas or Easter to a congregation of seafarers or doctors or university students? Then there must be a careful consideration of the elements which are essential to the expression of the good news; every detail must contribute in due proportion and at its proper place to the unfolding of the intention. Thirdly, if the whole is to make its impression, it must be so ordered and rendered that without distraction the worshipper becomes immediately sensitive to its significance, is caught up into its movement, and experiences as a direct intuition the revelation which it is designed to unfold.[37]

In order to achieve all this, Raven stressed the Cathedral's need for what he called "a controlling officer" and such it had in the person of its first Dean. Again Raven brought into parallel the architect and the liturgist:

> The Cathedral was endowed by its architect with the beauty which can of itself tranquillize, unify and inspire; it also possessed on its Staff an artist whose medium is public worship ... At their best, building, ministers, helpers, and congregation combined to create a single and perfectly integrated effect by which every individual was lifted up into a communion of adoration.[38]

There followed an explanation for the character and pattern of the Cathedral Sunday services. Holy Communion was celebrated at 8 am and at 12.15 pm. These were in days before a Choral Eucharist became the main Sunday morning service in churches and Cathedrals across the country and whatever may have been the hopes of the Dean and Chapter, Liverpool Cathedral adopted the standard pattern. "On Sundays after prolonged experiment the Chapter gave up the attempt to make a choral Eucharist the chief service of the morning. In the special circumstances of Liverpool in which the general type of churchmanship is strongly Evangelical, and where Mattins is accepted and enjoyed, the Choral Eucharist plainly does not appeal."[39] At Matins the choir did not sing all the Psalms for the day and the lessons were specially chosen and short. Choral Evensong with a teaching sermon was at 3 pm and the day finished with the plain congregational service at 8.30 pm. The timing of this service was chosen deliberately so as not to be in competition with the standard 6.30 pm services in the parish across the diocese. It was not the Cathedral's intention to draw people away from their own parishes in order to establish a regular Cathedral congregation: "... its services aimed rather at inspiration than at edification, at arousing desire more than satisfying it, at attracting outsiders more than ministering to a regular congregation."[40] Indeed, more and more the afternoon became the time for "special services for different sections of the community, doctors, teachers, nurses, seamen, postal workers, shop-assistants, and such like ..." It was this service in particular which gave scope to Dwelly's most imaginative liturgy.

The 8.30 was not a Liverpool invention, though Raven introduced it one week after the Consecration, but it was the service at which Dwelly and Raven made the most direct and powerful impact on many people, not all of whom would have considered themselves to be "church-goers". The service always began with half an hour of organ music. It was led very simply from the pulpit by one man. The service itself was plain and the address was the most important element.

Members of the Cross Guild wearing their distinctive robes unique to Liverpool Cathedral

The service was designed

> for young men and women working in shops and offices, living in
> lodgings, and strangers in the place; but it has made for itself a much
> larger circle, particularly of the undergraduate and the school-teacher
> class. The effort has been to attract and interest them so that they may be
> led to attach themselves to a parish church, and undertake there definite
> work for God.[41]

Some statements in the first chapter of this study indicated that, in the main, the Cathedrals of the nineteenth century lacked real understanding of their role. Chavasse had been quite certain about his reasons for wishing to establish a new Cathedral and it is interesting to place parts of Raven's book alongside the Bishop's speech in the Town Hall in 1901. Chavasse would have applauded the Cathedral's vision of its responsibility beyond its walls. Built by the people of Liverpool "the Cathedral could not become the church of a congregation or of a clique".[42] "It was recognized from the first that any narrow or exclusive interpretation of churchmanship would be inconsistent with the representative character of the foundation: it was the Cathedral of the people of Liverpool, cherishing its mother-tradition, the Anglican communion, but in no sectarian spirit; hallowing all seekers after God, and doing everything possible to make them welcome."[43] It is interesting that two Unitarian Ministers preached in Liverpool Cathedral in the 1930s and Chester Cathedral could not welcome a service for Unitarians in 2005. The Cathedral's perceived breadth of obligation to all sections of the community was further reason for the number of "great civic and united services" and special services for the trades and professions and for the fact that members of Chapter accepted that they must be "actively identified with civic and social life on Merseyside". They were determined that the ministry of the parishes should not be upset or diminished by the establishment of Cathedral groups which were traditionally part of the social community of the parish. The Chapter were sensitive to the feelings of the local churches whose priests and congregations could have so easily felt under threat: "The glamour of the great shrine, its novelty, its opportunities might have been used so as to conflict with the interests of the diocese and eclipse neighbouring parish churches."[44] On the other hand, the Cathedral staff realised that there was territory which would benefit from their support and new ground was broken in the field of post-ordination training. The Bishop dispensed with the traditional Priest's examination and instead, for the first two years of their ministry, they attended weekly sessions in the Cathedral led by Dwelly and Raven. Indirectly, the two most influential members of the Chapter did have considerable influence in the Diocese through the young Deacons whom they met every Tuesday morning in the Cathedral.

The fourth question which Raven addressed related to the organisation of the corporate life of the Cathedral and how the members related to each other. There is no reason to think that he was not reporting with total honesty on the excellence of the working of the organization between 1924 and 1933 which had been led by "Friendship, genuine, free, and sensitive … the necessary condition for effective and creative co-operation". All matters were discussed openly and without pressure with "free and friendly co-operation".[45] These conditions prevailed throughout the period when the new Cathedral statutes were being formulated.

> The intention of the Statutes was threefold – to perpetuate the spirit of friendship and of corporate responsibility together with unity of execution; to embody in a constitution the results of the period of experiment, and to lay down as plainly as legal phrases will allow the general lines which experience had approved; to leave freedom for growth and expansion and sufficient elasticity to encourage rapid adjustment to changing needs. It was clear from the first that the Cathedral was to be governed by love and not by law …[46]

The eventual breakdown in the mutual respect and love was to have the most serious effects on the life of the Cathedral and the Diocese for a decade and beyond. In 1933 Raven had been able to sum up the results of nine years of the Cathedral's work succinctly and honestly.

> The Cathedral had developed a clear and coherent life of its own, charac-terized by a definite theological outlook, by services and by an order fully in harmony with that outlook and expressing it in terms of worship, by an acknowledged and intimate connection with the many-sided activities of its civic, social, and religious environment, and by a type of government relying wholly upon fellowship, loyalty, and corporate effort.[47]

Raven's short but highly significant book makes it clear that the new cathedral in no way felt itself fettered by outworn traditions and embraced Modernism with enthusiasm. Throughout his time as Chancellor, Raven was the academic figure-head but it was Dwelly who pioneered the styles of worship appropriate to the Modernism which was central to the cathedral's theology. Dwelly's founding of the College of Counsel and the choice of its members was part of the same movement. The College was instituted at the time of the foundation of the Chapter. A rubric in the service paper explained the reasons behind its formation: "… so that others from beyond the borders of the diocese may hither bring their contributions of wisdom and experience, to the end that contact with the wider operations of the Spirit shall in every generation be established and maintained." The first members brought wisdom and expertise from a range of backgrounds: The Earl of Crawford and Balcarres, General Smuts, Rt. Rev. George Bell, Sir Stanford Downing, Sir Frederick Radcliffe, Dr. John Masefield, Professor Conwy Lloyd Morgan, Professor John Linton Myres, Francis Eeles and Martin Shaw.

A short statement followed their first meeting on 16 November 1932: "It was recognized that Liverpool Cathedral had become a national possession, that it stood for something new in the life of the church that it had become a point of contact between religion and thousands of people untouched by the church, and this over and above its normal activities as the centre of the diocese."[48] This is an extremely important claim which can surely be substantiated by the popularity and success of the many special services which drew worshippers into the cathedral who may have had little contact with any church community.

A number of members of the Counsel spoke at services in the cathedral and although they came from widely differing backgrounds they had much in common in the way they thought about religion and the role of the new cathedral. A shortage of words will not permit adequate consideration of the statements though selected sentences will indicate some of their central ideas. Professor Myers believed that "… the ever enlarging and embracing attitude of Liverpool Cathedral was the most hopeful thing in the spiritual life of our day."[49] Bishop Bell stated that "… whatever else is done at Liverpool the Chapter will continue their consecration of the imagination."[50] John Masefield said that he felt that "… more than anything else, the artists of our day needed a place – a holy place where they could take their work."[51] General Smuts spoke of the importance of the relationship between science and religion: "But science is only one of the great values. We want religion in order to realize our foremost human stature, as by this service religion affirms that it is one with science. In recent centuries these have been in watertight compartments, the great change to which we can look forward in the not distant future is the drawing together of all great values."[52] Masefield, the writer and poet, emphasised the life-affirming functions of the new Cathedral able as it was to attract such a variety of people within its services: "… no Cathedral can be serving Life that does not draw Life to it, all the Life." In Cathedral worship "Here the arts are needed, for by the arts men are linked, as by intellect men are set asunder." "The Cathedral of Liverpool, the greatest of modern Cathedrals, is a Church of the Resurrection. It comes into the life of our time, in a decade when all life known to us from

LIVERPOOL CATHEDRAL

An Impression of its Early Years

Carter Preston's cover for Raven's book.

CHARLES E. RAVEN

childhood have to be remade, when the nation has to be re-created, with what difficulty we do not yet know, but no doubt with much."[53]

Dwelly had in the Cathedral community a range of talent supporting what he and Raven were attempting to do. They were drawing into the community a strong circle who supported their theological modernism in their own ways. Goss Custard and Edgar Robinson formed a powerful musical team, always able to rise to the Dean's requests, while, within the visual arts, Edward Carter Preston's stone figures and bas-relief memorials embellished Scott's design and he and his wife were centrally involved in the design and making of the Cross Guild robes.

From Consecration to the founding of the Dean and Chapter, Dwelly and the Bishop established a close friendship which itself must have encouraged the freshness and vitality of Cathedral worship. However, the relations between the Bishop and his new Dean broke down irrevocably. Such problems as the invitation to the Unitarian preachers and the temporary refusal to install the two Arch-Deacons are likely to be the results of the breakdown rather than the cause and no one has been able to explain the actual cause of the rift. A rift which was obvious and painful to the Bishop's young family. As Patrick David wrote to me later,

> as children we adored him – like a favourite uncle. With his interest in youth work and adventure training he had a way with young people. On holiday in the Lake District I remember climbing Helvellyn with him in a snowstorm when I was sickening for the measles and being encouraged 'Mountaineers don't give up'. I was about nine. On the same holiday in his car 'Would you like the steering wheel or the accelerator! One really could do that sort of thing in those days! Naturally I chose the accelerator! And then suddenly, having been a frequent visitor to our house in Liverpool, he stopped coming. At the time we gathered that he and our father had fallen out but we were too young to understand what it was all about. But we missed him a lot.[54]

It could not be understood either by Canon W. R. Matthews, Canon Theologian in Liverpool and later Dean of St. Paul's.

> This troublesome circumstance was the disagreement, or rather the almost intolerable tension, between Dr. David, the Bishop of Liverpool, and Mr. Dwelly, who had just been appointed the first Dean of the unfinished Cathedral, to the building and establishment of which both had given devoted leadership. I admired and loved both these men and

A Dwelly special service concerned with work on the Mersey Tunnel. Of particular interest in this photograph is the temporary wooden gallery against the temporary brick wall.

was naturally embarrassed because each would talk to me, while for years they were not on speaking terms with each other. I know it is almost unbelievable, but I must repeat that to this day I do not know the cause of this quarrel or what it was about.[55]

Peart-Binns judged that: "In the appointment of the Dean, David allowed his affection to override intellect where intellect should have won."[56] All had gone so well in the Cathedral and the diocese only so long as their friendship lasted. He saw fault on both sides: "David would not 'let go' of the Cathedral, failing to accept that he was no longer Dean as well as Bishop. Dwelly had an inflated sense of his own place ... Once Raven had left, Dwelly tended to regard the Principal Chapter as his curates ... and the General Chapter as David's mob ..." Even the charitable and scholarly Frederick Dillistone wrote: "To put it bluntly the Bishop found it difficult to keep his hands off the Cathedral."[57]

Liverpool Cathedral, under its new Dean and Chapter, continued to arrange immensely successful services, but a serious and public rift between Bishop and Dean must have diminished what they might have been able to achieve and litigation was seen as a stain on the Church.

To be in the Cathedral today it is hard to imagine the effect of the elaborate temporary brick wall.

In a city which had known serious sectarian strife, the Chapter of the new Cathedral carried the expectations of people from outside the Church of England. One of the services within the Octave of the Consecration was held specifically for Free Churchmen and the Bishop declared "your Cathedral and mine". "And now our Cathedral is open unto all. A home in the heart of the Diocese for every child of the Church."[58] The media took up the news in banner headlines when in November the same year the Bishop reiterated his invitation:

> Great step for Church unity by Dr. David. Cathedral of the open door. Welcome extended to all seekers after truth. The Bishop of Liverpool (Dr. David), formerly Bishop of Suffolk, at the last of the consecration services of Liverpool Cathedral, on Saturday afternoon, took an important step, without precedent in the history of the church, when, by certain monitions and question and answer, he declared the Cathedral of Liverpool open to all men of good will, without regard to creed or manner. Speaking from the throne, he invited the co-operation of the Free churches and the Greek Archimandrite in efforts for the reunion of churches. Dr. David recognized *and* invited cooperation of the University in search for and the spread of truth.[59]

Raven's comment that "creeds and traditions are finger-posts, not boundary fences" would seem to relate strongly to the Bishop's aspirations.

In 1933, Dwelly invited the eminent Unitarian scholar, Dr. L. P. Jacks to deliver three addresses at the 8.30 services and he also issued an invitation to the Rev. Lawrence Redfern, Minister of Ullet Road Unitarian Church, and Chaplain to the High Sheriff to preach at the Assize Service. There had not been complaints about the invitation to Dr. Jacks but as Redfern had been invited to preach at a regular Prayer Book Service, a battle of words broke out in the press. After this had settled, Lord Hugh Cecil petitioned the Archbishop of York to move against the Bishop. The bitter controversy which followed revealed much about Dwelly's personality, particularly the strength, dedication, determination, devotion to his friends, and also his theology, particularly his modernism and his determination that the cathedral be the centre for inclusive worship. In terms of ecumenism he was ahead of his time but some of his actions might be seen as injudicious and he may have been over influenced by Raven in some of his public statements.

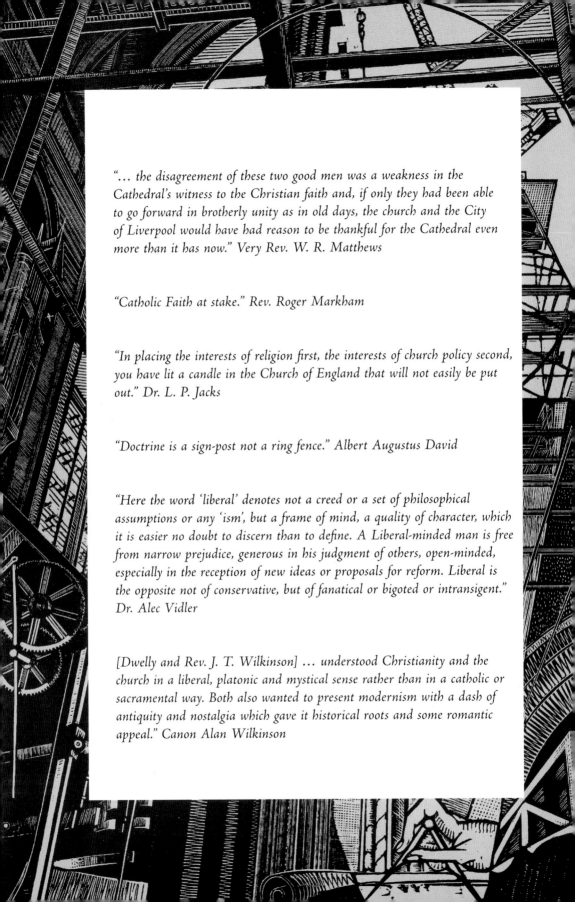

"... the disagreement of these two good men was a weakness in the Cathedral's witness to the Christian faith and, if only they had been able to go forward in brotherly unity as in old days, the church and the City of Liverpool would have had reason to be thankful for the Cathedral even more than it has now." Very Rev. W. R. Matthews

"Catholic Faith at stake." Rev. Roger Markham

"In placing the interests of religion first, the interests of church policy second, you have lit a candle in the Church of England that will not easily be put out." Dr. L. P. Jacks

"Doctrine is a sign-post not a ring fence." Albert Augustus David

"Here the word 'liberal' denotes not a creed or a set of philosophical assumptions or any 'ism', but a frame of mind, a quality of character, which it is easier no doubt to discern than to define. A Liberal-minded man is free from narrow prejudice, generous in his judgment of others, open-minded, especially in the reception of new ideas or proposals for reform. Liberal is the opposite not of conservative, but of fanatical or bigoted or intransigent." Dr. Alec Vidler

[Dwelly and Rev. J. T. Wilkinson] ... understood Christianity and the church in a liberal, platonic and mystical sense rather than in a catholic or sacramental way. Both also wanted to present modernism with a dash of antiquity and nostalgia which gave it historical roots and some romantic appeal." Canon Alan Wilkinson

SIX

Controversy

THE PROFOUND and long-term disagreement between Bishop and Dean was referred to at the end of the previous chapter in the words of W. R. Matthews and it is important that his opinion be reiterated here.

> I know it is almost unbelievable, but I must repeat that to this day I do not know the cause of this quarrel or what is was about. One fact, however, was only too evident – that the disagreement of these two good men was a weakness in the Cathedral's witness to the Christian faith and, if only they had been able to go forward in brotherly unity as in old days, the church and the city of Liverpool would have had reason to be thankful for the Cathedral even more than it has now.[1]

What is clear is that what became known as the Unitarian Controversy was not the cause of the breakdown in relations between the two men. At the start of the outbreak of local hysteria in the press, Dwelly and David were at one in their beliefs and their aspirations for their Cathedral. Joe Riley called one chapter 'Odium Theologicum' and was far-sighted in his judgment: "It is a story which is brutal and compassionate by turns; an episode when the letter of the law won a technical victory over the charity of men's hearts, but where the real victory is only now being fully realized."[2] The inference being that both Dean and Bishop were decades ahead of their time in concern for ecumenism.

The early stages in the build-up of controversy could not have been simpler.

Dwelly invited the eminent Unitarian, Dr. L. P. Jacks, to preach three sermons at the 8.30 in the summer of 1933: the Holy Ghost, the Holy Catholic Church and Death. There is nothing in the Dwelly archive to indicate that either the invitation or the sermons caused any concern within Anglicanism. But earlier in the year Dwelly had invited Rev. Lawrence Redfern, Minister of Ullet Road Unitarian Church in Liverpool, to preach at the assize service in October. The Unitarian Church was very strong in Liverpool, led by such families as the Rathbones and the Holts, and Dwelly was a friend of Lawrence Holt and his wife. Redfern was Chaplain to the High Sheriff. At the Assize Services in Lancaster, Manchester and Liverpool it was customary to invite the Chaplain to preach, but when the Chaplain was a Unitarian the invitation was usually reduced to a request to read one of the lessons. Redfern commented on the Liverpool invitation in *The Inquirer* cited by Alec Ellis,

> In Liverpool, however, there is good reason to believe that the Dean was greatly disturbed by this departure from normal practice, and was anxious to make good an omission which set aside the declared ideal of the Cathedral, which in the words of Canon Charles Raven (as he then was), 'should be above all sectional and divisive influences, and able to unite us all in whatever works for the true service of God and man … a centre of unity where all can sink their divisions in sole adoration of Him in whom is neither Jew nor Greek'.[3]

Redfern was grateful for the generous line the Dean was taking and sent a hand-written letter of thanks: "I appreciate it not merely for personal reasons but as a gesture of friendliness towards my people who have never been in love with the dissidence of dissent, but long to march with the great Christian host, of which our Cathedral is such a magnificent symbol."[4]

Dwelly had not consulted the Bishop before issuing the invitation to Redfern but obviously David was aware of who the preacher was to be before the service took place but we have no evidence that he attempted to change the arrangement or indeed made any critical comment about the arrangement. Alec Ellis has judged the sermon to be 'entirely non-controversial' and concerned with a desire for sound leadership through the troubled post-war conditions. Public controversy seems to have been triggered by a letter from Rev. Roger Markham, Rector of Aughton, in the *Liverpool Daily Post* on 25 October, under the headline 'Catholic Faith at stake'.

> I am sure I am not alone in protesting against a Unitarian minister being invited to preach in Liverpool Cathedral. Let me say at once that I do not blame the minister in the least, but I do very much blame those, be they

whom they may, who invited him to do so. To speak plainly, Unitarianism is a heresy which strikes at the very foundation of the Christian Faith by denying in any real sense the Incarnation of the Son of God. There is no charity in blinking the issue, either God in the Person of Our Lord Jesus Christ has taken human nature upon Him, or He has not. The Unitarians while professing (and I doubt not honestly) great reverence for Our Lord deny that He is one of the Persons or (to use the technical term) hypostases of the Holy Trinity. The whole conception of God and his relations to humanity is at stake. I believe that many of those who subscribed to build our Cathedral – and they were not as some people think, confined to the citizens of Liverpool – would have hesitated to give their money had they supposed that this, the mother church of the diocese, would be used as a place where those who did not hold the Catholic Faith, or indeed any form of Christian religion, would be invited to air their views. I can only say that I am astonished and distressed. If we humble parish priests cannot look to our mother church to lead and encourage us in maintaining and preaching the Catholic Faith, where can we look?[5]

For the rest of October and into November the local papers ran a sequence of letters, at least three from Markham. Not all the letters were antagonistic, as two on 27 October indicate: "Surely it is a very helpful sign, in these days, when two religious bodies are broad-minded enough to combine in a common purpose."[6] "The intolerance and bigotry shown by 'Churchman' is amazing. It is common knowledge that the cost of building Liverpool Cathedral has been subscribed to by practically all classes and creeds."[7] "Knowing that a previous request for a Unitarian minister to preach in the Cathedral had been refused, many welcomed the innovation last Sunday as a sign of hope for the future, but evidently the old spirit of intolerance still persists."[8]

Suddenly, the criticism relating to one preacher was broadened by a letter from the Rev. C. Ernest Proctor:

I would support the Rev. R. F. Markham's protest against much that is being introduced into the services of the Liverpool Cathedral. Though I

Though the Unitarian controversy raged in the press, much of the art in the Cathedral depicts aspects of the life of Jesus. The birth at Bethlehem is the central feature of the Lady Chapel Reredos.

may belong to another school of thought than that to which he does, yet, with him and many others, I am distressed to find truth often ignored, if not denied, and the Scriptures mutilated, misquoted, misapplied in these services. It is as if the composer of the forms of service had quite a different scheme of doctrine in his mind to that of the Christian scriptures, picked out from them only that which suited his ideas, and altered them to agree with his opinions.[9]

So then, the invitation to a Unitarian was attacked from both Catholic and Evangelical wings of the church and J. B. Lancelot Senior Diocesan Canon, was anxious to distance himself and other members of the Greater Chapter from what the Cathedral had done stating that they "have no sort of jurisdiction within the Cathedral, and, therefore, cannot be blamed in any way for the new departure which must have aroused misgivings."[10]

As the furore in the Liverpool newspapers was calming, there was national intervention which took the whole matter further by Lord Hugh Cecil whose family were the most powerful force within the House of Laity of the Church Assembly at Westminster. As Adrian Hastings has written, "It was indeed the lay Tory control of the Church Assembly which ensured that no odd outburst of some liberal cleric should unduly disturb the policies of the Establishment."[11] To have ignited the ire of Cecil's anti-liberal narrow orthodoxy was unfortunate indeed because he wielded immense power; Adrian Hasting: "Their aristocratic independence, political experience, wealth and public position at once effectively silenced other lay elements in the church and maintained a rein on Episcopal innovation. The Church of England in the 1930s, it is not too exaggerated to say, was controlled less by Lang and Temple in tandem than by Lang and Hugh Cecil."[12] Joe Riley wrote chillingly of Cecil's reputation, "Associates spoke of his forensic logic, often so rigid as to exclude a sense of charity. Cecil may have been on the side of personal liberty, but his vision was of a liberty strait-jacketed by unbending rules."[13] It was Cecil who ensured that the Unitarian Controversy really burst into flames by declaring his intention to begin proceedings against David and Dwelly under ecclesiastic law by petitioning William Temple, by this time Archbishop of York. Cecil's letter called upon the Archbishop to move against the Bishop of Liverpool "in respect of certain offences against laws ecclesiastical". He also demanded that David take action against his Dean:

> I therefore charge the said Dean with having offended against laws ecclesiastical in the matters aforesaid, and particularly against the canons of the year 1603, and modified in the year 1865 ... And I further charge the said Dean that, contrary to the laws ecclesiastical, he has, by

his action in the matters aforesaid, encouraged men to hold heretical opinions inconsistent with faith in the Incarnation of Our Lord Jesus Christ and in His Deity, or at the best to think lightly of the error of such heretical opinions.[14]

David was strongly supportive of his Dean but he made clear the difference between the "regular" Prayer Book services in the Cathedral and the non-liturgical "special" services. There is no archival evidence of expressed animosity between Bishop and Dean at this point and the Bishop had no intention of taking action against the Dean, even though as Bishop he would have to face a formal meeting in front of his fellow Bishops of the Northern Province. The *Liverpool Echo* for 5 January 1934 carried an article in which the Bishop quoted from his letter to Lord Cecil.

> … the Dean has accepted my ruling and expressed his regret that he, having treated the Assize Service as a 'special' service, invited a non-licensed preacher thereat without consulting me. Thus my only difference with the Dean has been removed and will not arise again.
>
> In regard to the 8.30 p.m. and other 'special' services he and I fully agreed that in view of the sacred call to a larger unity it is of the highest importance to maintain the liberty we have claimed, and, as seems expedient, to exercise it. I am not prepared to admit that such liberty is contrary to Canon Law. The other ground on which you ask me to condemn the Dean, namely, that 'he has encouraged men to hold heretical opinions' suggests that he had invited Unitarians to uphold their faith in the Cathedral against ours. No preacher invited here has ever transgressed the honourable understanding not to question Anglican doctrine, nor should we in any case invite one whom we could not trust to restrict himself to common ground. In view of this explanation, you will not be surprised to learn that I do not propose to proceed against the Dean.[15]

The Bishop was open about his attitude to the problems and his sermon at the 8.30 on 7 January was reported in the *Daily Post*. The whole piece is sensitive and balanced; while giving full support for creedal statements of doctrine and dogma, he saw the dangers inherent in clinging exclusively to them. "… it is very necessary that we should take clear account of the dangers to which the use of words in the expression of our faith exposes us. Religious history amply demonstrates the evils that flow from the misuse of formulae, and similar evidence is not wanting now."[16]

He continued to express publicly his intentions and those of the Cathedral:

We intend to go on teaching not only our own faith, but also the traditional expression of our faith, and we will defend it when it is attacked. But we will not behave to other men of other confessions as if they were always on the point of attacking ours. Until they attack it we will not regard them as our enemies, and therefore enemies of truth.

When we are forced to defend the truth enshrined in our creed, let it be in quietness and confidence, not in fear, as if it were something fragile and precarious, dependent for its safety upon our little victories over one another; not in anger, as though every man who questions the letter is thereby denying the spirit within. And when the difference concerns the Person of our Lord, let us specially remember that words can but faintly and faultily describe what He is.[17]

The words of a prominent layman, Captain Eric Rigby-Jones from the Cathedral Commoners were reported in the press:

This is not merely a question of Unitarians in the Cathedral. The Dean did not of sole purpose invite a Unitarian. He invited a man or men who bear in their life and work the marks of the spirit of Jesus. The charge now brought against the Bishop and the Dean challenges not only a few specific acts but the whole concept of the eternal spirit and of the consequent character of the Church. The issue is not just a trivial local matter. It goes deep into the issues vital to every Christian, and affects our whole vision of God, of His purpose, of His Church. This is why in my opinion the Bishop and the Dean cannot compromise upon it. To do so would not merely be to restrict the liberty of Liverpool Cathedral and damage its usefulness. It would be to surrender our faith, to deny its character, and to be false to the vision which the whole Church has seen and accepted.[18]

At the June meeting of Northern Convocation, Hensley Henson, Bishop of Durham, placed the motion before the house that "accordingly, this House is of opinion that, in the exercise of discretion approved in 1922 with regard to invitations to any preachers at special services, the Bishop should not extend such invitations to an person who does not hold, or who belongs to a denomination which does not hold, the 'common Christian faith' in Jesus Christ as 'Very God of Very God, Who for us men and our salvation came down from heaven and was made man'."[19] Both Bishops of Durham and Liverpool cannot have forgotten that it was Hensley Henson who had preached at one of the services in the Octave of the Consecration which welcomed Free-church ministers into the Cathedral. In his sermon he had said, "Your presence here

Jesus depicted in the Reredos behind the High Altar.

158

is profoundly significant. That it should be possible for the Bishop to say with such fitness that this Cathedral is 'yours and mine', is of the happiest augury. Only a united church, led by the spirit of truth, will gain audience. Primary responsibility rests with us, Anglican and Free churchmen."[20]

Albert Augustus made a formal report to his Diocese in an edition of *Liverpool Review* in which he explained the ruling which he had been forced to accept but he forthrightly stated his position.

> As I have already said, I shall conform to the decision. In making it, however, the House found itself (reluctantly, I think) compelled to declare by implication that Unitarians are not for that purpose to be reckoned as 'members of the Christian communion'. In this exclusion I do not, and shall never acquiesce. On the debate itself, I would make a first and final comment: it was largely a defence of a Christian doctrine which nobody attacked.[21]

Up to this point in the sequence of events, I judge Dwelly's influence on his Cathedral as entirely beneficial. He had taken a liberal stand over the people he invited to preach in the new, twentieth century Cathedral in Liverpool. He may have been unwise to invite Redfern without discussing the matter with the Bishop but I believe his decision to issue the invitation stemmed from Christian charity and concern for a well-respected local minister from a different denomination. The decision is completely in line with Raven's[22] *Liverpool Cathedral – An Impression of its Early Years* which was completed by August. Whether or not Raven wrote the work because of the problems that had arisen at the cathedral, I do not know. I have seen no written evidence but I strongly suspect that the publication of his ideas at that precise time was influenced by the furore which was developing. From the first, Dwelly was determined never to be held back by what he regarded as conservative, restricting convention. As the Rt. Rev. Gordon Bates, one time Precentor at Liverpool wrote to me, "Dwelly helped to create the uniqueness of Liverpool Cathedral and gave those who followed him the freedom to carry on and to develop this uniqueness. He saved us from 'conformity' and for that I remain very grateful."[23]

There is more material in the Dwelly archive relating to the Unitarian controversy than to any other subject but for the purposes of this study I have to be highly selective and yet deliver an accurate picture of many reactions. John H. Harris was almost certainly not known to Dwelly and wrote from Lee-on-Solent:

> If Sir, by your deviations from strict orthodoxy in the mode of your services in the Cathedral, by your preachers or by your inspiring brass

bands, which latter are the butt of unkindly ridicule on the part of many little Anglo-Catholics etc, you are filling your vast Cathedral with reverent and love inspired human beings, then Sir, you are accomplishing great things for that new and yet eternally old Christianity that is slowly and yet surely emerging in our day.

The late and good Studderd-Kennedy, Shepperd of St. Martins, and your own great Charles E. Raven, are the torches that have and are making their fire and strength felt over the land …[24]

"Dick" Shepperd in an edition of *The Quiver* offers the not inconsiderable weight of his support to Dwelly and Liverpool Cathedral:

> I do not know anything more calculated to enlarge our conception of God and His purposes than that Christians should increasingly be in debt to their partners in another boat. And why in the name of God should not a cathedral be used occasionally for all our sakes as the place where the other partners can give their contribution?[25]

Shepperd expressed his concern that Cecil, "so eminent and influential a Churchman" has taken such a narrow line. "It will be said that, in answer to the vast problems that cry for large Christian treatment, all that we have to contribute is an act of ecclesiastical bigotry."[26] Shepperd had a great regard for Jacks's intelligence and scholarship, having read "nearly everything he has written". The situation had become ridiculous. "Are we really to read him with profit, but stone him if he approaches our churches and cathedrals? It was grand for Liverpool people to hear him."[27]

Unfortunately, after the York Convocation the problems did not subside because Dwelly and Raven refused to let them subside. I cannot pronounce authoritatively on this matter but from the evidence of the letters in the Dwelly archive, Raven was the driving force in the next development, even though he had, of course, resigned as Chancellor in order to take up the post of Regius Professor of Divinity in Cambridge. From a clutch of letters, most only partly dated, there is evidence that he rather than Dwelly decided upon the next course of action. In January 1934 he wrote:

> I have just reread the chief speeches at Southport [Church Congress, 1926]. William Temple's might have been written for our special purpose. Spirit is fellowship – many movements outside the Church show it – we must respect, support and share in such movements – we must not exploit or condemn them – only in the whole church will the fellowship with the whole Christ be revealed. We could print this speech

as a pamphlet: personally I should do so: it leaves him completely and irrevocably committed.[28]

Another letter reminds Dwelly of what he and the Cathedral have tried to do:

> Guided by our Bishop we have tried to be faithful both to the maintenance of our Anglican heritage in the Book of Common Prayer, the rubrics and canons, and to our special opportunities as a new Cathedral in a great and grievously divided community. Time after time you have helped us to establish links with doctors, scientists, artists, musicians and men of affairs. Few events have been in my experience more obviously right than such occasions on which General Smuts and Sir Oliver Lodge preached to us; and the occasions have been very many. They have, I believe, not merely been rich in spiritual power for ourselves, but have given new status and influence to the Church of England, going far to justify its claim to be indeed the Church of the nation and not a sect.[29]

On Sunday 17 June, Canon Davey, the Canon in Residence for that day, read aloud from the pulpit a letter from Dwelly and Raven to Dr. Jacks, and also the letter written by Jacks in reply. Both letters are restrained yet powerful expressions of passionately held views. In view of the Bishop's unwillingness to discipline Dwelly over the Redfern sermon and the invidious position in which he was to find himself at the York Convocation, it was unfortunate that the Bishop was not even informed that the letters were to be read publicly from the Cathedral pulpit. Relations with the Bishop were further damaged as were the relations between the Cathedral and the Diocese. Raven's hand in the letter was clear enough – stylistically very similar to his *Liverpool Cathedral* publication of the previous year. Another letter gives some insight into the authorship of the letter: "... I produced a draft, the Dean saw, corrected and revised it. It was then submitted to one or two others. In its final shape it represents an agreed statement from those who signed it."[30] The letter expressed in the first sentence "our deep sense of regret and remorse" but the main body of the letter went beyond personal apology and became a strongly worded statement as to the whole character of the new Cathedral in Liverpool. As such it is a significant document about the theology of the new twentieth century cathedral. The attack on Temple and the Bishops was bound to cause hurt and anger. Although much of what followed was well argued and in temperate language, the anti-Episcopal charge at the beginning was politically inexpedient. The letter proceeded to outline in a restrained manner the dangers inherent in demanding strict creedal conformity, both in the past and in the present:

... while we recognize the right of any society to impose tests upon its members, and are not inclined to dispute the value for ourselves of the traditional creeds, we must make it plain that the attempt to foreclose the present inquiries by reference to ancient formulae seems a method damaging to intellectual honesty and hard to reconcile with any belief in a progressive revelation or any true concept of the nature of God's dealings with mankind.[31]

The argument proceeded by placing the new Cathedral in the intellectual tradition of F. D. Maurice, Charles Kingsley and F. J. A. Hort and by stressing that what they had been trying to do was in line with the spirit which was the guiding force for the Cathedral from the time of its consecration when

> ... most representative leaders of the Church of England united to assure us that a great opportunity lay before us, that the Cathedral built with the goodwill of a modern industrial city must strive to rise above narrow and sectional interests, and that in a day of fresh beginnings our loyalty to the Anglican communion should express itself in a reverent and courageous adventuring. Not less plainly was this advice emphasized by both the present Archbishops at the Church Congress held three years after the consecration in our diocese. By that time the general programme of our Cathedral had been settled. Our Special services and our invitation to preachers of other denominations were a matter of common knowledge. Our doctrinal position was fully explained at the Congress by our bishop and members of our Chapter.[32]

The letter shows the determination of Dwelly and Raven to stand by their principles.

> To quibble about ancient formularies, to appeal to outworn precedents, to refuse all movements as dangerous and all change as disloyal is to deny the faith, to betray the cause, to reject the opportunity ... We cannot and will not go back upon the road along which you have helped to lead us.[33]

A letter from Dr. Jacks was read at the same service. His words were courteous and deeply charitable towards his hosts but he expressed his ideas and fears forthrightly.

> In placing the interests of religion first, and the interests of church policy second, you have lit a candle in the Church of England that will not easily be put out ... If, henceforward, you are to be restricted, in the choice of Cathedral preachers from outside, to Nonconformists

The fanlight in the West Window. The rose window on the south side of the Central Space.

whose membership of the Visible church is guaranteed by unequivocal acceptance of the Creed of Nicaea, I am afraid you will find the area of selection not very large to begin with and continually diminishing as time goes on; you may even encounter doubtful cases among eminent members of the Church of England.[34]

At the end of the letter Jacks commented that had he been invited to preach at York Minster or Durham Cathedral he would have begged to decline, "feeling myself too out of place". "But somehow it was different when the invitation came from you in Liverpool. I reflected that Liverpool has a somewhat different manner of life, and a different outlook on the universe, from that of our ancient cathedral cities, and something of the Liverpool spirit, which I lived long enough in the city to imbibe, took possession of me."[35] These sentiments line up with many thoughts about the new Cathedral recorded in Chapters 1, 3 and 5 but the Bishop reported to his clergy: "My correspondence and interviews revealed not only strong feeling about a particular event, but also a certain dissatisfaction with the Cathedral generally in relation to the Diocese."[36]

Dwelly, together with Raven, exerted very strong influence in establishing and striving to maintain the liberal spirit and traditions of the Cathedral. Examination of the ministry of Edward Patey, third Dean, gives ample evidence that the Dwelly influence of experiment and open-ness was long maintained. Ecumenical growth might well have been set back by some of Dwelly's words and actions at the time of the Unitarian controversy. However, a service held in the Cathedral on 6 June 1937 was evidence of Dwelly's all-embracing vision for the Cathedral community. Official approval for this service was formally acknowledged in the Minute book of the Principal Chapter.

"The Chapter records with great appreciation the Empire Broadcast Service of Affirmation held on this day in the Cathedral shared by Clergy and Ministers from all denominations in the City and Diocese, the first actual personal witness together by Christians since the Reformation."[37] Dwelly was assisted in the devising of the service by an eminent Free Church minister, Rev. J. T. Wilkinson. The friendship of the two men was recorded by his son, now Canon Alan Wilkinson Dwelly had passionately wanted to appoint Wilkinson to some position in the Cathedral. And he wrote, "all my hopes so carefully builded are dashed … Not only is the blow to me the greatest I feel I have failed a friend for you so generously cooperated in my scheme."[38]

Alan Wilkinson considered the religious inclinations of his father and the Dean and found much in common. He described the Dean as being

... an innovative and romantic genius who could be affectionate, seductive and pastoral, but also difficult and obtuse ... Dwelly's understanding of Christianity and the Church was liberal, platonic and mystical rather than creedal, Catholic and sacramental, and this was exactly my father's outlook. Dwelly was less interested in the Eucharist and the statutory services than in pioneering, devising and staging colourful dramatic pageants of worship, expressed with original ceremonial and accompanied by fine music. On these occasions the lavishly produced and typographically elaborate service brochures, together with Wardour Street English which Dwelly wrote so well, presented modernism with a dash of antiquity and nostalgia so beloved by the English in church and on national occasions.[39]

The ecumenical broadcast service was immensely popular and 4,300 people who wished to attend could not be accommodated.

Other disagreements between Dwelly and the Bishop and Dwelly and the Archdeacons were public and bitter but they did not carry the theological significance of the Unitarian controversy. They did, however, make for very uneasy relations between the Cathedral and the diocese. Peart-Binns in Smout believed that Albert Augustus made a mistake in agreeing to the appointment of Dwelly as Dean; he "allowed his affection to override his intellect".[40]

"David's relations with Dwelly were founded on great affection, and all worked well so long as that intimate relationship lasted and Dwelly was eager to carry out what were really David's decisions. But, intellectually, and in all personal matters, they had little in common; and when the intimate relationship broke there was no longer common ground."[41] Dillistone declared, "To put it bluntly the Bishop found it difficult to keep his hands off the Cathedral; Dwelly on his part was determined to exercise the authority which had now been officially designated to him."[42] Probably both Cathedral and Diocese were damaged and it might well be argued that the split between the two, which developed in the 1930s, has still not been mended. "God's Dwelly House" was seen as remote and cut off from life in the parishes but not from the life of the city.

Despite the continuing animosity between Bishop and Dean, Dwelly through his great ecumenical services showed his determination that the Cathedral should not be the exclusive province of Church of England conformity. Several services to be considered in the following chapter are evidence of Dwelly's beliefs and the way in which those beliefs were manifested.

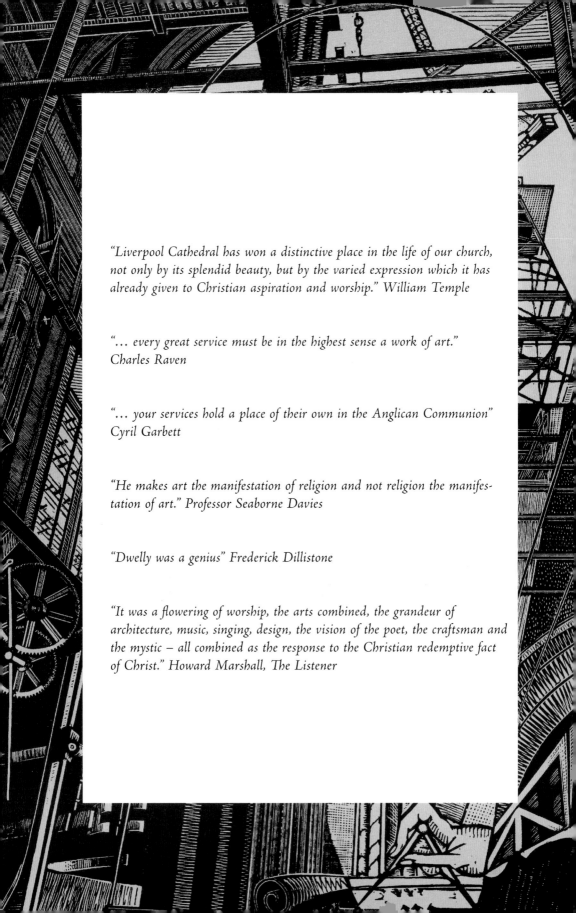

"Liverpool Cathedral has won a distinctive place in the life of our church, not only by its splendid beauty, but by the varied expression which it has already given to Christian aspiration and worship." William Temple

"… every great service must be in the highest sense a work of art." Charles Raven

"… your services hold a place of their own in the Anglican Communion" Cyril Garbett

"He makes art the manifestation of religion and not religion the manifestation of art." Professor Seaborne Davies

"Dwelly was a genius" Frederick Dillistone

"It was a flowering of worship, the arts combined, the grandeur of architecture, music, singing, design, the vision of the poet, the craftsman and the mystic – all combined as the response to the Christian redemptive fact of Christ." Howard Marshall, The Listener

The liturgical artist

I T   H A D   B E E N   openly acknowledged back in 1924 when the Bishop stated the need for "a service worthy of the occasion" that the new Cathedral needed an excellent liturgist. After 19 July 1924 it was obvious that the Cathedral had the services of a priest who possessed liturgical genius. Though Dwelly exhibited qualities of pastoral skill, leadership, and administrative ability, it was his liturgical skills which have left their greatest mark on the Cathedral and a wider canvas within the Church of England. A sermon preached by Cyril Garbett, Archbishop of York in 1945, twenty years after Dwelly's appointment to the Cathedral provides a useful statement from which to begin an examination of Dwelly the liturgist.

> Our Cathedrals cannot accept too high a standard for the art which should be used as a handmaid to worship.
>
> And the same principle applies to corporate worship as well as to the actual building and its adornment. There was a time when there was fear of using music colour and beauty in the worship of the church. It was thought that they might distract the worshipper from the solemnity of the act in which he was engaged. The result was that art became increasingly secular when it found the doors of the church closed to it. But we are learning again that all art should be consecrated to God, and that it should be used as an offering to Him. Here directed by the skill of your Dean, your public worship has been made beautiful with music and symbolism. In the richness of their colour and pageantry, as well as

A genial Dean Dwelly.

in variety and originality, your services hold a place of their own in the Anglican Communion. The prayers and praises used are both old and new; the worship of the historic liturgies is combined with prayers for modern needs in present day prose. And the appeal is made to the eye as well as to the ear, and to the imagination as well as to the intellect.

Your services have become popular in the best sense of the word. By this I mean that they have significance not merely to a small group of faithful who have been brought up to appreciate the ordinary worship of the Church, but to people of a great city. Men of different professions and interests find in the special services of the cathedral worship which is relevant to their daily work and problems. Our worship should not be separated by a gulf from the ordinary life of ordinary men and women. No Cathedral should stand apart from the life of those who live around it … This is the purpose of some of the great civic and special services held here, they are opportunities of dedicating all public and private work to him, and in return those who worship receive from him ideals and help which will raise their daily business to a higher level.

We must never forget that worship becomes selfish and self-centred if it begins and ends with the building in which it is held. If here on special occasions the offering of work is made to God, it is made so that day by day it may be done for his glory. Worship within the house of God should flow over into daily life. Your cathedral with all its majesty and beauty would stand as a rebuke unless its influence spread far and wide."[1]

The other significant statement against which the services should be measured is the statement made almost at the end of Dwelly's ministry by the University of Liverpool as they conferred on him the honorary degree of Doctor of Laws.

Into the superb edifice of the Cathedral which makes infinity so imaginable to us, Dean Dwelly puts animation which is always equal to the dignity of its purpose and its environment. Here is the great master

Dwelly receiving his honorary degree from the Vice Chancellor of the University of Liverpool.

of liturgical English to give perfect expression to the bidding prayer. Here is the creative artist of colour and symmetry to convey that majesty and wonder of creation and revelation which made the stars of the morning sing with joy. Providence was indeed kind to all worldly impresarios when it made Dr. Dwelly a Dean and left secular pageantry to their inferior talents. He makes art the manifestation of religion and not religion the manifestation of art. He habitually confounds the vulgar heresy that sanctity is greater where elegance is less: but he equally defeats those who would reduce fine ritual to the level of aesthetic mummery of pagans and atheists. Dwelly, the Cambridge Master of Arts, is always in harmony with Dwelly, the Oxford Doctor of Divinity.[2]

In any examination of Dwelly services it would be wise to hold in mind the Archbishop's focus upon music and symbolism, colour and pageantry, variety and originality, and popularity through relevance, as well as the University's notion of animation – headings which fit comfortably into the list which this study first applied to the Consecration Service: preparation, organization, structure, choreography, text, music, symbolism, service papers. Fortunately service papers enable current examination of services from the Dwelly era to be undertaken. Almost without exception, the service papers from 1926 to the outbreak of the Second World War are preserved in annual bound volumes. From 1939 to 1953 only the special service papers have been collected and it remains uncertain whether all of them have been saved and bound. A clear distinction has to be made between the regular services each Sunday and the large number of special or vocational services.

On a standard Sunday, a simple service sheet gave the basic details relating to the five regular services. Holy Communion was said at 8 am and 12.15 pm, Choral Matins was celebrated at 11 am. Choral Evensong was at 3 pm and the Congregational Service at 8.30. There were three weekday services: Holy Communion and Morning and Evening Prayer. In 1930 Evensong was Choral on Monday, Tuesday, Thursday and Saturday. All of these regular services were conducted according to the *Book of Common Prayer*, the only variation being that they did not sing all the set psalms for the day and did not sing the Nunc Dimittis at Evensong. It is not possible to state whether the set lessons were read in full but, judging by the shortness of the psalms, I suspect that lessons were shortened. Dwelly's handling of biblical material in special services will be considered later in the chapter.

An Easter morning service was broadcast by the B.B.C. throughout the 1930s and several of these services attracted lengthy detailed comment in the press. *The Church of England Newspaper* 1931, devoted considerable space to a critical description of the service by a correspondent many of whose words are relevant at this point. Such lengthy and informed and sensitive comment on a service celebrated seventy-five years ago has to be quoted in full.

> It is well known that Liverpool Cathedral during the past few years has been the scene of much liturgical experiment … Here is a development of Anglican worship which deserves the closest study and the warmest sympathy of all Churchmen, whatever their school of thought. No one who is dissatisfied with the traditional worship of our cathedrals and larger parish churches can afford to ignore the experiments of Liverpool. The word experiment, however, is barely adequate to describe what has practically become a tradition, for the principles governing the ordering of the rites and ceremonies appear, at least to the visitor, to have become already firmly rooted in the minds of those who take part in them and of the congregations which assist at them.
>
> Though the orders of service, with their prophecies, responses, litanies, benedictions, hallowings, and the like, will be unfamiliar to the visitor, yet they have not that distressing air of novelty (in the bad sense of the term) which causes the word 'stunt' to rise to the lips. They are a legitimate development; continuity with the main stream of Catholic liturgy is immediately perceived; they are rooted in Holy Scripture and the old service books …
>
> If this element of continuity is apparent in the rites, it is also present in the ceremonial, though here again its details were unfamiliar. The obvious practical intent of all the comings and goings within the choir and presbytery, and the absence of ceremony for the sake of ceremony, could not be missed. That the most practical ceremonial is also the most beautiful was strikingly proved by these two great festival services on Easter Day. The great sweeping movements of various processions, the stately pacings to and fro of the groups of clergy and other ministers as they went about their business, the precision of every movement which somehow did not create an air of self-conscious formality, the almost austere restraint governing the whole – all these belong to an order of things which has characterised the purest stream of Catholic ceremonial, and they are lessons which all who have the ordering of public worship should study diligently.
>
> When people complain that ceremonial distracts them and robs them of interior quiet, one should not always put this down as a Puritan objection. Perhaps it is the aim and spirit of the ceremonial which is at fault. That some ceremonial, though unfamiliar, can have a quite opposite

Easter Day in the Cathedral showing the meticulous planning of the choreography and the importance of the members of the Cross Guild.

effect and positively deepen one's sense of recollection and make the heart ready for prayer in an almost magical way, was the experience of one stranger at Liverpool on Easter Day, and apparently also of the majority of the congregations who came to worship. 'Let not him who seeks cease until he finds, finding he shall wonder, wondering he shall enter the kingdom and having entered the kingdom he shall rest'. The worshipper who heard the choir sing these words, as the Bishop entered and knelt before the High Altar, was enabled by all that was going on to go through that very experience.

How well, too, this repose of spirit was assisted by the colour of the ministers' ornaments. The quiet golden reds of the choir men's cassocks, and the soft greens and purples of the vergers' gowns and the chanters' mantles – all this helped to deepen the sense of peace and tranquility so precious but so rarely attainable at great church functions.

And the music. When reports of great services at Liverpool Cathedral are spread abroad, it is not usually the music which is specially commented upon. Yet it can be said with deliberation that the Cathedral possesses an absolutely first-class choir, ably directed by a musician of exceptional competence and sensibility. Too often is the worshipper sadly disappointed during a visit to some large church or cathedral where it is reported that 'the music is so beautiful'. Even if this is true in the abstract, Church music is too seldom quite unliturgical, being a mere performance more or less related to the devotional direction of the service and the 'note' of the fast or feast celebrated. Very often, too, what is called beautiful music is merely intricate music or even merely loud music. The music at Liverpool was strictly liturgical in character and sung with an understanding and skill far above the average. They sang such good things too – Bach, Palestrina, Byrd, Handel, Vaughan Williams and Martin Shaw all had their share, in addition to the composers of the well-known Easter hymns. The Cathedral also is fortunate in its music director, who is responsible for much arrangement and adaptation of old music to meet the special liturgical needs of the carefully planned rites. A most rare and pleasing feature of the singing was the light and shade in volume of sound. Easter Day is commonly regarded as an excuse for an immense noise and little else besides. Here we knelt quietly and were led up to our more vociferous praise by the gentle invitation of the choir singing pianissimo 'O come let us worship … in His presence is fullness of joy,' passing to those exquisite words of the Rosy Sequence, 'With Mary in the morning gloom I seek for Jesus at the tomb' in the proper plainsong melody.

Perhaps the reader is tired of so much superlative in this description. If so, an apology is offered, though without sincere contrition. Let him hold out a little longer while the pilgrim attempts to present two pictures which will long remain vivid in the mind.

In the first, the Bishop stands at the entrance into the choir facing the people, the clergy and other ministers grouped magnificently around. Valiantly and with genuine exultation, he chants forth' 'The Lord is risen. The Lord is risen indeed. Alleluia!' Then he proceeds to a four-fold blessing in old Galican style, each section being punctuated by an exultant Amen from the choir. In the second, the service is over and the whole concourse within the sanctuary moves forth down the choir, led by the bishop who, crozier in hand, strides out at their head. Never was the true function of the episcopate more dramatically set forth.[3]

For those worshippers who wanted plain Prayer Book Services, Morning and Evening Prayer were read at 9.30 am and 5.30 pm and there were celebrations of Holy communion at 6. am, 7 am, 8 am, 9.45 am, and 12.15 pm. The day closed with the traditional 8.30 pm service. The two big choral services were at 11 am and 3 pm: they were similar to each other but not identical. The congregation were given an explanation of the nature of what was to follow in a paragraph at the head of the service paper 1932.

The Festival of Easter calls for an offering of worship so wide and manifold as to justify the provision of a form of service added this day to Holy Communion and Morning Prayer. It begins with a selection from various sources of suggestions on which we may prepare ourselves for that which is prepared for us. Then in a procession from East to West, moving to the Resurrection Hymn, is brought an ancient threefold Easter Blessing answered by the *Hallelujah Chorus*. Then follow readings from the Epistle and Gospel, with the Easter Anthem between them, leading up to the Te Deum, the Creed and collects. After an Anthem, written for the Cathedral by John Masefield and Martin Shaw, come our now familiar Intercessions, set to music by Palestrina; the Sermon, with Hymns before and after a reminiscence of the Eucharistic Thanksgiving, and, when the final blessing has been given, a Hymn sung by the Congregation alone as the Dean's company leaves the Choir."[4]

All the preparation and organization which went into the structuring of the service are obvious when the service is studied after the event but at the time the text, choreography, music and symbolism would have animated the whole service through its dramatic flow. The service was, in the best sense, theatrical.

Current Cross Guild members keeping up the Dwelly ceremonial traditions.

Even before the first words of the service, the huge and dignified processions of Choir, Clergy and Cross Guild would have entered moving though the Sanctuary and Presbytery into their seats in the choir to the accompaniment of the organ. The words of the Preparation sung by Cantors and Choir were from various sources. They were mainly quiet and contemplative but holding within them a great sense of anticipation.

The bishop addressed the people from the High Altar in the words of the Easter Bidding: "Let us arise and unto the Lord bring a song instead of myrrh, and he shall meet us in the garden of the soul, even the Sun of Righteousness, who ever throweth open gates of new life, giving light and life to all mankind."[5] This was followed immediately by the singing of *Jesus Christ is risen today*, almost certainly accompanied by organ, drums, trumpets and tubular bells and with a dramatic build up to *Now above the sky he's King* and a dramatic silence before the final lines. During the singing of the hymn, the Bishop attended by the Chapter and Cross Guild moved west through the choir to stand at the chancel steps for the Lord's Prayer, General Thanksgiving and the Easter Blessing, the whole movement culminating as the congregation stood and the choir sang *Hallelujah Chorus* from Handel's *Messiah*. The effectiveness of the whole sequence is without question. Shortened reading from the Epistle and the Gospel for Easter Day were separated by the choir's performance of Martin Shaw's setting for the Prayer Book *Easter Anthems*, composed specially at

An annual naval service.

Dwelly's request for use in the Cathedral. After the Gospel the Choir sang *Te Deum Laudamus* composed by Vaughan Williams for Liverpool Cathedral and dedicated to the Bishop. John Masefield had written *They buried him, and then the soldiers slept* for the Consecration and they were subsequently set by Martin Shaw. The intercessions, regularly used in the Cathedral, were set to the music of Palestrina then after the Grace everyone sang the hymn *The strife is o'er* before the Bishop's sermon. Two further hymns and a blessing completed the service.

Any consideration of the text of a Dwelly service must be seen in the context of the Cathedral, with all the resources which he had available to him, then the word "animation" used in 1954 by the University Vice-Chancellor takes on its full significance. The whole service was indeed a drama of Easter which must have powerfully involved the whole Cathedral company. Alan Wilkinson wrote of Dwelly's "pioneering, devising and staging colourful dramatic pageants of worship expressed with original ceremonial and accompanied by fine music."[6]

The popularity of these great festival services was proved by the number of worshippers who filled every seat and by the fact that the B.B.C. regularly broadcast the Easter morning service.

Whitsunday services were planned by Dwelly in a similar style and structure was approved by the Rev. Colin Dunlop, later to become a Bishop. He wrote to Dwelly from Chichester on 18 May.

> You know how greatly I enjoyed my visit to you this Whitsuntide and how grateful I am to you for all your kindness. It was to be a never-to-be-forgotten weekend. Before coming I rather wondered whether I should like the services as much as I liked them at my first visit when everything was so novel. I am bound to say that this time I liked them even more and was better able to appreciate the details which go to make up the whole, which at a first visit are swallowed up in the general impression. The music in particular seemed to me to be superb and so truly liturgical, in that it never swamped the devotional aim of the service but always, both as to its character and quantity, assisted worship, without blurring the liturgical outlines of the service."[7]

He did not blandly praise everything because he felt that the use of Anglican chant for the Psalms in a service with so much very fine music was a let-down.

His comments on the robes might well have been made by a discerning visitor to the Cathedral today. The original cross guild robes were in use until about ten years ago when they were renewed in the same style but not quite the same quality of material.

> There is no doubt in my mind that the whole colour scheme of your service has been amazingly enriched and simplified (both) by the unbleached linen of the surplices ... the unbleached material makes the garments hang far better, and the sight of the clergy and choir entering the Cathedral is extraordinarily beautiful. And it makes both the robes of the ministers and the prevailing colours of the Cathedral fabric and furniture, all of the same order of colouring.[8]

To Dunlop only the scarlet of the Bishop's chimere and white sleeves of his rochet spoiled the unity of the whole scheme. The same criticism was voiced years later when the Rt. Rev. Rupert Hoare became the fifth Dean.

Dunlop's comments on the Eucharist were particularly interesting because it is known from Raven's remarks that Dwelly had not attempted to make any modifications to the way in which the service was treated and Dunlop was disappointed: "... the service which least embodied the excellencies which art has come to associate with Liverpool Cathedral worship. I know you will forgive me when I say that it seemed to be conventional in the bad sense."[9] His thoughts about future services in the completed Cathedral are interesting because they are very close to what does happen today – though without a baldachino. "I believe it would be a great step forward for the High Altar to be set up in the Central Space under a baldachino raised on a number of steps leading up from all sides. Then at a celebration the people would be gathered all round the Family Table, and this would devotionally be a great gain."[10] It was to be into the 1950s, under the leadership of the second Dean, that the Cathedral made this move. It must be remembered that Dwelly lived in the age before a celebration of the Eucharist was regarded as the central Sunday service. That Dunlop was prepared to make adverse criticism, gives me greater confidence in the sincerity of his positive comments.

The Christmas Day services were not as elaborate as those at Easter, though very popular carol services were held on the Sundays before and after Christmas Day and in 1932, when Christmas Day fell on a Sunday, on that day at 3.00 pm. The carol services did not follow the King's College Cambridge pattern of nine lessons and carols but relied almost entirely on the music. My earliest memories of services in the Cathedral in the early 1950s are of the carol service before Christmas when people arrived from 1.00 pm onwards in order to find a good seat. These services remain popular today and draw large congregations on two Sundays and on the Saturday before Christmas when there is a recital of all the Christmas music being sung that year.

Even before Dwelly's appointment as Dean, a great number of special services were held each year: Easter 1930 to Easter 1931 is typical.

April	Assize
1 May	College of Nursing
3 May	Cathedral Builders
11 May	Central Liverpool Girl Guides
24 May	Wolf Cubs
25 May	The Health of the People
31 May	Admission of Lay Readers
3 June	World Alliance for Promoting International Friendship through Churches
15 June	Annual Service for Nurses
21 June	Belvedere School Jubilee
2 July	President of the Senate of Hamburg and Burgomaster of Amsterdam
6 July	Child Welfare Organizations

Choristers before the start of a Harvest Service.

12 July	Marriage
13 July	Jubilee of the Diocese
7 September	Music and Readings
14 September	Centenary of the Liverpool and Manchester Railway
21 September	Ordination
September	Funeral
28 September	Installation of Canons
3 October	Funeral
5 October	Salonica Reunion
12 October	North East Division Girl guides
17 October	Funeral
19 October	Annual Medical Service
22 October	Liverpool College Commemoration Service
26 October	Liverpool and District Post Office Staff
2 November	Assize

9 November	Armistice Commemoration
9 November	Royal Artillary Association
11 November	Solemn Observance of Silence to the Honour of Heroes
11 November	United Peace Dedication Service
16 November	Civic Service
30 November	South Liverpool division Girl Guides
13 December	Toc H Service of Light
21 December	Ordination
21 December	Carols
25 December	Christmas Day Service
28 December	Carols
31 December	Watchnight
18 January	Epiphany Carols
18 January	University Carols
27 January	Funeral
1 February	Assizes
25 February	Funeral Margaret Beavan
27 February	Gwyl Dolewi
15 March	Refreshment Sunday and Mid-Lent Carols

This year, chosen more or less at random, is typical both of the number and the variety of special services and does indicate what Cyril Garbett was to call the popularity of the Cathedral's services in that they related directly to "different professions and interests". The worship was certainly not "separated by a gulf from the ordinary life of ordinary men and women". This chapter can be held to a reasonable length only by the selection for examination of a relatively small number of varied services. Severe war-time paper shortage meant that a number of services were unable to have printed sheets and there is an unfortunate gap in the Cathedral archives.

There are many examples of Dwelly special services but I have not discovered any document in which Dwelly himself explained the principles to which he was working while devising any of these services. Fortunately, a series of books was planned by Cambridge University Press under the general title of *Problems of Worship* under the general editorship of Dwelly and W. R. Matthews, Dean of St. Paul's. The war seems to have destroyed the venture but the first volume *English Prayer Books – An Introduction to the Literature of Christian Public Worship* was written by Stanley Morison, typographical adviser to Cambridge University Press and Sanders Reader of Bibliography in the University. The section of the book entitled 'Present Day Vocational Services' is based entirely on Dwelly's work in Liverpool. By way of introduction he referred to what

Cosmo Lang had said at the rehallowing of St. Mary Redcliffe in 1933. "He then drew attention to the advantage of a special service that was not a 'mutilation of Evensong'. More recently, his successor has laid stress upon the need for the Church of England to welcome its people by means of specially written 'supplementary' services. In fact highly successful services expressing the intercessions and thanks of particular groups of men and women banded together in work of social value have been held."[11] Within the same paragraph he made reference to Dwelly's *Kinship with the Sea* service of 1930. "The value of such a service that has been written in direct contact with those who have experienced the needs for which liturgical petition is made needs no apology. Vocational services so drafted have survived the test of use in a large building and that, not in one year only, but in several."[12] Then follow three paragraphs[13] which are clearly transmission of the account he had from Dwelly. Although they relate specifically to naval services, the principles hold good for the whole range of vocational services. Correspondence from Morison reveals how accurately he wished to communicate Dwelly's ideas.

> Twenty years ago, a service of thanksgiving was held for men of the sea in the cathedral of a port from which the ships go out. A fine congregation of officers and men of the Royal Navy paraded. The chaplains and the choirs sang handsomely to the accompaniment of coughs from officers and men. The select preacher faced a congregation whose attitude was respectful rather than attentive.
>
> Next year the same thank-offering was made. The failure was equally plain. Somebody at the time disposed of the service by describing it as a function at which 'nothing real happened'. The failure promised to be as customary as the service itself but for the fact that one of the clergy was 'lunched' by some of the mariners. He asked them if, in the experiences of their lives, they were spontaneously moved to feel thankful to God. Yes, all men of the sea had cause, from time to time, to ejaculate a thank-offering; and so, at another meal-time, written thank-offerings were forthcoming. At a later meeting agreement was reached that there should be two prayers: the official one, read by captains at sea, should be read first by a captain; and a second prayer, leading up to the Lord's Prayer, should be said by all. Strings of collects were never favoured, but the thank-offerings and petitions as drafted became a permanent part of the revised service.
>
> In the course of years the Benedictions of the Sea have increased in number, and in degree of correspondence with the vocations of the men. Thus the mainstay of the service was what was said and sung by men with

experience of the ships and the sea. The choir was dispensed from the task of singing elaborate responses and the single anthem was relegated to a position in the preparation. The sermon gave place to a business-like gathering-together of reflections which culminated in the seamen's petition to God, for help in relating their whole life with the beauty of the sea and all to His love and His providence. The form was easy to follow.[14]

Morison had examined several naval services; the quotations which follow are from the 1943 service. Morison has written about the nature of the preparation for the service with consultation with those for whom the service was created and we know that Dwelly worked very closely with Sir Percy Noble and Sir Max Horton when Liverpool was the headquarters of Western Approaches and crucial to the success of the Battle of the Atlantic. Dwelly and Horton became great friends as is reported by Rear-Admiral W. S. Chalmers in *Max Horton and the Western Approaches*.[15] Cathedral and Naval processions would have been impeccably conducted but the choreography of the service was very simple with concentration being upon the words.

The service opened with the whole congregation singing *Eternal Father strong to save*; the hymn known to the whole congregation. From the start everyone would have had a sense of personal involvement. The choir were present but their function was simply to lead the congregational singing. Dwelly's words, spoken by the Chaplain of the Port, would have sounded appropriate to all present.

> Terrible and magnificent is the sea in its proof through the ages of man's courage and strength, his endurance, his stern self-reliance, his gradual mastery of sea craft, his widening skill in ship construction, his dawning knowledge of science, of astronomy, meteorology, and engineering, his inventions, recordings, questings; his gatherings of infinite sums of knowledge and resource, bringing into being the great fleet of ships that sail the oceans of the world today.
>
> Magnificent the unswerving fortitude, the enduring loyalty, the selfless sacrifice of the men of the Sea, who keep watch over the great sea lanes. Safeguard the true freedom of the seas, giving battle for the ultimate world brotherhood of mankind, with our sovereign Lord the King.
>
> We of the British Empire and Commonwealth together with officers and men of the navies founded in sea tradition are gathered in our Cathedral church to give thanks to Almighty God for the Kinship of the Sea.[16]

The hymn *Praise, my soul, the King of Heaven* preceded the single Bible reading.

The reading is typical of Dwelly and might have distressed the purist as he joined together verses from different books of the Bible into one continuous reading without explanation; the italics are mine.

The Spirit of God moved upon the face of the waters. [*Genesis 1.2*]

And God divided the waters which were under the firmament from the waters which were above the firmament. [*Genesis 1.7*]

And the gathering together of the waters called the seas. [*Genesis 1.10*]

The waves of the sea are mighty, and rage horribly; but yet the Lord, who dwelleth on high, is mightier. [*Psalm 95.4*]

He layeth the beams of his chambers in the waters.

He maketh the clouds his chariot, and walketh upon the wings of the wind. [*Psalm 104.3*]

His way also is in the sea, and his paths in the great waters; and his footsteps are not known. [*Psalm 77.19*]

They that go down to the sea in ships, and occupy their business in great waters; these men see the works of the Lord and his wonders in the deep. [*Psalm 107.23,24*]

How he maketh the storm to cease so that the waves thereof are still [*Psalm 107.29*]

And so he bringeth them to the haven where they would be. [*Psalm 107.30*]

I was in the spirit on the Lord's day, and heard behind me a great voice. [*Revelation 1.10*]

And the voice was the sound of many waters. [*Revelation 1.15*]

And I turned to see the voice that spoke with me. [*Revelation 1.12*]

And I heard a great voice out of heaven, saying: Behold the tabernacle of God is with men, and he will dwell with them. [*Revelation 21.3*]

And he showed me a pure river of water of life, clear as crystal, proceeding out of the throne of God. On either side of the river was there the tree of life, which bare twelve manner of fruits, and yielded her fruit every month; and the leaves of the tree were for the healing of the nations. [*Revelation 22.1,2*][17]

Dwelly has succeeded in welding together a range of material from various biblical sources, giving them a unity through imagery and cadence. He did not attempt to use the Psalms and the set readings for the day, which though meaningful to the regular worshippers, might have made little impact on most of the congregation that afternoon.

The single anthem was short and highly atmospheric and dramatic being the opening pages of *The Sea Symphony* by Vaughan Williams, a setting of words by Walt Whitman. The opening is explosive:

Behold the sea itself,
And on its limitless heaving breast, the ships.

The Holly Bough placed in the Sanctuary at the culmination of a carol service

O my brave Soul!
O farther,
Farther sail![18]

The imagery around which the Benedictions were written was close to the lives and experiences of the sailor and chosen to focus the vocational minds of all present more effectively than most traditional prayers.

> Blessed the unending beauty of the seas and oceans,
> The ineffable, wondrous colour of sky, cloud and sea;
> The birds, the fishes, the sounds.
> The view of distant coast and hinterland from a ship's deck,
> The breathless loveliness of a tropic dawn,
> The cold blue grandeur of the iceberg.

> Blessed the Beauty of the Sea.

> Blessed the headlands, the lighthouse,
> The mountain, the Cathedral tower,
> The point of departure on a long trans-ocean voyage.

> Blessed the first sight of land,
> The merging of a mountain from the clouds,
> The looming of the light of a city at night,
> The flashing beam of a lighthouse,
> The tree-tops rising over a clear horizon,
> The land-fall at the Voyage's End.

> Blessed the landfall at the Voyage's End.[19]

After the Benedictions the entire company joined together in saying Nelson's prayer, known to all naval men.

> May the great God whom I worship grant to my country, and for the benefit of Europe in general, a great and glorious victory; and may no misconduct in anyone tarnish it; and may humanity after victory be the predominant feature in the British Fleet. For myself, individually, I commit my life to Him that made me, and may His blessing alight on my endeavours for serving my country faithfully. To Him I resign myself and the just cause which it entrusted to me to defend. Amen. Amen. Amen.[20]

The service ended with a blessing from the Bishop and the singing of the hymn *Onward Christian soldiers*. The service was not long or elaborate; the sentiments which it expressed were meaningful to the company; old and new material was fused comfortably into a style which had dignity without being remote. The celebration of a naval service continued after the war as a service to commemorate the Battle of the Atlantic, and the sixtieth anniversary service devised by Precentor, Canon Ken Riley, was broadcast on national television.

Dwelly's first sea service has already been mentioned, *Kinship with the Sea*, 9 February, 1930. That service opened with the choir singing a long Dwelly Biblical conflation referred to as The Psalms of the Sea, though the material was not drawn solely from the psalms. Fifteen pages of words and music in manuscript have been preserved. The music likely to have been the work of Edgar Robinson, the choral conductor.

The heart of the service was the performance of something Dwelly had referred to as a masque, though there is no dramatic movement. It was an original work with a text by John Masefield set to music by Martin Shaw. Entry to the service was by ticket only but the morning service, open to all, had also celebrated the city's Kinship with the Sea. The service paper for the afternoon service ran to 32 pages produced in the distinctive Liverpool Cathedral style – very high quality cream paper, with a distinctive cover printed in black and red. The font size of the text varied and made generous use of 'white-space'. The service paper was far more than simply the words for the service: it was in keeping with the size and character of the Cathedral, the dignity of the ceremonial and it was something which members of the congregation wished to keep as a reminder of the service.

Stanley Morison also made reference to the Dwelly service[21] commemorating the twenty fifth anniversary of the Royal Air Force, 1943, and the way in which members of Fighter and Bomber Command had been involved in the drafting of the service. They had stressed the importance of the whole team rather than the singling out of individuals for praise. The pilots and navigators appreciated how much they owed to whole teams of people on the ground who never expected glory. The whole company of the Air Force spoke the Benedictions and the response was made by the Dean and members of Chapter. The use of a single verse sung by the choir must have been very powerful.

> Blessed the call of duty in the air and blessed the need therefore of fine human qualities.

> R. Blessed the call of duty.

> Blessed the call for courage, and initiative to which there is no parallel and blessed the call for physical perfection and dexterity.

> Blessed the call for mental gifts whose multiplicity and ingenuity are like

Junior choristers with candles and Christmas trees.

to the aircraft armament, wireless, oxygen plant and complicated panel of the machine.

Blessed the airman's quiet and efficient fulfillment of his duty.

Blessed the reluctance to speak of self and blessed the modesty after gallant performance.

Blessed the ready patriots who without looking for reward offer their lives and their limbs.

The Choir shall sing 'One of our Machines did not return'

> So to the entrance of that fiery gate,
> Borne by no current, driven by no breeze,
> Knowing no guide but some compelling fate,
> Bold navigators of uncharted seas,
> Courage and youth went proudly sweeping by,
> To win the unchallenged freedom of the sky.

Blessed even in the dangers of taking off in the half light.

Blessed even in the adventure of night flight.

Blessed in the groping efforts, the finding of the bandits, day and night, sneaking in through clouds and protectively coloured.

Blessed in the cold patrol of the wastes of the seas.

Blessed, for ever blessed, the finding of the lost, after descent into the sea by parachute.

Blessed be God in every coming of the deliverer, blessed the most sure promise of the coming of the Son of Righteousness with healing in his wings, even he who taught us to say: OUR FATHER.[22]

Morison drew significant conclusions from his experience of Dwelly's liturgical developments:

> The Anglican Dean's comparison of liturgiology with stamp-collecting implies scorn for the frivolity of thought recognizable in men who satisfied an appetite for ceremony-mongering and dressing-up while evading the real problems of Christian worship. It now looks as if the millinery and play-acting stage has passed. Liturgiology can no longer be identified with a programme to restore public worship into conformity with such conventions as east windows, oak screens, elongated chancels

and four-poster altars. We are likely to find religious bodies looking forward, rather than backward; spending less time on the 'beauty' of liturgical worship and more on the task of rendering it congregationally efficacious ... Today there is a new realization by those who profess a religious affiliation that public worship needs to be made more vital for more people.[23]

"Vital" and wholly appropriate worship had been devised by Dwelly in 1929 for the *Scout Jamboree Services*, 11 August 1929. The twenty two page service book contains the text of the three services. The 3 pm People's Service of Thanksgiving was short and created for adults while the 4.45 pm service was for the Scouts themselves and made effective use of rousing hymns which they could enjoy singing: *Jerusalem, Mine eyes have seen the glory, ,All people that on earth do dwell, Praise the Lord, ye heavens, adore him, I vow to thee, my country, Pioneers* and *Praise, my soul, the King of Heaven*. Visually the service was arresting in that the flags of the sixty five visiting nations were paraded by the scouts right up to surround the Bishop in the Sanctuary. The single reading and the prayers were short and the Scout Law and Promise formed a central feature. The choir were present but sang only one piece of special music – a blessing to the music of Martin Shaw. Dwelly, Chaplain of the First Windermere Sea Scouts, preached to parents and friends at the 8.30. The service paper gave notice that for a fortnight parties of scouts, not exceeding 250 in number, would be shown round the building and taken over the roof. On five days there were to be services "one every hour, and one for each several Nation, Race, Dominion and Colour. Interpreters will be provided. An illustrated Guide Book will be given to each Scout. Only the music of the Nation in attendance will be used. A copy of the Guide Book is retained and it is stylistically the work of Dwelly. Unfortunately nothing remains from the hourly services.

In the context of the history of the Cathedral building, a sequence of services in July 1941 was arranged to mark the occasion when the Dean and Chapter formally took possession of and moved into the newly completed central space. The temporary wall blocking the eastern under-tower arch was demolished and the vast central space became available for services. *Solemn Entry in Time of War* invited Dwelly to use his choreographic skills to highlight the symbolic significance of the event. At the heart of the service was symbolic movement.

> Then the Building Committee, by the action of their chairman, shall put the Dean and Chapter into possession of the new portion of the Cathedral, passing over that place in the Crypt where during an enemy air raid a celebration of holy communion was begun in the older part of

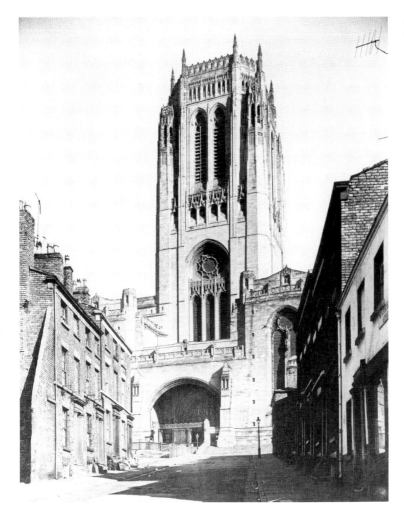

A view of the tower through Washington Street, now long demolished,

the building and completed at a carpenter's bench in the new; consummating the consecration of the Choir at the first Eucharist in the Nave. During the procession the choir shall sing the hymn:

Lord, thy glory fills the heavens;
Earth is with its fullness stored;
Unto thee be glory given,
Holy, Holy, Holy, Lord.

When the action of the chairman has been duly acknowledged and the formalities of entering into possession completed, the chairman shall take his place in the westernmost part of the Cathedral, near to where the Building Committee purpose the building of the great bridge of the Nave, and the Dean shall say:

At first let us rejoice in his assurance, knowing that his promise never fails, Wheresoever two or three are gathered together in his name, there he is in the midst.

A space of silence shall be kept.

Then the Dean shall continue:

It is written, then came Jesus and stood in the midst, and said, Peace be unto you. And they worshipped him.

A space of silence shall be kept.

Children shall then enter into the procession.

When the leading boy has crossed the threshold, the reading shall continue:

Jesus called unto him a little child, and set him in the midst and said, Verily I say unto you. Except ye become as little children, ye shall no wise enter into the kingdom of heaven.[24]

These simple words and actions were as powerful as anything Dwelly ever produced. The drama of the whole was enhanced by the careful use of periods of silence and the singing of the simple, well-known hymn. The choreography 'spoke' the significance of the whole ceremony in terms of architecture – moving into the new portion, of history – the remembrance of the interrupted Eucharist, and of theology – with the words of Jesus and the movement of the single choir boy.

An account of the incident referred to in the ceremony is preserved in Chris Wagstaffe's handwriting. On Sunday 8 September 1940, the overnight raids had been so bad that most of the roads approaching the Cathedral were closed and prevented most of the congregation from attending. During the recitation of the Apostles' Creed at Matins celebrated with less than a dozen people, the air raid siren sounded and the service was finished and Holy Communion celebrated down in the Crypt.

Another outstanding war-time Dwelly service took place in September 1944, when war-torn Liverpool welcomed Clifford Martin as its third Bishop. The enthronement service was not one of splendour and pageantry but it was deeply spiritual and must have had a profound effect on the new Bishop. Here was another example of the importance of preparation for a Dwelly service. In an obituary notice in the *Liverpool Daily Post* in May, the Bishop wrote appreciatively of the way in which he and his family had been made ready for the enthronement service.

> A few weeks before my Enthronement the Dean arrived at our home bringing with him a cathedral hymn book. This he handed to our three young daughters with the instruction: 'Go into your Father's study and choose the hymn you would like to have sung in the Cathedral when he is enthroned.' So he drew them into the Cathedral company, as he did our son, then a lad of seventeen. John was given the task of accompanying his father at every stage in the Enthronement ceremony. All this was Dr. Dwelly's idea. It was part of his genius. Worship, according to his idea, was not something imposed upon the people but drawn out of them, so that they learned to offer their best to God.[25]

Everything about the service must have been both a challenge and a support to the new Bishop: the service seemed to be *for* him rather than being for the packed congregation. The Bishop was carefully prepared by Dwelly for the enormity of the occasion so that with calm and quiet he could appreciate its full significance.

> Before my Enthronement the Dean asked me to go to the Cathedral not once but several times "to walk over the ground" as he called it. In this way he helped me to become used to my part in that great ceremony and on the day to do it without flurry or anxiety.[26]

The finished service in September 1944 showed a perfect balance between the theatrical and the spiritual. The war still raged and the service was punctuated by times of silence "to seek the blessing of God on those bearing the burdens of the war, winning victories for the free spirit." Those people who had been present at the Consecration would have remembered the knocking on the door, but now the Cathedral was a third larger than it had been then. The rubric in the service paper, pointed to the significance of the movements. "At five-thirty in the afternoon the bishop shall knock three times at the door which opens from the carpenter's workshop into the Cathedral church. He shall knock with the same ivory mallet that was used by the late King Edward VII when he laid the foundation stone of the Cathedral. The Dean shall order the doors to be thrown open. As the door is opened, the Keeper of the Door shall say in a quiet voice the words: Do justly. Love mercy. Walk humbly with thy God."[27] These words were repeated quietly several times in the service and at different significant parts of the building.

The Dean, delivering the Staff into the hands of the bishop, shall say:

With this Staff may the Lord give thee grace to do justly, to love mercy, to walk humbly with thy God.

When the Bishop is come to the throne he shall be asked:

What doth the Lord require of thee?

The Bishop:　　To do justly

　　　　　　　To love mercy

　　　　　　　To walk humbly with my God."[28]

Movement and music underlined the significance of the Bishop's journey through his Cathedral.

At the Font, before he approaches the Nave of the Cathedral, the Bishop shall call to mind the love of Jesus, how he took little children in his arms and blessed them and how to them he said – of such is the kingdom of heaven; and then he shall call to mind the command of Jesus to the Apostles to go into all the world and make disciples, baptizing them, a boy, Alan Topping, singing:

Alone, yet not alone, my God, I journey on my way; what need I fear when thou art near, O King of night and day.[29]

The Bishop's lone walk towards the east was not accompanied by fanfares and loud music but by the choir singing a simple anthem by Sterndale Bennett – *God is spirit and they that worship him must worship him in spirit and in truth.* There was no celebration of the Eucharist at the service but parts echoed the words of the Eucharist and there was a very short reading from the Epistles by the Bishop: "I bow my knees unto the Father of our Lord Jesus Christ, of whom the whole family in heaven and earth is named, that they may be filled with all the fullness of God." All the incumbents in the Diocese together read the lines of the Gospel: "That same day at evening, Jesus came and stood in the midst and Said: Peace be unto you. As my Father has sent me, even so send I you: Lo, I am with you always."[30]

There was concern amongst many Free Churchmen that, after the Unitarian problems, Dwelly issued no invitations to them to participate in any way in Cathedral services. After the Jubilee Service for King George V, The Rev. Nichol Grieve wrote to complain about Dwelly's stance over the service. A Free Church Minister had taken a role in the Jubilee Service at St. Paul's Cathedral with full approval of the Archbishop of Canterbury. Grieve commented that in the past Liverpool Cathedral had given a lead over ecumenical matters but the mood appeared to have changed: "For many of us have been proud and grateful that among all other Cathedrals Liverpool seemed to be taking a lead, even on striking out new lines, to further the fact and witness of unity, but this honour is here no longer. She seems to be lagging behind others."[31]

A meeting was held with a group of Free Church Ministers and Dwelly in February 1937 and some handwritten notes were taken by one anonymous minister. They revealed the Free Churchmen's respect for Dwelly's high aspirations at the same time as urging his practical help: "So that I would plead earnestly and affectionately with Dr. Dwelly not to be content with engaging the Holy War for the University of the Spirit on the one level only, though that may be a very high plane, as it always is, in his case, but to come down also to a more pragmatic level – the level of stimulating unity by such means as are still open to him, and us, working together."[32]

Dwelly had established a strong working relationship with the Rev. J. T. Wilkinson, President of the Free Church Council. Dwelly and Wilkinson together designed a united service entitled *Affirmations of those who call themselves Christians* to be held in the Cathedral on Sunday 6 June 1937 and broadcast in the Empire Programme of the BBC. Dwelly wrote to all the Free Church Ministers and Wilkinson wrote to them all on 16 April underlining the significance of the service: "Such an occasion of our united affirmations in worship, as that to which he invites us as Free Churchmen, should be regarded as a sincere and valuable opportunity. It forms a new kind of witness to the unity of our common faith. Further, as the service is to be broadcast throughout the Empire, it is unique. The listeners will number many millions."[33] 161 clergy attended together with 1,955 representatives from churches and chapels, mainly from the choirs: another 4,300 people applied for tickets and were unsuccessful.

On 25 May a meeting of Free Church Ministers examined the order of service and J. T. Wilkinson wrote directly to the Bishop to report on the tenor of the meeting.

> I think you will be particularly pleased to hear that the deep strain of mysticism running through the service captured the hearts of all and (as afterwards I found in conversation) was even something of a revelation to not a few who were present. The arrangement of the passages of Holy Scripture was very much welcomed, and the suggestion that these could provide a basis of thought and prayer and study in preparation for the service itself was warmly accepted ... I found also that the setting out of the historic links from Cranmer's time to our own day, showing those

who had given their minds to affirm truth in order to the uniting of a divided church aroused an enthusiasm, which is perhaps best expressed in the words of one of the keenest minds present, who said that he felt we had now got down to something 'really central and constructive' in the matter of unity."[34]

Wilkinson raised similar ideas in a newspaper article reporting on the service – unfortunately the title of the paper is unknown: "Whilst unity in faith and order may go far, unity through worship may go much further. There is an essential mystical unity in the soul's experience of God through Christ allowing a vast comprehension within which can be abundant variety of form and expression. Its essence is in a familiar saying of Meldenius: 'In things essential, unity; in things doubtful, liberty; in all things charity'."[35] Wilkinson used the word mystical four times in his full report. One dictionary definition of mysticism seems wholly appropriate to the content and character of this service: "spiritually true or real in a way which transcends man's reason" There was an undoubted reality in this service; one anonymous newspaper called the service unique and epoch-making. The Merseyside Free Church Centre Annual Secretaries' Report was forthright in its approval: "Never before had such a service been held in a Cathedral, and it is impossible to estimate what its far-reaching effects may be in the direction of unity of the Churches."[36]

The service paper, 6 June 1937, is a significant devotional document, 24 pages long. In choreography or pageantry it is by far the plainest Dwelly special service. A great deal of work must have gone into the production of the lengthy printed text with material drawn from many sources as a close examination of even one part would reveal. It might best be described as a verbal meditation on Christian unity with careful and dramatic use of hymns sung by the whole congregation, after practice. The whole was carefully structured so as to lead the congregation through a range of thoughts and emotions in a very gentle manner. Throughout his career, there is evidence of Dwelly's use of hymns or single verses stitched into the fabric of the devotions rather than being used at set points to rouse the congregation into vocal action. The Rejoicings at the start the congregation focused on "our common Master Christ" before bursting into just three verses, one with descant of *All hail the power of Jesus' name*. Three verses of *When I survey the wondrous cross* became the most powerful response to Christ's sacrifice. A Litany of the Ingathering of the Spirit made mention of 26 people whose lives and work helped reveal something of the spirit of God. The list was wide ranging with such names as Thomas Cranmer, Hugo Grotius, Thomas Browne, Linnaeus, Leibnitz, John Wesley, Thomas Arnold and was concluded with the singing of two verses of a hymn by Charles Wesley:

Let saints on earth in concert sing with those whose work is done;
For all the servants of our King, in earth and heaven are one.

One family, we dwell in him, one church, above beneath;
Though now divided by the stream, the narrow stream of death.

The words of The Recollection, very carefully laid on the page, lead to the anthem.

WORSHIPPING

ACKNOWLEDGING HIS GRACE
RESTING IN THE ORIGIN OF OUR BEING
BREATHING HIS SPIRIT HIS PEACE HIS JOY

REPUDIATING PREOCCUPATIONS WITH THE TRANSITORY
AWAKENING SURRENDING HALLOWING PENETRATING
CONTEMPLATING THE PROCESSES OF HIS CREATION
SEARCHING THE REALMS OF HIS SPIRIT
DISCERNING LOVELINESS IN HIS LIGHT
HEARKENING UNTO HIS VOICE
SEEKING HIS WISDOM

ADVENTURING IN HIS SPIRIT AND ACQUIRING IDENTITY
APPROVING DELIVERING PROTECTING THE EXCELLENT
RECEIVING WONDERING RECOLLECTING PARTAKING
WALKING HIS JUST AND MERCIFUL WAYS
OBEYING HIS VOICE DOING MY DUTY
NOURISHING THE JOY OF OTHERS
CHERISHING COMPASSION
TRIUMPHING IN GOD
MAGNANIMOUS
CONTENT

Such density of text demanded a time of meditation which must have been encouraged and supported by the Cathedral Choir and a soloist singing Mendelssohn's *Hear my Prayer* and *O for the wings of a dove!*

The Principal Chapter met half an hour after the end of the service to place on record in the Minute Book their feelings as to the significance of the event.

The Chapter records with great appreciation the Empire Broadcast Service of Affirmation held on this day in the Cathedral shared by Clergy and Ministers from all denominations in the City and the Diocese, the first actual personal witness together by Christians to their common experience of God which has been held since the Reformation.[37]

Eight newspaper cuttings are held in the archives, unfortunately without date or name of journal. Only one is adversely critical: "There is no predicting in which direction liturgical eccentricity will next erupt in Liverpool Cathedral." Sir John Reith had expressed a personal interest in the service and Rev. J. T. Wilkinson gathered hundreds of written responses to the service; one Methodist minister recorded his perceptions which counterbalance the vituperative newspaper correspondent. "… a simple brotherliness and utter lack of any spirit of condescension, … the real bond of unity. On my left was a little deformed Pastor, humble, unordained and almost poor; opposite me was a Salvation Army Officer; behind me was the Bishop. One felt that there had never been anything quite like it since Gentile and Jew first mingled in the early Church."[38] There was no sense of Church of England triumphalism in their great Cathedral. There were no obvious leaders in the service: groups of clergy spoke together and many of the prayers were responsorial in character – typical of many of Dwelly's prayers. This service was a significant liturgical development in Dwelly's ministry but probably even more significant in the context of the controversy generated by Cecil's responses to the Unitarians. The size of the Affirmations service tends to obscure the fact that there were seven other services in the Cathedral that day. Holy Communion was celebrated at 8 am and 12.15 pm. Morning Prayer was said at 10 am. There was a special service at 11.00 am attended by the Officers and Men of the First Minesweeping Flotilla and Officers and Ratings of R.N.V.R. There was a Red Cross Service at 2.45 pm with an address by Dwelly. Evening Prayer was said at 6 pm and the day ended with the 8.30 pm.

The following year the Affirmations service was followed by *A Service of Recollection*, another similar in content and character, to commemorate the two hundredth anniversary of John Wesley's experience in the Aldersgate Chapel on 24 May, 1738. That an Anglican Cathedral should decide to celebrate this event in an immense service, with congregations inside and outside the Cathedral, is evidence of Dwelly's ecumenical determination to honour and remember the founder of Methodism. The first page of the twenty four page service book declared, "HE THAT HATH UNIVERSAL LOVE IS OF A CATHOLIC SPIRIT" The service was divided into ten sections, most of which were introduced by Wesley's own words from letters, sermons or journals. As in the Affirmations service, much of the text is responsorial in character with groups rather than individuals leading the litanies. And as in the former service there was the recalling of a list of names of significant examples of Christian discipleship, as well as John and Charles Wesley such people as George Whitfield, John Newton, Hannah More, William Wilberforce and Charles Simeon. The hymns were all by Charles Wesley and such words as *Ye Servants of God, your master proclaim, Love divine, all loves excelling, Come, O thou traveller unknown* fitted perfectly into the unfolding of the structure of the whole. *Forth in thy name, O Lord, I go* could not have been more appropriate as the final hymn after which the congregation left the Cathedral to join the crowds outside in St. James' Road shortly before the end of the main service.

Less than a month later came *1538 The Open Bible 1938* "being the commemoration of the placing of the open Bible in the churches of our land four hundred years ago". The Cathedral was host to representatives of two hundred and fifty four churches and chapels – including Unitarians, from Liverpool, the Diocese and the Wirral. The Benedictions highlighted the names of many people who were responsible for the translations of the English Bible. The service was yet a further example of the Cathedral serving the whole community and seeing its responsibilities spreading beyond the Anglican Communion. 30 October 1938 marked a service with both ecumenical and international significance: *The Order of Service being a partaking of the Benedictions and Praises customary with Christians of the Eastern Communion.* The music was sung by the Russian Choir of Paris who sang traditional material from the Orthodox tradition to the music of Rimsky-Korsakov, Balakirev, Azev, Panchenko, Kastalsky, Gontcharov, Loovsky, Bortniansky and Rachmaninov.

Among the annual sea services *The Masting of Nelson* on the School ship HMS. Conway on 11 September 1938 must have been one of the most memorable. The 24 page service book had a striking cover designed by Carter Preston and printed in red and black on 'cathedral cream' card. Carter Preston had carved the new figurehead for the training vessel moored for some years in the Mersey. John Masefield, Poet Laureate and friend of Dwelly had served on HMS Conway and had been invited to read the New Testament Lesson. There were relevant quotations in the service from the works of Robert Herrick, John Chapman, Edward Carpenter, Walt Whitman and Robert Browning. The whole of Liverpool's development as a city had been entirely dependent on the sea and so a celebratory service of this nature was appropriate and relevant. The prose style was dignified but modern and fresh. The whole service was memorable.

The Listener for 14 April 1937 carried the text of a broadcast by Howard Marshall under the title "The Church in Action. What is Being Done in Liverpool Cathedral" The talk is particularly important in that Marshall had spent hours with Dwelly and reported his comments verbatim. He had been present for the morning service on Easter Day, part of a congregation of 2000.

Whilst admitting to his own lack of musical education, he commented very positively on the richly complex service of which he had been a part.

> I could see the purpose behind it. It was a flowering of worship, the arts combined, the grandeur of architecture, music, singing, design, the vision of the poet, the craftsman and the mystic – all combined as the response of the Christian to the redemptive fact of Christ.[39]

The Dean had felt it necessary to give his interviewer basic information which lay behind the forms of worship in the Cathedral.

> It is perfectly clear that we have to provide for two quite distinct classes of people – those who are liturgically minded – those, that is to day, to whom the Easter morning service appeals greatly – and the other class who don't want liturgical services but instead something very simple and related to everyday life.[40]

Marshall admitted to his lack of experience of complex styles of worship and that he was not an enthusiast for looking at churches and climbing long flights of steps but for him a tour with the Dean behind the scenes was a revelation and for him even more impressive than the service. "It was like stepping into a new Renaissance. Here once more were craftsmen and scientists and engineers and inventors working together. And the building was alive, growing like any other living thing, growing, as they would tell you there, to the greater glory of God."[41]

Marshall was impressed by the size of the congregations attending the 8.30 service and some of the activities which had come about because of the service and the way in which the needs of people were being addressed. Unemployment was a serious social issue in the thirties and the Cathedral was talking with people and beginning to provide practical help. "The cathedral, in fact, is working like the leaven in the lump – quietly, unostentatiously, but always active, coordinating the lives of people in the district, drawing them together, seeking a common and communal purpose relating it all to an eternal truth." Dwelly stated his concern over people and their problems:

> Many of the problems of the day would be solved if the outlook of artists and scientists could be fused into one creative vision. And as with the actual building of the cathedral so with the life of the diocese and the city in which it stands. Here again you have so many different forms of endeavour – different kinds of business being carried on – every sort of activity of man. And all the time at Liverpool Cathedral men are looking for unities in these various manifestations of life.[42]

The Dean saw the great importance of the way in which the Cathedral welcomed its thousands of visitors and helped them towards an understanding of its whole purpose.

> We try to make them feel that cathedral worship is not just a matter of what the parson is doing in taking the prayers or what the choir is doing. But here, in this worship, you have the whole of the arts and the crafts represented – the glass-workers, the sculptors, the engineers and inventors and so on. And we try to get them to feel that their own job is represented in this offering of worship which contains work from so many different sections of the people ... There is no true act of worship without an offering of mind or will or experience. Our work is to gather the affirmations of our time as they are to be found in every walk of life ... as our people are seeking with people of all kinds, we discover the unities, the worth-while things – the creative spirit if you like – and we come into the cathedral to affirm these things. We will affirm in a special service, for example, what one branch of science has discovered for the good of humanity; or the beauty that certain artists have brought into people's lives. And in affirming these eternal principles, these creative activities, we believe we are helping to prepare for that new spirit which we are persuaded is coming into the world.[43]

No clearer reasons for the time and energies devoted to the special and vocational services can be given than that expressed in Dwelly's broadcast words: "With all its faults the cathedral is the encourager of goodwill. It attempts to establish an actual communication of friendship with men who seem to be moving in bewildered ways and, as far as possible, to give them support, understanding, sympathy and encouragement."[44]

Central to this chapter has been the theology and the artistry of the first Dean. The bound copies of the service papers were wholly his responsibility. The primary and secondary source comments on Dwelly and the services are now part of his archive. There are some photographic records in the cathedral archives giving visual report on set moments in the choreography. As will be examined in later chapters, the essence of Dwelly's liturgical achievements did not die with him but is still retained and developed today. A number of personal memories are still vivid. The treble who sang the solo at the font in 1944 at the enthronement Service of Bishop Clifford Martin received a letter from the Bishop in January 1976: "It is only quite recently that I discovered that yours was the voice where as a young choir boy in Liverpool Cathedral Choir, you sang 'Alone yet not alone' while I walked the length of the Cathedral in

Henry Goss
Custard with his
pupil, the young
Noel Rawsthorne.

preparation of my enthronement ... The beautiful clarity of your voice has never
been forgotten by me and the words you sang have been an inspiration to me
ever since."[45] The musical tradition inspired by Dwelly can still be examined first
hand. From joining the choir in 1930, Ronald Woan went on to become Master
of the Choristers and though he retired in 1983, he is still part of the cathedral
community. Noel Rawthorne joined the choir at ten, became assistant organist
under Goss Custard in 1949 and organist six years later. Ian Tracey, currently
Organist and until recently, Master of the Choristers since his appointment as
organist, at the age of twenty-five, was trained by Noel Rawsthorne.

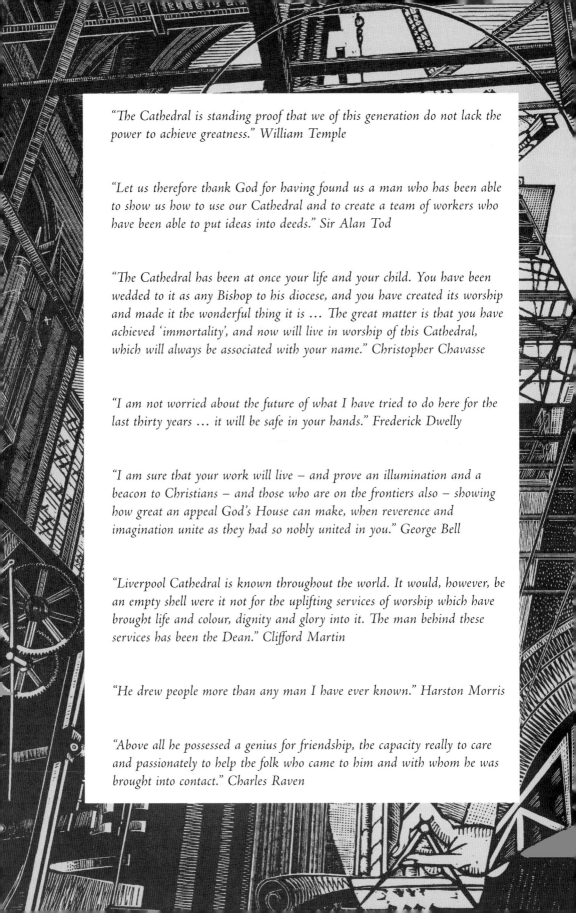

"The Cathedral is standing proof that we of this generation do not lack the power to achieve greatness." *William Temple*

"Let us therefore thank God for having found us a man who has been able to show us how to use our Cathedral and to create a team of workers who have been able to put ideas into deeds." *Sir Alan Tod*

"The Cathedral has been at once your life and your child. You have been wedded to it as any Bishop to his diocese, and you have created its worship and made it the wonderful thing it is … The great matter is that you have achieved 'immortality', and now will live in worship of this Cathedral, which will always be associated with your name." *Christopher Chavasse*

"I am not worried about the future of what I have tried to do here for the last thirty years … it will be safe in your hands." *Frederick Dwelly*

"I am sure that your work will live – and prove an illumination and a beacon to Christians – and those who are on the frontiers also – showing how great an appeal God's House can make, when reverence and imagination unite as they had so nobly united in you." *George Bell*

"Liverpool Cathedral is known throughout the world. It would, however, be an empty shell were it not for the uplifting services of worship which have brought life and colour, dignity and glory into it. The man behind these services has been the Dean." *Clifford Martin*

"He drew people more than any man I have ever known." *Harston Morris*

"Above all he possessed a genius for friendship, the capacity really to care and passionately to help the folk who came to him and with whom he was brought into contact." *Charles Raven*

EIGHT

"The first human milestone"

URING THE YEARS 1939–1945, Dwelly encouraged the naval
officers and men to regard Liverpool Cathedral as the Parish church
of the Western Approaches and Dwelly's influence within and upon
his Cathedral during those years must not be under-estimated. I made use of
the limited archival resources of the period in chapter 12 of *Frederick William
Dwelly: First Dean of Liverpool*. Words will not permit an adequate account of
the war years in this context but certain aspects of those years must be noted.

By the time the bombing of the strategically vital north west port began,
Dwelly had quite literally moved into the Cathedral twenty four hours a day. An
inhospitable little room part way up a turret at the east end became his bedroom:
chillingly cold in winter and stifling and airless in the summer – it was to be my
office for nearly ten years. Chris Wagstaffe lived in an airless and claustrophobic
area at one end of the old sacristy safe. Choral conductor, Edgar Robinson,
moved into a vestry and Rodney Street surgeon, Hugh Reid took up residence
in the Song Room. Clerk of Works, Owen Pittaway, and his family were tucked
away in the crypt. The size of the building made it a prominent target and
navigation aid to enemy aircraft and the green patina of the copper roofing had
to be painted grey so as not to reflect bright moonlight. Because of shortage of
manpower, as well as restrictions on vital building materials, building during
the war was severely curtailed but never ceased. The upper tower walls were
incomplete and necessitated continued work. The final finial was completed in
March 1942, though the tower roof itself could not be undertaken until steel

GOD BE THANKED FOR WESTERN APPROACHES 1941 1945

and cement became available after the end of the war.

On 6 May 1941, the Cathedral building site received several hits by incendiary devices which destroyed the contractor's offices, the setting-out shed and stone-cutting saws. High explosive bombs followed, two of which caused considerable minor damage to the glass and stone-work of the Lady Chapel. One much larger bomb fell directly onto the roof of the south east transept. What happened was recorded in the words of someone identified only by the initials W. J.

It broke through the roof and entered the space between roof and ceiling of the transept. By happy chance the bomb struck the top of the inner brick wall supporting the central beam of the transept, and, being deflected downwards, burst through the outer wall and exploded in the air high above street level. There the chief damage was to the tall windows of the transept. The havoc that would have been occasioned had the bomb been deflected inwards so that it penetrated the ceiling to explode inside the transept is best left to the imagination.

It may be placed on record that the Dean, subsequently continuing his tour of the Cathedral and finding that the tower had survived, tried to sing the 'Te Deum'. In his own words – "it simply would not come.' Just then a blackbird somewhere in the trees outside burst into song. That was the 'Te Deum'.

The bird's liquid notes heralded the dawn. The raid having ended, the watchers at the Cathedral were able to look over the city to watch the light rising in the east. The fires left by the raiders were still blazing against the duck-egg blue of the western sky.[1]

The Dean Cathedral was used as an air-raid shelter by many of the local residents because it was regarded as safer than the brick and concrete public shelters in the neighbouring streets. On a number of occasions, Sir Giles

Scott also stayed in the Cathedral as the Dean's guest and both recognised the uniqueness of their situation. Despite physically living in difficult conditions in the Cathedral, Dwelly continued his work in the wider field and from archive letters and telegrams it is clear that he was practically involved in helping foreign nationals who had been interned on Merseyside and in the Isle of Man. He took George Bell, Bishop of Chichester, to speak with some of the 2000 German nationals interned at Huyton, just outside Liverpool. Dwelly became a close friend of both Sir Percy Noble and particularly Sir Max Horton when he was Commander in Chief Western Approaches. When Horton was made a Freeman of the city he said,

> And there are others I would mention who deal in a different plane and helped in a different way. I refer, in particular, to our Dean of Liverpool Cathedral. What mortal man or priest could do to aid and strengthen us, he did – and I wish publicly to acknowledge the debt I and Western Approaches owe to him.[2]

Even during most difficult periods, Dwelly continued to arrange and lead many special services as can be seen by an examination of such services during the summer and autumn of 1942.

14 June	The United Nations' Celebration.
5 July	Commemoration of the Establishment of the Air Training Corps.
12 July	The Girls' Training corps.
19 July	Sailors' Day
26 July	Annual Thanksgiving for the consecration of the Cathedral.
26 July	National Fire Service.
3 September	Day of Prayer in Time of War.
13 September	Civil Defence Wardens' Service.
20 September	The Royal Airforce commemoration of the Battle of Britain.
October	Celebration of the Prayers and Praises of the Western Approaches.
11 October	Service for Rangers and Guiders
25 October	The Assize Service.
1 November	In Thanksgiving and Prayer for the Czechoslovak People.
13 December	Day of Mourning for the Victims of Massacres of Jews in Nazi lands.

Bound alongside this paper is a service in Hebrew and English issued by the Office of the Chief Rabbi.

Throughout all the difficult times during the war and in the immediate post-war years of austerity, Dwelly knew that he could look in two directions for unfailing support. Christine Wagstaffe had been a member of his young Galahads group at Emmanuel, Southport. When, in 1925, he became a Residentiary Canon, he brought Chris with him to Liverpool as his secretary and her life was spent devoted to him and to the Cathedral. She was a very strong personality who, as Dwelly became older, became totally supportive of him and very defensive on his behalf. She knew how his mind worked; she understood his prose style; she could sign his signature. Her significance will be underlined when letters written at the time of the Dean's impending resignation are considered. His

A service in the Central Space as a result of bomb damage to the windows in the Chancel.

other devoted work force was the Cross Guild who had been trained in his ways since they were young choristers, later to become central to the choreography of all the main services. By Dwelly's own admission in 1955, he could not have remained so long in office without their support.

Important primary source material is held in the archive in the form of letters written to Dwelly and to Chris Wagstaffe at the time of his retirement, and in the form of sermons and obituary notices after his death and at the time of the unveiling of the Dwelly Memorial in 1960. The material provides a significant evaluation of his work and influence at the end of his ministry.

In 1952, Canon Bezzant resigned his Chancellorship in order to take up the post of Dean of St. John's College, Cambridge and there was concern about the character of his replacement. Colin Dunlop wrote to Dwelly in December 1952.

> I do hope the bishop will appoint someone whom you will really like and trust. It ought to be someone who could learn and then succeed you – a Coadjutor Dean – You do deserve a good sensible disciple who could perpetuate and develop your work in days to come. There is so much a man could learn from you over a course of years and then turn to good account later on.[3]

There are twelve letters in the archive from Bezzant written between 1952 and 1954 and a recurring topic concerns the appointment of a new canon. It is clear that Dwelly wished the Bishop to appoint Ralph Dawson, Vicar of St. Edward's in Cambridge, whom Dwelly had known since the years when he was Bishop's Chaplain. Dwelly and a number of people around him were anxious to protect the traditions and standards which the Dwelly regime had established and fostered. Eventually Frederick Dillistone was appointed, the man who was to succeed Dwelly as Dean. In September 1983, Dillistone wrote to the Rev. Alan Wilkinson who was interested in undertaking some research into Dwelly's ministry, "When I first met him in 1952 he was already a shadow of his former self: Parkinson's Disease robbed him of his powers and he was shielded from the outside world by Miss Wagstaffe."[4] In another letter in December 1986 he wrote, "... after the war there began that decline in his powers which was sad to watch."[5] Dillistone admitted that he knew Dwelly only during his fading years but they worked together for three years and Dillistone was able to experience the character and quality of Dwelly services despite his fading powers: the services had not diminished in quality. Dillistone wrote an unpublished article entitled *The Language of Movement* to mark the centenary of Dwelly's birth and parts of it form an important evaluation of his achievements.

He recognized instinctively the power of ritual both to express corporate emotions and to create community spirit … it was Dwelly who became the inspired creator of movement in the worship of the Cathedral. Giles Scott was the genius behind the architecture, Carter Preston behind the sculpture, Goss Custard behind the music, such men as Charles Raven and Thompson Elliott behind the preaching, but it was Dwelly who saw the possibilities for dramatic movement provided by the aisles and open spaces and who gathered around him a team of young lay men prepared to be trained for distinctive roles in ceremonial processions …

The result has been that no feature of the worship of the Cathedral has been more impressive than that of the colour and orderliness of these processions. What may at first sight seem an undue proportion of the total floor-space has been kept open for free movement: the absence of fixed pews has made it possible to relate movements to the particular character of whatever service is being solemnized …

Dwelly recognized the immense importance not only of movement but also of colour. Those taking part in the processions wore robes designed to harmonize with the distinctive shade of the red sand-stone out of which the fabric of the Cathedral was constructed. Dominant colours selected for choir and guild were russet, green and that belonging to ripening ears of corn, all suggestive of the life of nature in the countryside. Dwelly, it seems, was eager to bring symbols of the natural order into the worship of God as Creator and this he tried to achieve through design, through colour and through movement.

   It was … in … 'the cosmic language of movement' that he made his outstanding contribution to worship in the Church of England. To some degree processions had been introduced into Anglican liturgical worship as a consequence of the Oxford Movement but generally speaking those followed mediaeval patterns, with a focusing of attention on what was being carried or on the dignitary whom the procession was designed to honour. In Dwelly's vision, all the participants had a part to play in the dramatic framework which, like that of the great cosmic recurring cycle, encircled the words and actions of the Service itself.

   In his book *Gothic Architecture and Scholasticism*, Erwin Panofsky has written: 'Ceremonialism permits a group to behave in a symbolically ornamented way so that it seems to represent an ordered universe: each particle achieves an identity by its mere interdependency with all the others'. Dwelly tried to design ceremonial which would combine ordered movement with variations relating to varied changing circumstances …[6]

Between 1982 and 1986, Dillistone was in correspondence with Rev. Alan Wilkinson (son of Rev. John Wilkinson Dwelly's close Nonconformist friend) with whom he cooperated closely in the 1930s. In the summary of a conversation between Dillistone and Wilkinson in 1982 he wrote, "[Dwelly] was the combination of a 17th century Cambridge Platonist and a 19th century Romantic with a flair for dramatic movement."[7] In a letter on 31 August 1983 he wrote, referring to Dwelly and John Wilkinson, "They were drawn into a close friendship and working relationship because (it seems to me) both of them understood Christianity and the church in a liberal, platonic and mystical sense rather than a catholic or sacramental way. Both wanted to present modernism with a dash of antiquity and nostalgia which gave it historical roots and some romantic appeal."[8]

The Dillistone–Wilkinson correspondence centred upon Wilkinson's interest in a piece of research in which Dwelly would have featured strongly and Dillistone gave his condensed judgements of Dwelly's achievement in several letters.

> 5 September 1983: "[Dwelly] seems to have had little concern for the traditions or institutions of the wider church. I yield to none in my admiration of his genius for creating splendid ceremonial within a richly aesthetic framework. He did more in an innovative way than has generally been recognized in the C.of E. But like many geniuses he had his own circle of friends, admirers and disciples. As you so rightly and penetratingly put it, his whole cast of mind and outlook was liberal (in a restricted sense), platonic and mystical. Charles [Raven] and he were very different men but each was a nature mystic and both sat lightly towards any kind of authoritarianism in matters of worship or doctrine. Yes and both were within that general movement which we call romantic."[9]

> 13 April (no year indicated): I have often thought of Dwelly as a *producer* but I think it is more accurate to regard him as an outstanding *director*. In many respects the church can be very near to the theatre. It was Dwelly's genius first to direct a remarkable civic pageant at Southport and then to be entrusted with the ceremonies of Consecration at Liverpool in 1924 – something he did with outstanding success. From 1924 to 1945 he carried on the role of Director with the able assistance for part of the time of Raven who supplied the more intellectual component of what he was doing.
>
> I have never lost the conviction that Dwelly was a genius in the development of the arts in the new Cathedral. Scott was his ally in the building but it was Dwelly who directed the inside drama.[10]

Bishop Albert Augustus David after his retirement returned to preach in the Cathedral on 29 March 1949 and delivered his judgement on the significance of what the Cathedral was able to achieve:

> No longer can it be said that the days of great architecture inspired by religious faith are all in the past. Modern art moved by modern faith and interpreted by modern craftsmanship has still something to offer not unworthy to be compared with the masterpieces of the Middle ages. The Cathedral is standing proof that we of this generation do not lack the power to achieve greatness. Within these walls we may take fresh courage as we face colossal tasks of other kinds crowding on us now – tasks of rebuilding the national life of our country and the broken life of the world.[11]

Dillistone's assessments are significant in that he worked with Dwelly in the Cathedral for three years and then expressed his judgments thirty years later. David's words are important from his station as former Diocesan Bishop and from the fact that he had known and worked with Dwelly from the days of the Life and Liberty Movement. Some of what happened in Liverpool Cathedral in the 1930s had caused concern for David but he was still forthright in stating the achievements of the Cathedral.

Dillistone had informed Wilkinson that Mervyn Haigh had actually persuaded Dwelly to resign though there is nothing still in the archive to support that statement though there is no reason to doubt Dillistone's opinion. It had become obvious that despite the support of Chris Wagstaffe Dwelly could no longer remain in post. In the summer of 1955, Eda David, widow of Bishop Albert Augustus, wrote to Chris Wagstaffe, "I felt when I saw the Dean in June, that he had already gone from us into a world of his own – I hope he will find peace and rest when all the turmoil of leave-taking is over."[12] In September of the previous year, Neilson had written to Chris, "I presume that you are saving him from every exertion in every way and that you think it better for him to carry on as long as possible because you fear his successor may not be in sympathy with the tradition you have established."[13]

On 9 June 1955, Dwelly's letter of resignation was written to Prime Minister, Anthony Eden. The carbon copy of the letter in the archive is signed not by Dwelly's fine nib but with the broad nib of Chris Wagstaffe. It will probably never be known who made the actual resignation decision.

Dwelly wrote to the senior Cross Guild members on 18 June to thank them for their support without which he said he would have had to retire "over a year ago". He expressed his confidence in their ability to maintain the tradition they had together established. "I am not worried about the future of what I have tried to do here for the last thirty years – it will be safe in your hands."[14]

Any exploration of the influence of the Dean on the new Cathedral must take account of the many archive letters to Dwelly and to Chris Wagstaffe at the time of the resignation announcement. I have no way of knowing how many of the letters they received have been retained. Inevitably such letters would have been written in positive support of his ministry but there are so many, and from so many different people, from Bishops to choir boys and cleaners, that their unanimity of praise has to be regarded.

There are a number of letters from Bezzant from the period, but the most poignant was written to Chris. "What a decision to have to take! But I can, I think, fully understand what it means, as I am sure it would not have been made unless you were convinced that it is right. But after 30 years! It's like the end of life, isn't it?"[15]

Bishop Colin Dunlop, who had known Dwelly's work in Liverpool even before the establishment of the Deanery, wrote, "But what a lot you have to look back on with thankfulness and pride. Few Deans can ever have had so much as you and it has been hard slogging work all the way I imagine … I just cannot imagine the Cathedral without you."[16]

Dean W. R. Matthews wrote, "I hope that you can reflect on the wonderful work you have done for your great Cathedral and be glad and I hope you will reflect upon the number of people who are your grateful friends."[17] Matthews had been a Canon Theologian at Liverpool before he became Dean of St. Paul's.

A letter from Bishop George Bell stated, "The Church owe you a deep debt for the pioneer work you have done in worship, in drawing industry, art, learning, education, commerce to find in that great Temple their benediction and inspiration from Almighty God. I am sure that your work will live – and prove an illumination and a beacon to Christians – and those who are on the frontiers also – showing how great an appeal God's House can make, when reverence and imagination unite as they had so nobly united in you.[18]

Bishop Christopher Chavasse wrote, "The Cathedral has been at once your life and your child. You have been wedded to it as any Bishop to his diocese, and you have created its worship and made it the wonderful thing it is – The great matter is that you have achieved 'immortality', and now will live in the worship of the Cathedral, which will always be associated with your name. A hundred years from now, and more, people will still be talking of 'Dean Dwelly of Liverpool'.[19]

Bishop Herbert Gresford Jones had been a member of chapter since 1935. "For it is your own genius, your own sympathy, your own inter-relation to so many diocesan minds of what our Anglican worship may be – made Liverpool what it is."[20]

Much of *The Liverpool Cathedral Choristers' Guild Magazine* for Autumn 1955 is devoted to a series of short tributes to Dwelly introduced by an anonymous editorial, clearly written by one of the senior members of the Cross Guild and it is remarkably forward-looking:

> The future must, of course, be a *moving* future. It must define and enter new paths whilst retaining and strengthening the old ones; it must, in short, move along lines which Dr. Dwelly himself made plain. Hence the need for Guild members to remember the Dean's past, to appreciate the importance of the present, and to cultivate an outlook for the future …
>
> It must be admitted, of course, that his period of office has not been completed without the appearance of controversy. A word against convention can normally be expected to provoke discussion. Chesterton's verdict on Bernard Shaw – 'he did not compel agreement: he compelled thought' – applies equally to Dr. Dwelly. What is surprising is that after the thought that he compelled we so often found ourselves with a new approach to our subject. It is doubtful whether the influence of his short, dynamic sermons has ever been fully realized.[21]

What is so significant about this piece is that it is not focused upon a nostalgic past but upon a developing future and contradicts the notion that thoughts of Dwelly made people look to the past, and traditions which could never be changed. The whole of Dwelly's ministry was evidence of his understanding of the necessity for growth and development, in the words of one special service "Liberty to Grow."

In the same journal, Bishop Christopher Chavasse expanded upon part of his personal letter to the Dean.

> Few Deans of Cathedrals, or for that matter Diocesan Bishops, are known beyond their neighbourhood, or remembered after their departure. But certain names become almost household words in the church, and achieve an immortal status. During the present century the names of Dean Bennett of Chester and Dwelly of Liverpool are outstanding for what they have accomplished in making Cathedrals power houses of worship in a modern-day diocese.[22]

Short formal recognition of the importance of the Dean's achievement was made by the Cathedral Executive Committee at their July meeting:

> For twenty-four years he has occupied this position with the utmost distinction, and the series of great services, imaginatively planned and faultlessly executed which have made splendid use of the resources of

Liverpool Cathedral, but have had a profound influence on the whole Anglican Church in its approach to ceremonial worship.[23]

The catalogue of praise for Dwelly's liturgical skills and powers of leadership is impressive and satisfyingly supportive of the central ideas of this study but what has emerged most clearly from many of the letters is the strength of feeling, not just for the liturgist, but for the man. There were letters from Chard, Windermere, Cheltenham and Southport as well as Liverpool. The magnetism of his personality and his devotion and dedication to his friends shines through. "Your name always brings back such happy childhood memories of Cheltenham. How adept you were at writing your name in treacle on bread and butter! I still have my school-girl autograph book, in which you wrote a quotation from Robert Browning. The date February 1916."[24]

Gratitude and genuine grief underlie so many of the words used in the letters. Typical is one of the letters from Eda David.

> I was not surprised at the announcement in the papers when I saw the Dean last week, I knew it must come soon. Please God, when he has complete rest, he may get back some of his strength and vigour – I can imagine what leaving that lovely place will mean to you both and I don't like to think about it. But the past few months must have been an awful strain for you and it must have been an agonizing decision to make. I am so grateful that I saw two lovely services and Canon Dwelly in his place in the Cathedral. It will be the last of many lovely memories. You will write now and then to tell me how Canon Dwelly is. I feel very anxious about him. Much love, my dear."[25]

The letters directly to Chris Wagstaffe are powerful and significant because they indicate how vital her support to Dwelly had been, especially in his later years. Ronald Woan has reported on the way Chris Wagstaffe's behaviour in public seemed almost not to register the signs of his degeneration and she did everything to support his public ministry. The extent of her total devotion was acknowledged gratefully by many who understood, including Bishop Clifford Martin.

> I feel equally heavy heart for somebody else but I mustn't say more because she wouldn't like it. Let me just say this. Thank you and bless you for the wonderful job done with courage and devotion. Few people may know what we all owe to you but one who knows something of it is Yours affectionately, Clifford Liverpool.[26]

The Rev. Lionel Jacobs knew the Dean and Chris Wagstaffe well and understood the significance of her role in the Dwelly years.

But any appreciation of the Dean must also include another appreciation and that is of you, yourself. No one will ever be able to evaluate what you have meant to him and his work. And my little note is just to say a very deep appreciation of all you have been and have done for him.

I know you will say that this has all been LIFE to you, and that you would never have offered any less help than you have done. But that does not alter the fact that the LIFE of the Cathedral owes you a debt of gratitude again quite beyond repayment. The way you have devoted yourself to this task calls out the admiration of all who possess some knowledge of the inner life of the Cathedral.[27]

Mary Dwelly had died in 1950 but after retirement Dwelly and Chris Wagstaffe continued living in the house in Grove Park. There was to be no improvement in Dwelly's physical and mental state and he became more and more dependent on Chris and wandered about the house calling her name in a disturbed condition if he could not find her. Those few of the Cathedral community that remembered Dwelly's final years in office and short period of retirement have been reticent even to talk about it. On 9 May 1957, the first Dean of Liverpool died at home, the cause of death being given as hypostatic congestion of lungs and cerebral arteriosclerosis. A wax death mask was taken soon after death by his sculptor friend Edward Carter Preston: the mask was used later in the carving of the Dwelly Memorial to go in the south choir aisle of the Cathedral. Carter Preston's daughter has reported that her father considered that commission the saddest he ever undertook.

Reliance on obituary notices might seem questionable in an academic work as it is unlikely that anything of a detrimental character would have been published but because all except one of the pieces I have used were written by people of standing who knew him well, I believe their opinions ought to be registered. My attention has focused itself on assessments that link closely from one writer to another even though they were written independently.

Bishop Clifford Martin's comments go to the heart of Dwelly's total significance for the worshipping life of the Cathedral and are supportive of the main ideas behind this book: "Liverpool Cathedral is known throughout the world. It would however, be an empty shell were it not for the uplifting services of worship which have brought life and colour, dignity and glory, into it. The mind behind these services has been the Dean."[28] In another piece, the Bishop listed what were for him the three crucial names in the development of the Cathedral. "The idea of a Cathedral exceeding magnifical had its origins in the mind of Francis James Chavasse; the design in stone and wood has come from the architect Giles Gilbert Scott; a tradition of worship to match the beauty of the building has been given to us by Frederick William Dwelly."[29] Two of Charles Raven's comments made in different pieces are in parallel with the Bishop's judgments: one declared Dwelly to be "… the man who has given to Sir Giles Gilbert Scott's wonderful building its characteristic spiritual quality."[30] And another: "The character and achievement of the great Liverpool Cathedral … owe more to him than to any other of its friends and servants."[31]

Dwelly's artistic sensibility and the use he made of artists and their arts were highlighted by most of the writers and preachers. Canon Harston Morris said in a sermon on 19 May 1957, "… he brought his studied and expert knowledge of beauty in all its forms – architecture, music, colour, ceremonial, liturgy – and in the application of these things to the worship of Liverpool Cathedral, he set a standard which will be permanent in that Cathedral and which has influenced the church throughout our country."[32] Raven wrote of Dwelly's "gathering a great company of artists and craftsmen and fellow-workers in every field and maintaining the inward life of the Church that combination of dignity, richness of detail, and unity of design which Sir Giles Scott had given to its architecture."[33] Clifford Martin's words about the artistry of a Dwelly service expressed even in a simple procession have been frequently quoted. "You have to go to Liverpool Cathedral if you want to see how to walk to the glory of God. Every procession is an act of worship. Every boy in the choir, even the smallest of them, is helped to think of himself as an important factor in a common act of praise and prayer."[34]

It is fitting at this point to make reference to an article in the *Liverpool Daily Post* written at the time of his retirement and claiming to have been written "by a correspondent who has been in close association with the Dean". There is evidence that this is so and almost certainly someone connected with Cathedral music. "When he became Dean, both the choir and the music library were reorganized and strengthened. He played a large part in the restoring to the Cathedral Service lists the treasures of Tudor Music and, at the same time, he was active in the encouragement of the singing of the best works of contemporary composers … No one did more than Dr. Dwelly to raise the status of the choir."[35] The same correspondent, with clear inside information, stressed Dwelly's deep interest in and concern for the overall education of the choristers and the Cross Guild.

> He has heard recently how this young man is in Whitefriar's studio designing stained glass, how another is doing research in metallurgy at the University of Liverpool; or has been playing his oboe in the National Youth Orchestra at a concert in Amsterdam; reading for the Bar; just back from National Service in Singapore; graduated in Fine Arts in the

University of Cambridge; obtained a Master's Ticket in the Merchant Navy, or has gained an F.R.C.O. On Michaelmas morning, too, one of his old boys particularly gifted in the study of the form and order of festival services and a graduate of the University of Cambridge, was ordained Deacon.[36]

Raven might have provided an intellectual underpinning to some of Dwelly's achievements – something which the two of them recognised, "He was a man of artistic rather than academic gifts, a loving student of poetry, of sculpture and painting, of music and colour."[37] One anonymous reviewer wrote, "He had a considerable though not an orderly or academic knowledge of liturgiology, and a great flair for combining material from ancient sources with that of his own and others devising." Raven also commented on this special ability to bring together: "It was this brilliant combination of qualities, a knowledge of liturgies and church music, an instinct for ritual and drama, and an insight into the lives and needs both of individuals and communities …[38]

There was acknowledgement that Dwelly filled his Cathedral regularly with worshippers, something he had been able to do throughout his ministry. The Bishop was grateful for what was happening in his Cathedral: "The fact remains that among all the Cathedrals in this country, Liverpool is among the very few exceptions which draw large congregations not only for special services but on normal Sundays as well."[39] The Very Rev. V. Spencer Ellis, Dean of St. Asaph, acknowledged Dwelly's ability to reach out through his services to those who did not necessarily regard themselves as active church-goers. "Perhaps less understood was his zeal to compel those afar off from 'organised religion' to come in."[40] The anonymous writer in the *Liverpool Echo*, 9 May, 1957, appreciated what might now be called the Cathedral's outreach. "Dr. Dwelly's creative genius in adapting the historic and traditional worship of the Church of England to the vast Cathedral and the modern mind, and his appreciation of the ever-widening range of public bodies desirous of engaging in corporate worship in the Cathedral were, perhaps, the greatest features of his service as Dean of Liverpool."[41]

The shortest sentence in one of Raven's pieces is the most telling, "But above all he was a friend." Harston Morris wrote about "his power of attractiveness. He drew people more than any man I have ever known. The affection which was felt for him by every member of the Cathedral staff – clergy, choir, vergers, cleaners. He was so full of thought for them"[42] "His kindness and help to his friends were unlimited," declared one anonymous writer. The Bishop acknowledged that some people may have found him stern, austere and difficult but for the Bishop the real Dwelly had the most loving nature and was brilliant in all his work and relationships with children. Ralph Dawson, Bishop's Chaplain, wrote of "his deep interest in and affection for people" and his "remarkable acts of kindness and of exceptional thoughtfulness and generosity. It was people he cared for more than causes."[43]

Limitations on length have made it impossible to examine any obituary notice in its entirety but I intend that this selective process be balanced by the inclusion of two sermons quoted in full so as to show how two people who knew him well attempted to evaluate his life and his ministry within the limitations of sermons in the Cathedral. The Dwelly Memorial in the south choir aisle was dedicated on Sunday 11 December 1960 with visiting preachers at both 11 a.m. and 3 p.m. The afternoon address was given by Gerald Ellison, the Bishop of Chester, and it is an important theological statement about the Dean and his ministry.

> 1 Corinthians 4: 2: "Moreover, it is required in stewards, that a man be found faithful."

> It is particularly fitting that we should make commemoration of the life and work of Frederick William Dwelly on this, the third Sunday in Advent. Today, in the Collect, Epistle and Gospel, we are directed to consider and pray for the sacred ministry of the Church. We asked that those called to be ministers and stewards of the mysteries of God may discharge their functions faithfully. How better can we make this prayer a reality than by thanking God for one of his servants who so pre-eminently was faithful in the stewardship entrusted to him.

> I am greatly privileged to be allowed to recall the ministry of Dean Dwelly on this occasion, and yet I am conscious of great difficulties in doing so. There are many who knew him longer and worked more intimately with him than I did. The breadth of his interests, the intensity of his concerns, the multitude of his friends, must mean that I shall omit some facet of his personality which appealed to some particular person. I can only speak from my own experience and record what I learnt from my friendship with this great and lovable man, since first I fell under his spell twenty years ago.

> Can it be doubted but that the mainspring of his life was the intensity of his vision of the glory of God? I fancy that in his personal religion he was aware of God first as transcendent. He was acutely conscious of the greatness of God, his majesty and power and beauty. So, in his liturgical compositions and in the services which he designed, there is the constant note of praise, the outpouring of thanksgiving and devotion to the Almighty God who has given so liberally and to whom man must respond by the uplifting of his heart and mind and soul.

Centenary
Service
Liverpool
Cathedral
February·5
1·9·5·0

Liverpool
Cathedral

March 29·1949

1951

The Hallowing
of the Bells to the
Praise and Glory
of God

It was because Dean Dwelly felt so intensely the awefulness of God that he could never be satisfied with anything less than the best in the offering of worship which man brought him. Shape, colour, sound, movement, all integral parts in man's offering to God; and as such, all must strive for perfection. Himself a person deeply sensitive to beautiful things, he called upon craftsmen of all kinds to offer their skill for the worship of God, and he taught and trained others to bring what they possessed into the treasury of the divine offering.

So it was that he made Liverpool Cathedral renowned throughout the world for the splendour and beauty of its worship. It was indeed providential that as this great building arose, so Dr. Dwelly was there to breathe life and spirit into its walls. In a memorable sermon preached here, Dr. Garbett, then Archbishop of York, pointed out how fortunate it was that the opportunity presented by the new Cathedral was matched by the liturgical genius of its first Dean, so that within the new setting it was possible for sound liturgical experiment to take place. That experiment was original, but loyal to the ethos of Anglican tradition. It was to be an enrichment to the whole Church.

Liverpool Cathedral came to be a by-word for perfection in worship. No detail was too unimportant to merit the most careful scrutiny and preparation. In a building which called for splendid ceremonial, Dwelly designed and put into effect the act of worship worthy of Him to whom it was offered. The music must be of the finest, the language fitting for the occasion. The colours of robes and furnishings must harmonize. The movement of officiants must be dignified. So, with infinite preparation and patience, the tradition was built up, one generation taught another, the great Cathedral became a great house of worship and prayer.

Of course, Dean Dwelly had his critics and his detractors. There were those who regarded him as an eccentric, or dismissed him merely as a great stage manager. In lesser hands these criticisms might have had some justification. But in fact Dr. Dwelly was not an amateurish experimenter. He was a learned liturgical scholar, he had a considerable knowledge of the works of the mystics, he was deeply versed in literature and poetry, and he was an artist to his finger-tips. So, in the planning of a service, the designing of some furnishing for the Cathedral, he knew instinctively what was wanted, how far to go, what was right. What in less skilful hands or with a less discerning mind what might have become vulgar and offensive, was, under the Dean, uplifting and deeply satisfying.

For Dean Dwelly did not expend his great talents on the Cathedral and its services merely for their own sake. Always they were to be a worthy offering to God, something through which man approached the most High, and through which God spoke to his children. He saw God both as transcendent, high above in glory, to be approached humbly; and as immanent, revealing himself through his creation, through the skill of men's hands. Dr. Dwelly saw every good material thing as a sacrament, as a vehicle of God's truth, and he used the opportunities given to him with skill and imagination. I remember hearing tell of an incident familiar probably to you who know the Cathedral, which expresses so well his insight. He was designing a great service, and was hard put for robing accommodation at the West end of the Cathedral. 'I'm afraid, Mr. Dean, there is nowhere available except the carpenter's shop.' The carpenter's shop! Immediately the Dean's imagination caught the significance, the symbolism of Christ's earthly life was woven into the fabric of the act of worship. Such an incident shows us why it was that Dean Dwelly took such a delight in beautiful things. He saw them both as an expression of the being of God himself, and as a vehicle by which man could offer himself to God.

The Cathedral and all that it stands for is the wider, the more public expression of Dr. Dwelly's genius, and through it millions of people have been brought by him to God. A smaller number, though doubtless large enough, were privileged to be his personal friends, to enjoy his boundless kindness and to profit from his generosity. His affection was without limit, and those of us who were his friends know the lengths to which he would go to bring comfort and happiness to those who needed him. His was a love which overflowed, a love which knew no measure, a love which exceeded the bounds by which common sense or prudence might have limited his self-giving. We shall never know the number of people who had reason to be grateful for his kindness and understanding; those in need who were helped; those who were sad and were made stable; the young men guided as they planned their careers. All that can be assessed is that we, as individuals who knew him and were inspired by him, can never be sufficiently thankful for what he taught us and what he gave us.

Many people have attempted to define genius, and we will not try to do so again. But certainly one of its attributes is the power to take ordinary and familiar things, to uplift and enrich them and to give them a new quality. In this respect Frederick William Dwelly possessed the gift of genius. Things which were for other people routine and commonplace acquired a new life, an uncommon look, when he had touched them. And when this gift is further dedicated to the glory of God, then the inspiration and power of such a life becomes irresistible. Such was the influence which Dean Dwelly exercised. He captivated men and carried them on to God. That was the way he understood and fulfilled his stewardship. For such faithfulness we thank God.[44]

The actual unveiling ceremony had taken place at the morning service. The service paper, with a cover design by Carter Preston, might have been written by Dwelly himself. Three elements were repeated from the funeral service three years before: the opening poem "Strange is the vigour of a brave man's soul", the hymn "Who would true Valour see", and the Anthem to the music of Bach "God liveth still". Charles Raven was the obvious choice as the preacher, who had worked with him as part of the Chapter and been a close friend for thirty years.

In the 10th Chapter of the Gospel according to St. John and the 10th verse are the familiar words 'I am come that you might have life and have it more abundantly.' So Jesus describes the purpose of his mission as Life Giver, and on this Third Sunday in Advent, when we commemorate the Ministers and Stewards of God's mysteries and thank God for their work

EDWARD ROBERT BICKERSTETH
✝ SURGEON ✝ 1828 · 1908 ✝

and example, it is peculiarly appropriate that we in this great city and in this great Cathedral church should commemorate Frederick William Dwelly, our First Dean, who was more than any other responsible for the implanting of the characteristic life of this Cathedral and for its care and development during the formative years in which he presided over our Chapter.

He was a man uniquely fitted to his time; a man dedicated to God in Christ and to his own ministry in the Church of England; a man exquisitely sensitive to all the appeals of art, music, poetry, literature, drama, liturgy; exquisitely aware of the intuitive capacities which he possessed and singularly gifted in his approach to people of all sorts, able to get along side of them and interpret almost without spoken word their needs and express his willingness to help. But in addition, he had singular gifts of administration, gifts of ingenuity in devising means for recording and storing and making available all the experience that he gathered, whether from his reading or his conversation, from his scholarship or from his contacts with men and things. But above all, he possessed a genius for friendship, the capacity really to care and passionately to help the folk who came to him and with whom he was brought into contact. He was for us a steward of the good gifts of God in this place and we owe him the building up of the community of this Cathedral which has stood the test of economic depression, of world war and of radical changes in its personnel and resources.

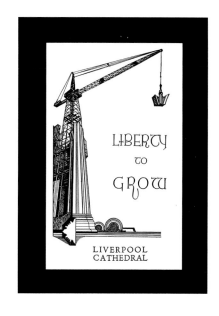

LIBERTY to GROW

LIVERPOOL CATHEDRAL

Of his life I need say very little. He was born and brought up in the West, in Somerset, without any special advantages of birth or prestige or privilege. Schooled for business, given a sudden conversion which transformed his whole way of living, going to Cambridge, to Queens' College – taking a degree without any special academic distinction – being ordained for a curacy at Windermere, then going on for a short

Opposite Dwelly depicted in the Scholars window on the south side of the Nave.

"THE FIRST HUMAN MILESTONE" **223**

time to Cheltenham, and finally coming after the First World War as Vicar of Emmanuel Church in Southport, where many of you surely will remember his remarkable ministry. He and his wife made themselves known and beloved by a wide circle of parishioners. With all kinds he was constantly trying not only new experiments in methods of church service, but new adventures in the bringing of Christian help to the neighbourhood as a whole. They loved him as he loved them. I shall never forget how one of them, a man of high standing in Southport, spoke to me of him, "We loved him. We knew that he cared for us. We knew that he would stand beside us whatever happened. We knew that if he was at the ends of the earth, he would come to our help if any disaster occurred."

That was the tribute to his many-sided service to his folk. And when he came to us at the consecration of this great Cathedral in 1924, bringing with him the trust of the Bishop, to order the great consecration service, we discovered not only the manifold range of his activities and knowledge, but his astonishing capacity to adapt himself to changing conditions, to improvise, to direct, and without the slightest self-aggrandisement, quietly, competently, devotedly to steer us all into the fulfilment of a design of which he was a master-planner. That great service gave to the Church of England something new, an artistry in worship which should

Ronald Woan with the choir at Christmas.

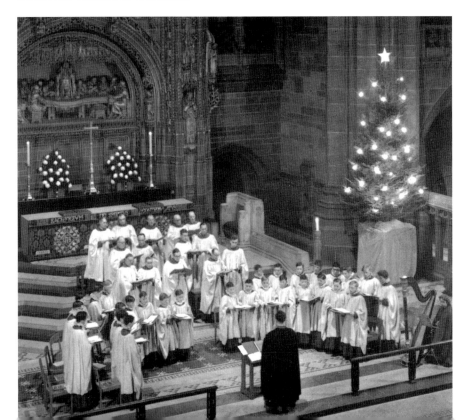

I think have been used by the church as a whole far more widely than it was, but which for us here and for the world-wide population that has passed through this Cathedral and city and taken part in these great services, an inspiration, an opening of the eyes, a quickening of the soul, a strengthening of the mind and an inspiration towards the common purpose and the common service.

He had the most extraordinary artistic gift of sensitiveness and intuition. You can see it in his discovery of musicians like Goss Custard, or if I dare say so Benjamin Britten: of artists like the sculptor of this Cathedral, Mr. Carter Preston who is responsible for the memorial that we are soon to dedicate: of poets – he brought John Masefield here: – of statesmen – some of you will remember Field Marshal Smuts speaking from this pulpit: of doctors and scientists and thinkers, and men of letters: of industrialists and politicians: of soldiers, sailors and airmen – the great Admiral of the Battle of the Western Approaches Max Horton not least – indeed all sorts and conditions of men, craftsmen, and singers, visitors, tourists, all and sundry. To all of them he had an instinctive approach, and I think that all of them, all of us, knew that we were joyful in his presence and that we went away from it better men and better women. He gave life and life abundant. And if he had singular difficulty in explaining the reasons for his intuitive judgments, he was always conscious of the need to consult others and by the end of his life when he gave his pastoral theology lectures in Cambridge, he startled me by the brilliance with which he handled an academic audience and academic subjects.

He was a man who grew continually in the range and extent of his resources. Yes, but of course, those resources were held together by a unity of purpose which gave them at once a sense of solidarity. People could perceive beyond the immediate interest which brought them into his company. This was his consuming passion to make this Cathedral a house of God, a member of the Body of Christ, an instrument for the operation of the Spirit of God. And so he welded together into a living community all these diversities of gifts, all these diversities of people. He was capable of producing community, because his own many-sided interests and experience were held together by a single sublimating and integrating motive.

'En Christo – In Christ.' That was the motto of the great 8.30 services in which I had the privilege of being his colleague. Fullness of life, the first that Jesus came to give, must be held together by unity of purpose but unless it combined with a measure of practical and administrative ability, the dreams will not of necessity come true. They need to be translated and I suppose not the least remarkable feature of Fred Dwelly's equipment was his mastery of means, the ingenuity with which he adjusted the available machinery to the purpose that he had in hand, the way in which he drew in human beings and found means of using their particular gifts, however small, however queer, in the common service, the ability to work and plan and adjust and organize until the dream came true. I suppose that the greatest quality in the life of the Apostle St. Paul is that he was pre-eminently the dreamer whose dreams came true. I suppose it is significant of our faith in the incarnation that the eternal purpose of God can be transmitted and transmuted into the stuff of our daily lives. Thus, as the great prophet of this last year or two (Teilhard de Chardin) is telling us in his latest book, we can divinize, make divine both our activities and our passivities; and so in action and in the intimacies of our lives we can fulfil the will of God and share in some measure, dare we say it, the very nature of God.

A word or two about the cost involved and the sum of his achievement before we dedicate ourselves and his memorial. The cost of such self-giving, joyous as it was in the paying, freed from any sort of self-pity or I think any thought of self-aggrandizement, nevertheless was inescapable. Every prophet, every minister of the Gospel must be both a challenge and an inspiration; and in his case the challenge was manifest. He met with a certain amount of real malice, a good deal of misunderstanding and, of course, the immense difficulties which this city and our country had to confront at the time of the slump, just before I left Liverpool in the 'thirties', when the threat of war grew near and supremely during those years of blitz and terror, when its first Dean lived night and day in this Cathedral and when it so narrowly escaped almost total destruction.

Those years, though at the end of them, when he visited us in Cambridge, he seemed to have lost nothing of his vitality and his friend-liness and his charm, nevertheless, those years had brought their inevitable collapse. Fullness of life leads to a Cross. That is the price which we have to pay if the fullness of our life here is to become life eternal. And of the Cross which he suffered in his last years, this is neither the time nor the place to speak. Some of us watched the paying of it and will not easily forget the pain that it involved. Yes, but let us think rather of the splendid loyalty of the band which he had gathered together of workers in this great Cathedral, of the staff, the Cross Guild, the Choir, the Sidesmen,

The coffin in the Presbytery at Dwelly's funeral.

the Vergers, and indeed of all those linked up with the direct service of the sanctuary, of Chris Wagstaffe and his own close friends among clergy and laity, of the splendid service which they rendered in maintaining the quality of life which he had seen and encouraged and indeed inspired, maintaining the quality of God manifest among us, taking new forms and gaining new resources, and employing new and splendid means. The cost was worth the pain.

And the purpose of it? There is one supreme need in the world at this moment, one manifest need. It is of course the need for community. In our over-individualistic western world, as in the fear-dominated regions of communism, community is far to seek. Yet life is community; the fellowship of the Holy Spirit is the end product of the ministry, the teaching, the passion, the death and resurrection of Jesus. And community is what this Cathedral church has always stood for and enabled. One world or none. That is the choice before us. We have the tremendous encouragement of a new partnership between science and religion, between the ancient traditions and the modern outlook, the partnership which is near ready for sealing. We have an increasing partnership between the churches dedicated to the name of Christ and I think a new understanding of religion in all its phases. We could achieve a world-wide community for the first time in history.

We have already, and shall within another generation at most, unlimited resources. If we can free the use of nuclear energy from its prostitution, its purpose of destruction, if we can see in proportion the rather childish business of interstellar exploration, if we can realize that we could quadruple the resources of the earth, overcome all drudgery, eliminate most disease, produce a condition in which the threat of increasing population was no longer overshadowing us, we might have, as Rutherford foresaw, a century in which mankind could sit down together to discover how this earth can become a home for the sons and daughters of men. We could see the dream which Paul, the Apostle, dreamt that mankind might 'come home to the oneness of the faith, that is to the sensitive awareness of the Son of God, to a mature manhood, to the measure of the stature of the fullness of the Christ.' In his name we are dedicated. To that dedication our friend the first Dean gave himself. In that name we would dedicate ourselves. So in that great day of the Lord we may fulfill our high calling in God and his Christ, in memory of our past and in aspiration for our future: and to God be all glory.[45]

I believe that it is beyond doubt that, by the end of his life, the influence of F. W. Dwelly on the worshipping life of a vast, newly established twentieth century Cathedral was immense. The evidence stands in the texts of the services which he devised and in descriptions and evaluations of his work in the words of a wide range of people: Archbishops, Bishops, Deans, Canons, Priests, Musicians, Admirals, the Media, life-long friends, unknown names. Eminent figures within the Church declared that Dwelly's influence extended far more widely than his Cathedral and diocese and that his influence would be felt beyond his life-time. Bishop Christopher Chavasse, son of the founding Bishop, had understood his father's aspirations for the new Cathedral and had a clear understanding of what Dwelly had achieved. "The great matter is that you have achieved 'immortality',

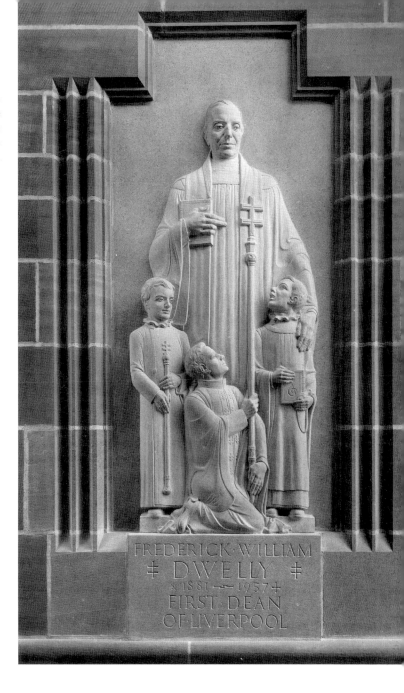

The Dwelly memorial in the South Choir Aisle, the work of Carter Preston who had taken a death mask of his friend.

FREDERICK·WILLIAM
✠ DWELLY ✠
✠1881 ✠ 1957✠
FIRST·DEAN
OF·LIVERPOOL

and now will live in the worship of the Cathedral, which will always be associated with your name. A hundred years from now, and more, people will still be talking of 'Dean Dwelly of Liverpool'."[46]

The final chapters of this study must address the difficult task of finding and examining evidence for Dwelly's long-term influence on his Cathedral and beyond.

"Tradition is only useful if it remains the servant. But tradition likes to take over and become boss, if given half a chance." Edward Patey

"Nostalgia has no place in religion but history does." Ken Riley

"… we had to meet head-on two dangers … The first was the danger of cutting loose from the great heritage from the past. The second was the danger of being imprisoned in the past, and so being paralysed by it." Edward Patey

"Although he was no longer here when I arrived, I could sense his presence. Everyone from the Cross Guild to the cleaners were still hung around Dwelly. They had the tradition almost built into them." Basil Naylor

"Dwelly helped to create the uniqueness of Liverpool Cathedral and gave those who followed him the freedom to carry on and develop this uniqueness. He saved us from conformity and for that I remain very grateful." Gordon Bates

"I found in the light of my experience what a very forward looking person Dean Dwelly had been, twenty years or more before Coventry Cathedral was opened. Many of the experiments regarding community and worship and liturgy, which we were operating at Coventry, he had already pioneered." Edward Patey

"Dean Dwelly's liturgical achievement, which still shapes the tradition of this Cathedral, was to connect such a heavenly vision with the daily experience of the people of this city and diocese in good times and in hard times." Rupert Hoare

NINE

Dwelly tradition:
death mask or spirit

B EFORE THE END of the previous chapter of this study, almost all the words quoted about Frederick Dwelly, his ministry and his influence, apart from obituaries and memorial sermons, were written or spoken during his life-time. As Ceremoniarius, Canon Residentiary, Vice-Dean and Dean his influence upon the new Cathedral was direct and indisputable. The remaining chapters are an attempt to assess Dwelly's influence on the worshipping life of the Cathedral over the years from his death up to the centenary of the laying of the foundation stone and an attempt to discern Dwelly's possible influence beyond Liverpool Cathedral.

Any attempt to examine fully the worshipping life of the Cathedral from 1955 up to 2004 would go way beyond the word limits of this study. I have chosen to take account of the work of twelve men who have all played vital roles in the Cathedral's development. Frederick William Dillistone, Dean 1956–1963, Basil Naylor, Canon Chancellor, 1956–1982, Edward Patey, Dean, 1964–1982, Derrick Walters, Dean, 1983–1999, Nicholas Frayling, Precentor, 1983–1987, subsequently Dean of Chichester, Ken Riley, Treasurer and Precentor, 1983–1993, subsequently Dean of Manchester, Mark Boyling, Precentor, 1994–2004, subsequently Dean of Carlisle, Rupert Hoare, Dean of Liverpool 2000–2007, formlerly Principal of Westcott House and Bishop of Dudley, Ronald Woan, Director of Music, Noel Rawthorne, Organist, Ian

Tracey, Organist and Master of the Choristers. The only one of these men I did not know was Basil Naylor.

At Dwelly's resignation in 1955, no one had any memory of the Cathedral without his presence and influence. His final years were hurt by physical and mental degeneration and the Cathedral had been in danger of becoming remote from the life of the diocese: "If there is any objective criticism to be made about the Dwelly period, it was that the cathedral atmosphere became rather too aloof during the later years when the Dean was in ill health."[1] Basil Naylor commented, "I think the cathedral company tended to think of themselves as a separate section away from the diocese. There was a tendency to become like a Vatican Chapel rather than the mother church of the area."[2]

Dwelly had been part of the Cathedral for thirty years: whoever took his place was inevitably going to be compared with the first Dean. Frederick Dillistone had been Canon Chancellor for three years and was known and liked by the community. The post-war years were difficult. The Chapter was not at full strength, money was short, it was difficult to regain the momentum of building and the whole of the chancel had to be re-pointed. Dillistone was calm, dignified, a considerable scholar, respected and loved by the community. He read the mood accurately and acted wisely, not attempting to change traditions which were healthy and sound but steadily determined to make the Cathedral and its worship more open to the diocese. His colleague, Basil Naylor, summed up the new leadership: "It needed a man of great humility to work with people who were themselves so attached to the Dwelly days. You didn't want a man who was going to make noisy pronouncements or antagonize. Dillistone was unobtrusive but firm and made the cathedral a diocesan home again."[3]

Services from the Cathedral had been broadcast regularly during Dwelly's time but it was during Dillistone's leadership that television entered the cathedral. On 13 September 1959, ABC Television broadcast the Sunday morning Holy Communion service, considered by some of the press to have been a more demanding project than the televising of the coronation service in Westminster Abbey six years before. Dillstone commented,

> We approach this new departure with a great deal of uncertainty and even apprehension, but no single event in our history, has, as far as I am aware, aroused so much interest and led to so appreciative a response. At least we know that an effective TV programme of the cathedral and its worship is now possible.[4]

Far more significant than a television broadcast was the Chapter's decision to replace Matins with a Choral Eucharist on one Sunday a month. This had not happened in Dwelly's day and there was strong opposition but Dwelly's ministry was full of examples of experiment. In the thirties Raven had recorded that a Choral Eucharist had not proved popular but by the fifties liturgical development across the Anglican Communion was moving in the direction of placing the Eucharist as the central Sunday service and Liverpool Cathedral did not lag behind. The choreography for the new service was in the hands of Chancellor Basil Naylor who used the Cross Guild resources Dwelly had made available and showed that he too had a strong feeling for the importance of human movement in public worship. A nave altar, mentioned years before by Colin Dunlop brought the celebration closer to the people and the essence of Naylor's choreography still orders the Sunday 10.30 service.

Dwelly had a realistic grasp of the responsibilities of the first Dean. He certainly appreciated that his ministry had not been bound by ancient statute or simply by tradition. He had also been conscious of the danger that everything he did might become a strait-jacket for the future. Riley cites a pertinent Dwelly comment, "What you are proposing may be all right with Dr. Dwelly, but the first Dean of Liverpool has to be careful, because what he allows will stand as precedents for all time."[5]

Basil Naylor had clear vision of the mission of the Cathedral for his generation and a clear realisation that what the Cathedral was attempting to do in his day was in direct parallel with Dwelly's intentions.

> More and more groups are seeking to express themselves in a larger area than the normal city and urban life. A cathedral is mother, servant, and teacher, and our services reflect community interests. It was here that Dwelly achieved so much by breaking away from simply using the old prayer-book formulae. When services are suggested, we ask the people concerned what they want to say, and tailor the proceedings accordingly."[6]

This statement is directly in line with Dwelly's sentiments as expressed in Stanley Morison's *English Prayer Books*, 1945.

It was generally thought that Dillistone had been reluctant to accept the Deanery because its arduous duties impeded his work as a scholar and a writer. He was a popular man but the news of his resignation and return to the academic world of Oxford was no surprise. The anonymous writer in the *Liverpool Cathedral Bulletin* for December 1963 attempted to sum up Dillistone's cathedral achievements:

> To succeed Dean Dwelly was no easy task, but Dr. Dillistone, while carrying on the tradition of his predecessor, succeeded in giving permanent form to what had been a highly individual contribution to

Eucharist celebrated at the Nave Altar.

modern liturgical practice. At the same time he introduced a number of innovations of his own, notably the periodic choral celebrations of Holy Communion in place of Matins, and the broadcasting and televising of services. But it was in the sphere of music that the Dean made his greatest contribution to the life of the cathedral, as witness the great rendering of Berlioz' Grande Messe des Morts in November 1962, and the foundation of the Cathedral Music Club.[7]

Fortunately, Basil Naylor, who had succeeded him as Chancellor remained in post as an effective link through to Liverpool's third Dean. In terms of length of time in office, Naylor was second only to Dwelly and held the post for twenty six years. I am indebted to three men for their thoughtful memories of Naylor's ministry. Myles Davies, a current Residentiary Canon, and Mark Boyling, Dean of Carlisle and sometime Canon Precentor of Liverpool were both influenced by Naylor as he was for them Director of Post-Ordination Training. Ian Tracey,

Organist and Master of the Choristers, had been influenced by his ideas and personality. A young musician moving towards his position of leadership of Cathedral music needed the theological and liturgical experience of Basil Naylor as much he needed the musical experience of Noel Rawsthorne.

Naylor moved to Liverpool one year after Dwelly's retirement in 1956 having previously been Chaplain and Dean of St. Peter's College, Oxford with all its Liverpool connections through the Chavasse family. He resembled Dwelly in the way he responded to the Cathedral building: as Myles Davies stated from the Cathedral pulpit in November 2006, "Basil had an instinctive understanding of the building and was able to use it to great effect on so many great occasions."[8] This idea was paralleled by Ian Tracey in a letter to me in December 2006. "Basil, as a student, was fascinated by Dwelly's theatre and his use of the Great Space of Liverpool Cathedral. Basil always had a belief in the drama of worship – the drama of the birth and death, the resurrection all need to be re-enacted in our worship – I heard him say that so many times."[9]

A Cross Guild Team led by the Beadle.

Current worshippers at the Sunday Eucharist are probably unaware that the choreography was designed not by Dwelly but by Naylor; in the words of Myles Davies, "He created the choreography of the Cathedral Eucharist around the Altar in the Central Space. Like Dwelly before him, he saw the possibilities which this building offers."[10] Possibly his most memorable service in the presence of the Queen in October 1978 will be considered later. It was no copy of a Dwelly service but it was in the Dwelly spirit.

Ian Tracey commented on the way Naylor, in the Dwelly tradition, drew people into the Cathedral through special services.

> His big thing was to 'bring in' organizations (again a parallel with FWD). I heard him say so often that Jesus collected not the professionally religious and the churchgoers, but those on the margins and therefore services where people could come from organizations to say what it was they wanted to celebrate, be sorry for – to lay their professional selves before Almighty God and we were there to help them to explore this in words and music in a glorious space …[11]

Dwelly's sense of care for his Cathedral community was strong in Naylor as well and Tracey appreciated his concern for Cathedral music. "As a priest he had a real concern for his fellows – especially the choir and the cross guild – he saw them as the heart of the place (just as FWD did) – 'the living Cathedral' as he once said to me."[12] Tracey had vivid memory of Naylor's lecture to the Cathedral Organists' Association in 1987 under the title "Take a pinch of transcendence": "that's what he reckoned as musicians and liturgists we do in services. We provide the pinch of transcendental material."[13]

Dillistone's short appointment as Dean had proved to be a very wise appointment as he was temperamentally right to take over after the long Dwelly years. By 1964 the cathedral needed powerful fresh leadership to take the cathedral through to physical completion and beyond but even some of his friends found it hard to understand why Edward Patey agreed to take on the responsibility. His modest paperback, *My Liverpool Life* answered the questions.

> It is not usual to receive letters of condolence on accepting an appointment which would generally be seen as a promotion. Yet that is what happened when some of my friends read in the press that I was going to be Dean of Liverpool. They wondered why I should want to leave Coventry, with all the excitement and world-wide interest surrounding the new cathedral, to go to Liverpool where the huge unfinished sandstone edifice was already in danger of becoming a dinosaur surviving from another age, an

Edwardian *folie de grandeur* out of tune with the mood of the second half of the twentieth century.[14]

I am not old enough to remember the consecration of Liverpool Cathedral but I do remember the consecration of the new Coventry Cathedral in 1962 and the huge interest which was generated with thousands of visitors every day. Edward Patey was appointed as a canon in 1956, at the start of the building project, and he lived through six years of freshness, excitement and vitality. Coventry looked to the present and the future. "I found myself getting impatient with those aspects of church life which were more concerned with keeping faith with the past than with daring to move into the future."[15] It may be that Patey realised that there was one powerful unifying feature between Liverpool in 1924 and Coventry in 1962: "The fact that we were a new community starting afresh in a new building meant that we were not tied to the past or paralysed by tradition."[16] Patey's questions about cathedral in Coventry in the sixties were in direct parallel with those of Dwelly and Raven in the twenties and thirties. "What kind of worship, what style of community life, what forms of ministry, what methods of evangelism and pastoral care, what sort of prophecy would be fitting for a brand new cathedral in a city which was still in the process of rising renewed from the ashes of its past?"[17]

The Dwelly and Patey answers to these questions were not identical but what is relevant is that they were grappling to find meaningful answers to the same questions and Patey had the honesty to realise this and give due credit to his famous predecessor. I had long conversations with Patey in 1990 when I was working on *The Building of Liverpool Cathedral*, in which he admitted his initial misjudgement of Liverpool. It was not a dinosaur: Dwelly's ideas and practices had been way ahead of his time. "I found in the light of my experience what a very forward looking person Dean Dwelly had been, twenty years or more before Coventry Cathedral was opened. Many of the experiments regarding community and worship and liturgy, which were operating at Coventry, he had already pioneered. I discovered the sheer opportunity of the space here."[18]

While recognizing Dwelly as ahead of his time, it was also clear to Patey that there was a danger of the cathedral being caught in a Dwelly time warp. Carter Preston had used a death mask in the carving of the Dwelly Memorial. As I pointed out in a sermon in the cathedral on 8 October 2006, the Dwelly tradition must not be symbolised by the fixed inertia of death mask but by the vitality of the Dwelly spirit. It was this idea which Patey embraced: he was not interested in doing exactly what the cathedral had done thirty years before but he was determined to embrace the central ideas of his predecessor though in a fresh way appropriate to a different age.

Picturesque view of the completed Cathedral above the trees.

We already had a great tradition of dignified worship and courageous experiment stemming from the first Dean of Liverpool, F. W. Dwelly, who was far ahead of his time in his imaginative use of a great building. But although we were in a new cathedral, I sensed that we were already in danger of developing a tradition which preferred to look back rather than forward. For some of the cathedral company, 'what we did in the time of Dean Dwelly' was the yardstick by which everything was to be measured. Without jettisoning what good things had been inherited from the earlier days of the cathedral's life in Liverpool, and from much longer noble traditions of English cathedral worship, we had to ask new questions to the problem of relating the real needs of the rapidly changing secular society to the eternal truths of Christian worship and mission."[19]

Patey's understanding of the Dwelly tradition was deeper than that held by many of his congregation and he knew that he had to present fresh challenges and that he was not always going to be met with agreement. He never held back from challenge, however, and neither had Dwelly.

Interesting and important as cathedral buildings are, they must not be thought of as ends in themselves. They are instruments to be used ... Nor is it for them to reproduce unquestioningly the old cathedral pattern in a modern setting. A new cathedral is an empty shell until the builders have created life and purpose and vision within it. Pre-eminently cathedrals must be places where great worship is offered. There must be continual experiment if cathedral worship is not to become a mere fossilization of the past, a museum piece, an antiquarian hangover. It is obvious that it is at this very point that most cathedrals are hopelessly conservative."[20]

These sentiments in the sixties are so close to the ideas of Dwelly and Raven in the twenties.

The second bay of the nave was dedicated in May 1968 and an appeal launched to raise the money to complete the building. An editorial by Trevor Beeson in *New Christian* was so widely quoted that Patey felt he had to use the media to reply. He was a very media conscious Dean who wrote and broadcast frequently and effectively.

It was with some surprise that those of us who have responsibility at Liverpool Cathedral read in your Editorial that our building presents 'a major problem for those who are required to use it'. This is not how we see it here. Neither is it our experience that 'successive deans and chapters have battled against impossible odds to relate the worship and life of the cathedral to the city and port below'. The truth is that Liverpool cathedral is probably used and appreciated by as wide a section of the community as any cathedral in the country today. Again and again two or three thousand people crowd into the building for great acts of worship ranging from youth occasions (with beat or folk music), to civic services involving such aspects of community life as the fruit importers, social service organizations, the university, education, commerce and industry. The great space of the cathedral provides us with a unique opportunity for liturgical and dramatic experiment. There is, I believe, no cathedral in the country which so adequately provides the flexibility and adaptability which is an essential prerequisite of modern community worship ... Cathedrals, far from being hangovers from the past, are beginning to discover a new and exciting role in the contemporary scene.

Whatever your leader writer may think about Liverpool cathedral,

The Nave Bridge, not completed until after Dwelly's death. How meaningfully he would have used it!

those of us who have to work in it believe that Gilbert Scott has provided us with a marvellous instrument for the Kingdom of God. Far from 'battling against impossible odds', we believe that we have as fine an opportunity here as anywhere in the country for discovering the new relevance and potential of cathedrals in the twentieth century."[21]

Patey was not deluded about the impact the cathedral might be making upon the wider community particularly when the cathedral was seen in its geographical position in the city. Many of the wide tree-lined roads and solidly built big houses were in a state of decay and the cathedral was right on the edge of the area of the city which achieved such notoriety in 1981 during the summer nights of the Toxteth Riots.

It was easy to wonder whether this great building, for all its artistry in stone and glass and wood, with all its music in the best English cathedral tradition, was not just a monstrous piece of escapism in the face of all the surrounding problems. I often had an uncomfortable feeling that much of the worship we offered was at best a harmless irrelevancy, at worst a romantic escape from the real world …[22]

The sentiments expressed here are so similar to those of Dwelly twenty years earlier when he had written about the difficulties involved in making the vocational services relevant and not an occasion like the Service for Seafarers which someone had described as a service where "nothing real happened". But Stanley Morison had written, "Today there is a new realization by those

A procession through the Central Space in 1978 at the service to mark the completion of the building.

Part of the service for the installation of Bishop Stuart Blanch.

who profess a religious affiliation that public worship needs to be made more vital for more people."[23] Patey possessed that same determination that Dwelly possessed to ensure that as far as possible the services were relevant to the daily lives of those who attended. Patey was as determined as Dwelly to take the service forward even in the face of some degree of opposition of some of his more conservative community. "I wanted every group to leave the cathedral with the feeling that what had taken place had really been about them – and about God. Each service tailor-made for the occasion, involved hours of preliminary discussion and rehearsal."[24]

Dwelly's ministry was over before the Liturgical Movement in the sixties led the church towards making a celebration of the Eucharist the main Sunday morning service. In the face of some opposition, the Cathedral abandoned Choral Matins at 11.00 for Choral Eucharist at 10.30 with time afterwards for the congregation to meet each other over coffee. A movable nave altar was used to bring the celebrant much closer to the people and an elaborate and meaningful choreography was devised by Basil Naylor and remains little changed even today.

In a letter to me in 2004, Bishop Gordon Bates, Precentor, 1973–1983, makes some important statements about the Dwelly influence and traditions both in the past and in the present.

It has always seemed to me that Dwelly was a great inventor and entrepreneur; wanting to create a liturgy and style which was peculiar to Liverpool and which in no way aped any other style (Roman or Lutheran). Some people described him as a 'decorated protestant', but that seems to me to be wide of the mark. He wanted and he created a Liverpool Cathedral liturgical style that allowed God to be worshipped in other ways than just words and music. It was Bishop Clifford Martin, I believe, who said that if you wanted to see how to walk to the glory of God go and observe the processions at Liverpool Cathedral. The 'worship' started not with an opening prayer or hymn, but with the processions of choristers and clergy. That set the pattern for all that followed. Even now there is something left of the 'Dwelly style' in the processions from both ends of the Cathedral; though I must admit that some of the 'style' seems to have been curtailed somewhat, which seems a pity.

Then, of course there were the 'traditions of Liverpool' Dwelly created using as many young people (especially junior choristers) as possible. The very colour of the surplices and cassocks had to match with the colour of the stone; nothing was to 'jar' or seem out of place. That has been maintained and I hope always will. But what about the 'festival liturgies' of the Holly Bough and Christmas Tree processions at Christmas, the daffodils at Easter, the red tulips at Pentecost, the signing with water of the Consecration stone on the anniversary? These were what gained Dwelly the title 'decorated protestant', I suppose but that is not enough. They were meant to be special signs and symbols of the passing of the Christian Year which were to become 'peculiar' to Liverpool Cathedral. They were not copied from anywhere else and they were not for "export" to other places. They were (and, in a sense, still are) what singled Liverpool Cathedral out from other churches and other cathedrals. I suppose there was a period when these traditions were followed slavishly; nothing could be altered and nothing missed out from these processions and they did become a little 'twee': but the worshippers loved them and came from miles to witness them, so we kept them going, and they should still be kept alive. But more than that we began to create new 'signs and symbols' and felt free and able to do this because it had always been part of the traditions of Liverpool Cathedral. We could go on evolving the liturgies initiated by Dwelly and adding to them; and no one could protest because, of course, they had been the style of Liverpool since the

Awe inspiring view through the whole Cathedral from just inside the West Doors.

early Dwelly days. So whilst some people saw the 'Dwellyisms' as limiting and time warped, I for one saw them as useful examples and stepping stones to the introduction of new and amended styles of marking the festivals and the special events in Cathedral life. Traditions need to be a stepping stone to further development and never a block to further progress and vision.

I suppose that if I had felt I had to comply with everything Dwelly introduced and had been unable to make changes and introduce new liturgical styles at all then 'Dwellyism' would have become a prison, a very limiting shackle around me. But because Dwelly had always wanted to be 'creative' it gave those who followed him the chance to be creative and innovative as well. So all in all I am very thankful for this strange character, who must have been very difficult to work with (especially in his later years), but who gave to Liverpool Cathedral not only an inheritance of style and panache, but also gave those who came after him the license to be creative and innovative as well. Had it not been for the 'Dwelly legacy' then the liturgy and ethos of Liverpool Cathedral might have been just as uninspiring and pedestrian as many other Cathedrals in the country. Dwelly helped to create the uniqueness of Liverpool Cathedral and gave those who followed him the freedom to carry on and to develop this uniqueness. He saved us from 'conformity' and for that I remain very grateful.[25]

I regard these assessments as so important that the letter had to be quoted in full. It is such a significant statement because Bates knew the Cathedral for over ten years; he worked with Patey and Naylor – both now dead – and he moved away from Liverpool Cathedral to perform a much wider role in the Anglican Communion as a Suffragan Bishop in the Northern Province. He has also maintained a link with Liverpool and occasionally worships or preaches in the cathedral.

Patey was aware of what the church was achieving through the Liturgical Movement and the physical centrality of the Eucharist – a sense of the immanence of God. There was an ensuing danger of a loss of a sense of the transcendence of God, a sense so important to Dwelly in all his striving to produce worship worthy of God. Bates underlined the creativity of the first Dean and Patey developed the idea further theologically seeing the creativity of humanity resembling the ultimate creativity of God: "… it is man's creativity above all his other attributes which bears witness to the maker in whose image he is made." And, "We have still to explore fully the potential of our larger churches as the places in which great creative experiences can take place."[26]

Because of the pioneering creative spirit of Dwelly in the twenties and thirties, Patey was able to go so much further in the sixties and seventies when he was able to say to a wide variety of people, "If you are trying to be genuinely creative, come and share your work and experience with us. For here we honour God as the source of all true creativity."[27]

In 1966, I was able to witness, first-hand, Patey's encouragement of the creative when he invited students of the IM Marsh college of Physical Education to celebrate Christmas and incarnation in dance. There was conservative opposition and at least one annual donation to the Cathedral Friends and Builders was lost because the donor did not approve of "the cathedral being used for ballet dancing." I was on the staff of the college and assisted in a small way in the stage-managing and lighting of the suit of three dances. It was for me, for performers and for many of the congregation a profoundly religious experience which could only have been created in that setting. For Patey "… the criterion of any work of art or community activity which we present in church is not whether it is 'religious' or not, but whether its significance and enjoyment will be enhanced by its being mounted in a place of worship rather than in an art gallery, a concert hall or a theatre."[28]

Liverpool in the sixties was the cradle of an outpouring of creativity, particularly exemplified in pop music, the Beatles and the Mersey Poets. One letter of complaint to the Dean challenged him to behave "like a priest of Christ and not a beat age impresario". Patey was determined that the Cathedral should not be the province of only one cultural pattern and so the cathedral was the concert venue for both Yehudi Menuhin and Tangerine Dream, a German electronic rock band. The "liberty to grow" spoken of by Albert Augustus David in 1930 was used with determination thirty five years later.

Two services stood out in Patey's mind at his retirement. As well as the more traditional Carol services at Christmas, Patey had been developing services in a more folk and pop idiom aimed at young people. At the invitation of ABC Television in 1967, a service called 'How on Earth?' was recorded for television and broadcast on Christmas Eve. "We attempted to present the truths of the meaning behind the Christmas story, and the consequences of man's rejection of those truths in world hunger, oppression and nuclear threat."[29] The music was provided by the Bee Gees and the Cathedral choir; Kenny Everett read from the Bible in 'scouse' and actors from the Everyman Theatre presented a play. Inevitably the service caused immense controversy. As did 'A Festival of Peace' following the shooting of John Lennon but the third Dean was as used to adverse criticism and controversy as the first.

The most important service during the Patey years was held in October 1978

The Nave Altar below the Chancel steps.

A procession through the Choir at an ordination service.

in the presence of the Queen to commemorate the completion of the building. Some months before, the Dean sent a memorandum to all the members of the staff to seek their ideas for a service which would inevitably be linked in people's minds with the Consecration in 1924.

> We must, I think, find the right formula for this service, based on some central biblical or theological theme which can give unity and purpose to the celebration. The consecration of the cathedral in 1924 must have been an impressive and even formidable occasion. But in the intervening half century we have moved into a new kind of society and have developed a fresh understanding of the theology of church and community. We have, therefore, to ask very seriously what kind of celebration is appropriate to mark the completion of a twentieth century cathedral in a modern industrial diocese. It would be a significant step if we could find a way of making this a joyful, celebratory, popular and contemporary event, without sacrificing necessary dignity, and without blurring basic theological insights about the role of the Church in the world. We need

particularly to emphasize that although the cathedral was planned by a world which was passing, it is designed to be used by a world which is coming into being. The service must look to the future as much as to the past, and this must be reflected in the style employed."[30]

The service was devised by Basil Naylor: in keeping with the Dean's wishes but also redolent of Dwelly's service in 1924. The headings used to examine that service are equally appropriate again in 1978: preparation, organization, structure, choreography, text, music, symbolism, service paper. The service was shaped by the prayer of Sir Francis Drake and beginning, continuing and finishing are the three foundation ideas and building blocks. The second, and even more fundamental theme of continuous challenge is ever present as choir and chapter move steadily through the service from east to west: "so that when the Queen leads the congregation out of the cathedral at the end, she will be leading them to face the city, the community and the world, where alone what is professed in the cathedral can become real, positive and meaningful."[31]

The Prologue was read at the foundation stone by Philip Radcliffe Evans, grandson of Sir Frederick Radcliffe who had been present when the stone was laid. He used words of Bishop Chavasse from 2004.

> It is my earnest desire that the new Cathedral of Liverpool shall be built by all and for all, that it shall be the church of the people, where rich and poor meet together to worship God, and where the Gospel of our Lord Jesus Christ is fully preached. It must be the best that we can give, and its walls and towers rising high above our City must be a silent but majestic witness to God and the Unseen.[32]

These words were followed by Drake's prayer which led into The Beginning at the start of which the Bishop stood by the consecration mark in the chancel to read a prayer used by Bishop Albert Augustus David at the consecration service in 1924, a prayer almost certainly composed by Dwelly:

> Blessed be thy name, O Lord, that it hath pleased thee to put into the hearts of thy servants, and especially thy servant Francis James Chavasse, sometime Bishop of this Diocese, to erect this house to thy honour and worship. Bless O Lord, them, their families and substance, and accept the work of their hands; remember them concerning this; wipe not out this kindness that they have shewed for the house of their God and for the offices thereof, and grant that all who may enjoy the benefit of this pious work may show forth their thankfulness to thee by making a right use of the same, to the glory of thy blessed name; through Jesus Christ our Lord. Amen.[33]

The service continued as Precentor and Choir sang part of the *Rejoicings* composed by Martin Shaw and sung by the choir as part of the consecration service. Then followed the first three verses of *All people that on earth do dwell*, also sung at the consecration. During a pause in the hymn, the Roman Catholic Archbishop of Liverpool presented a copy of the Jerusalem Bible to the Dean and acknowledged by him. "It will be in constant use as we read and preach God's Word in this Cathedral, and will be to us a symbol of the mission we share, and of the growing friendship between our two Cathedrals at either end of Hope Street here in Liverpool."[34]

Some of Stuart Blanch's words in the sermon could not have been more appropriate in their pointing to the transcendence and immanence of God, concepts important to Dwelly's faith and his feelings for his cathedral.

> The stones of this great Cathedral from the quarry at Woolton have been shouting since 1910, shouting about the high and lofty One who inhabits eternity, but who is near to those of a humble and contrite spirit. This is one of the great buildings of the world, not simply performing a function, but reminding us of the greatness and majesty of God. In this temple we see the Lord high and lifted up. I have never been able to enter this Cathedral without a revived sense of the majesty of God and a revived sense of my own unimportance in the scheme of things. But strangely enough this has managed to combine a testimony to the high and holy One who inhabits eternity with a testimony to the God who is near to those who are of a humble contrite spirit.[35]

At The Continuing the processions moved to the middle of the central space during the singing of *Christ is made the sure foundation*. The thanksgiving was led by former Dean Frederick Dillistone and included a prayer written by Dwelly for Solemn Entrance in Time of War in 1941. The choir sang *Hail, sovereign Lord*, words which Sir Frederick Radcliffe had written to music by Holst. At The Finishing and the Future, during the singing of *Tell, out my soul*, the processions moved westwards, the choir to stand under the new window and the Queen and clergy to remain under the bridge looking westwards for the handing over of the final bay to the Dean and Chapter and the dedication. The choir sang a new setting of the Benedicite by John Madden from temporary stalls set up underneath the great Benedicite window. There is no doubt that the service spoke strongly to the congregation of 1978 and yet it was a clear acknowledgement to Dwelly and all who had been vital parts of the cathedral's history. The choreography now had a completed building only known to Dwelly as architect's drawings and the whole length of the building was used to effect.

Over the years, and particularly when there had been so many obstacles to the completion of the cathedral, the following day the leader writer in *The Telegraph*, 26 October 1978, wondered whether some people might have viewed the service and the day with some cynicism:

> In such a setting, does not her Anglican Cathedral look like a huge anachronism? Even some of the devout seem inclined to apologise for it, on the grounds that money (all of it raised by private subscription let it be noted) might have been better spent on works of mercy or on some more utilitarian places of worship.
>
> Such sentiments are wholly out of place. The Church proclaims her message by striving, as the architects of Liverpool Cathedral did, to build for as near to eternity as is humanly possible. We should surely by now have learned the error of supposing that Christian virtues will continue to flourish in a society which fails to nourish the faith from which they spring, and great ecclesiastical architecture is one of the most fertile sources of such nourishment. This cathedral will stand, even to the eyes of the unbelieving, as a symbol of what patience and devotion can achieve in the face of endless difficulties and some catastrophes. It is a triumphant proclamation of hope."[36]

The word anachronism appears in the opening sentence prefacing the start of the first chapter of this study. It is I believe significant that a national newspaper dismissed the idea on the day that the cathedral was dedicated.

The 1978 service was no 'death mask' service, reproducing the ideas of a long-dead Dean but was driven by the spirit of that great man. It was carefully planned around key symbols, it was relevant, dignified, imaginative, well-choreographed, supported by appropriate music, the language was simpler and the service book less extensive and ornate. It is in no sense a pastiche of earlier work but it is in the style and spirit of many of the great Dwelly services. I am not suggesting that Patey and Naylor were lacking in original ideas but rather that they recognised the rightness of the Dwelly style for a great occasion in a great building.

Trevor Beeson's description of the fourth Dean might almost have been written about Dwelly. "Endowed with a warmth and humanity that enabled him to get on with everyone, but also a courage and determination that would brook no obstacle to the realization of his vision."[37] When Derrick Walters arrived in the city in 1983 as the fourth Dean, he entered an exhausted and impoverished community of which he said, "I walked into this marvellous Cathedral and it was absolutely empty and it did seem we had an important

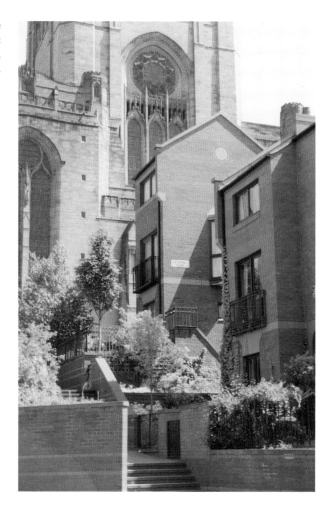

Interesting angles and levels of the new houses in front of the Cathedral: a project inspired by Derrick Walters, the fourth Dean of Liiverpool.

part to play."[38] Walters was not a great imaginative liturgist though devoted to traditional Choral Evensong and Mozart and Haydn masses but his support for the Organist and choir and the musical life of the Cathedral was strong. During his time the choir began to sing Evensong six days a week and with his support an annual music festival was held for two weeks in July. There were annual performances of Handel's *Messiah* and the Bach *Matthew* and *John Passions*. Festival performances with full symphony orchestra of such works as the Verdi *Requiem*, Mahler's *Symphony of a Thousand*, and Britten's *War Requiem* were outstanding and the performers felt themselves to be a living part of the great Dwelly Liverpool tradition. Undoubtedly these performances led the way for a full season of orchestral and choral concerts in the Cathedral, when the Cathedral became the concert venue for fifty eight concerts during the year when the Philharmonic Hall was closed for refurbishment. No Cathedral had ever attempted such a massive venture but it was completely in keeping with the imaginative vitality which had become part of the Liverpool Cathedral tradition.

Derrick Walters had studied at the London School of Economics and was a brilliant financial manager who put the Cathedral on a sound financial footing. He felt that the Cathedral and its community had a responsibility within the wider community, particularly amongst those living in decayed urban poverty. "While our primary role is to let the Cathedral help people in their encounter with God, you can't ignore the context in which we're working. It is desperately important that we create new jobs in the city because that's what gives people a sense of pride and meaning."[39] Trevor Beeson entitled his chapter on Walters in *The Deans* The Urban Regenerator. His building schemes on the urban dereliction in front of the Cathedral and on the Project Rosemary site a short distance away in Toxteth have no parallel in the world of English Cathedrals. Here was yet another example of the freshness and vitality of thinking which has always been associated with Liverpool Cathedral. His friend Professor Peter Toyne, Vice-Chancellor of Liverpool John Moores University said at the memorial service in the Cathedral in 2000, "He used his influence with people of influence to influence the lives of those with little or no influence. He had a rare gift to make the most unlikely people work together, which no one before him had ever been able to do. No cathedral can have done more for the city in which it is so magnificently set."[40]

Derrick Walters was well served by three Precentors, all of whom had a strong feeling for the building for which they devised worship: Nicholas Frayling, Later Dean of Chichester, Ken Riley, later Dean of Manchester, and Mark Boyling, later Dean of Carlisle.

Nicholas Frayling was appointed to Liverpool from a parish in London and had not grown up within the Dwelly tradition but he quickly absorbed the spirit of worship in Liverpool Cathedral. In a conversation with me in June 2004 he told me about his strong memories for some of the special services for which he had been responsible: the service to mark the deaths of 39 people in the Heysel football stadium; the liturgy for Holy Saturday and the Advent Procession: from Darkness to Light. The dramatic processional element of this service was not possible during Dwelly's time in an incomplete Cathedral but the service devised in the 1980s was central to the Liverpool–Dwelly tradition.

The whole of Ken Riley's ministry had been served in the Liverpool diocese and he knew the Cathedral well long before his appointment. I had known him for a number of years as my parish priest and was aware of his vitality and imagination and his intuitive feeling for the use of music in worship. He was no imitator but he responded to the great worship space Scott had designed with imagination, freshness and occasional audacity to which the Cathedral had become accustomed. In conversation with me in November 2006, Ken Riley put forward the suggestion that the Cathedral itself, Scott's masterpiece, encouraged creativity and freshness in those people who had the responsibility for the writing of services. He was also aware of the strength, for good or ill, of the Dwelly–Liverpool tradition. Creativity, imagination, design, language, poetry, symbolism, music, movement, use of space, relevance – the hallmarks of a Dwelly service – were all discernible in Riley's services. I often watched him standing at the eastern crossing, arms folded, looking through choir and presbytery towards the High Altar as he contemplated a new special service. In a great diocesan service to celebrate David Sheppard's twenty years as Bishop, the retiring procession moved through a snow storm of hundreds of floating balloons. The adventure motto of the Air Training Corps was made visibly startling as cadets abseiled from the corona gallery high above the main body of the congregation. The Fiftieth Anniversary of the Battle of the Atlantic and the Hillsborough Memorial service in 1989 were broadcast live on national television. Both services were relevant and right for two entirely different congregations and entirely different occasions.

When Mark Boyling succeeded Ken Riley as Precentor in 1994, he knew the diocese and the Cathedral well and had served four years as Bishop's Chaplain. Basil Naylor had been Diocesan Director of Ordinands during his first curacy and he always spoke very highly of his mentor as a liturgist and priest in tune with his Cathedral. He worked with the dictates of the building at the same time as being innovative. He did not change for the sake of change but improved detail whenever he could. His introduction of a husband and wife and their newly born baby into the Blessing of the Crib service was a powerful innovation. For part of his time as Precentor I was Cathedral Custos and met with him every month to discuss the physical needs of particular services he was planning and he was meticulous over preparation and organization, just like Dwelly. He had fresh ideas but often called on me to find service papers from the archives, not to copy slavishly, but to take account of what had been done before.

Twenty years after the Laying of the Foundation Stone in 1904, Frederick Dwelly devised the first services for the Cathedral. In 2004, to mark the centenary of the Cathedral's establishment, Mark Boyling produced his final services for Liverpool Cathedral before moving to the Deanery of Carlisle. One eminent member of the congregation at the 4 p.m. service on Monday 19 July

Dean Edward Patey and Bishop David Sheppard with the Pope.

was heard to say, "That service was eighty percent Dwelly." That remark was not a slur on Mark Boyling's creativity as a liturgist, but high praise that he had made his mark within the great tradition inaugurated by the first Dean. The service book was more elaborate in its production than anything since the 1924 service. Rich use of processions and meaningful movement rose from the heart of the Dwelly tradition. The litany prayers had something of the character of *Acts of Devotion*. There was a strong ecumenical presence in the service much in line with the openness of Dwelly and Raven seventy years before. The service was no Dwelly pastiche but certainly reflected the spirit of his ideas and his work was referred to specifically by the Dean. He spoke of him as "one whose liturgical genius had opened windows into heaven for those who worshipped in this great house of prayer. Dean Dwelly's liturgical achievement, which still shapes the tradition of this Cathedral, was to connect such a heavenly vision with the daily experience of the people of this City and Diocese in good times and in hard times."[41]

Ken Riley was invited to preach at the Cathedral Centenary Service on 19 July 2004 and much that he said was pertinent to this study. He was aware of what he called "the drag factor" within the church. "Don't get stuck in the archives. Don't get lost in the past ... Nostalgia has no place in religion, but history has."[42] Central to his sermon had been his re-reading of Raven's *Liverpool Cathedral – An impression of its early years.*

> Writing of those days, Canon Charles Raven spoke of the creative adventure – 'At Liverpool the venture of faith which has enabled the building of a new Cathedral on so grand a scale aroused a keen sense of expectancy. Sir Giles Scott had given expression in architecture to the hope for a church which should stand for fresh and creative vision. To reproduce ancient formularies, to imitate earlier artistic modes, would be to betray the hopes of the community.' It is that freshness, that creative searching for the appropriate word, worship and service for each

generation which has delivered Liverpool Cathedral from becoming a cocoon of nostalgia. And I dare to suggest that the creativity of which Raven wrote has now been taken up and is at the heart of English Cathedral life in general so that if things go wrong now, it is much more likely to be as a result of over-enthusiasm than of paralyzing inertia. So we are not ashamed of what the Dean will refer to later in the service as the Liverpool Tradition, for that tradition has always been about proclaiming the gospel afresh, ever-new, ever-young in each generation.[43]

These words and those of Bishop Gordon Bates quoted earlier confirm in my mind that the Dwelly influence is still strongly felt in Cathedral worship and that that influence is not at work to fix the Cathedral into a time warp.

> ... because Dwelly had always wanted to be 'creative' it gave those who followed him the chance to be creative and innovative as well ... Had it not been for the 'Dwelly legacy' then the liturgy and ethos of Liverpool Cathedral might just have been as uninspiring and pedestrian as many other Cathedrals in the country. Dwelly helped to create the uniqueness of Liverpool Cathedral and he gave those who followed him the freedom to carry on and to develop this uniqueness. He saves us from 'conformity' and for that I remain very grateful.[44]

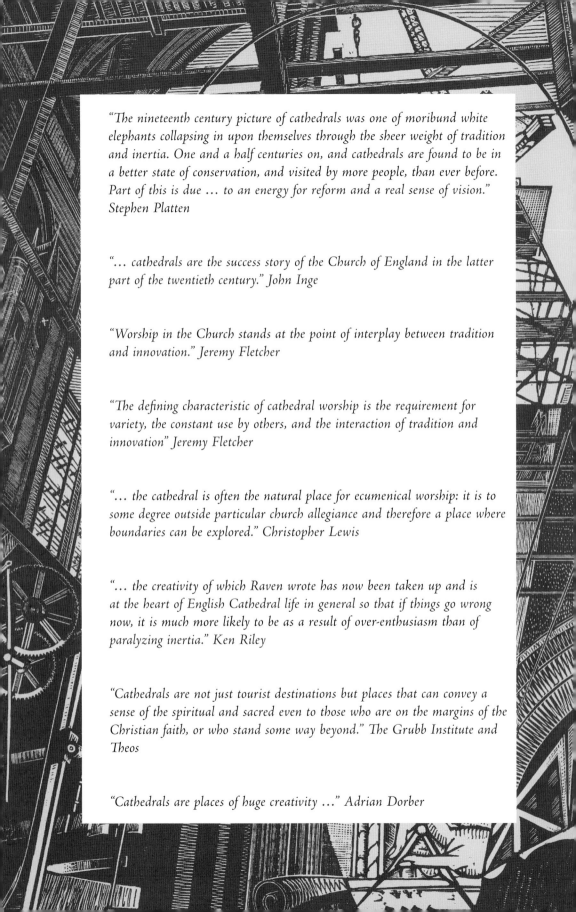

"The nineteenth century picture of cathedrals was one of moribund white elephants collapsing in upon themselves through the sheer weight of tradition and inertia. One and a half centuries on, and cathedrals are found to be in a better state of conservation, and visited by more people, than ever before. Part of this is due ... to an energy for reform and a real sense of vision." Stephen Platten

"... cathedrals are the success story of the Church of England in the latter part of the twentieth century." John Inge

"Worship in the Church stands at the point of interplay between tradition and innovation." Jeremy Fletcher

"The defining characteristic of cathedral worship is the requirement for variety, the constant use by others, and the interaction of tradition and innovation" Jeremy Fletcher

"... the cathedral is often the natural place for ecumenical worship: it is to some degree outside particular church allegiance and therefore a place where boundaries can be explored." Christopher Lewis

"... the creativity of which Raven wrote has now been taken up and is at the heart of English Cathedral life in general so that if things go wrong now, it is much more likely to be as a result of over-enthusiasm than of paralyzing inertia." Ken Riley

"Cathedrals are not just tourist destinations but places that can convey a sense of the spiritual and sacred even to those who are on the margins of the Christian faith, or who stand some way beyond." The Grubb Institute and Theos

"Cathedrals are places of huge creativity ..." Adrian Dorber

TEN

Cathedrals are the success story of the Church of England

THE FIRST CHAPTER of this study indicated that, even at the end of the nineteenth century, English Cathedrals remained unclear as to their function, uncertain as to their general health and unpopular in the minds of the general population. Lehmberg's comment was devastating: "… pockets of privilege, lethargy and decadence, in-bred and self-centred, staffed by lazy and pompous clerics, little concerned with ordinary people …"[1] In Raven's words, "… they had come to occupy a fixed position and are not easily moved from their routine."[2] By 2006, Bishop John Inge was able to declare that "… cathedrals are the success story of the Church of England in the latter part of the twentieth century."[3] As I have progressed with my research I have become alerted to the notion that the work of the first Dean of Liverpool might have had an influence way beyond the walls of his new cathedral. Many references throughout this study point to Dwelly's wider significance in the church.

"Ever so many thanks for that, your latest and most brilliant effort – I set it down in front of the A [rchbishop] at his desk and made him go right throughout … He was really impressed."[4]

"I hear you are most kindly looking at the Consecration Service. You have the Chelmsford Enthronement Form? I hear that was excellent – and your handiwork."[5]

"… you have given so much time and thought in these recent years to the

257

The procession at the start of John Moores University graduation ceremony.

A service with David Poulter, Director of Music, in the Lady Chapel in 2010.

drawing up of Special Services for special occasions that I would be grateful to have some hints or suggestions from you."[6])

"He has been consulted by most cathedrals when great ceremonies have been arranged."[7]

"Liverpool Cathedral has won a distinctive place in the life of our church."[8]

"Here is a development of Anglican worship which deserves the closest study … No one who is dissatisfied with the traditional worship of our cathedrals and larger parish churches can afford to ignore the experiments of Liverpool."[9]

"Your services hold a place of their own in the Anglican Communion."[10]

"Liverpool Cathedral is known throughout the world. It would, however, be an empty shell were it not for the uplifting services of worship which have brought life and colour, dignity and glory into it. The man behind these services has been the Dean."[11]

"During the present century the names of Dean Bennett of Chester and Dwelly of Liverpool are outstanding for what they have accomplished in making Cathedrals power-houses of worship in a modern-day diocese."[12]

"That experiment was original, but loyal to the ethos of Anglican worship. It was to be an enrichment in the whole Church."[13]

"Many of the experiments regarding community and worship and liturgy, which were operating at Coventry, he had already pioneered."[14]

"The creativity of which Raven wrote has now been taken up and is at the heart of English Cathedral life in general …"[15]

While I was at work on this chapter, I received unsolicited letters from two retired bishops who had grown up in the Liverpool Diocese and who had both recently read my biography of Dwelly. Rt. Rev. John Wayne wrote on 13 April 2007, "Liverpool Cathedral has been an inspiration to me all my life, and I love the very stones of it."[16] On 21 April 2007, Rt. Revd. Jonathan Bailey wrote,

> As a child and youth I went to the Cathedral from time to time with my parents, and took what I experienced to be normative for cathedral worship. The range of special

Vice-Dean in one of the gold copes.

services for varied constituencies, some of them very unexpected, stands out among my memories. It was only as adult life and my training took me elsewhere in the church of England that I fully appreciated just how different, and innovative Liverpool was among the 40 plus cathedrals. Your book holds the key as to why, and that is what made it such a compelling read for me.[17]

In a letter I asked the Bishop if he would expand on what he had perceived to be "different and innovative" and this he did by email on 26 May 2007. The Bishop consulted his wife, also ordained and also from Liverpool, and they were able to make a joint response.

> Together we agree we had grown-up to assume that Liverpool represented what a typical cathedral is and does. It was only as we spread our wings beyond Liverpool that we came to recognise how special our home cathedral was. Some points of difference we identified later.
>
> Acts of worship often focused on non-geographical secular constituencies such as medics, fruit wholesalers. In doing so, the constituencies concerns and service to the community were articulated liturgically in ways which reflected an incarnational theology with its implicit or explicit message that, for example, God was concerned about how the fruit trade did its business. Susan's early experience included the annual St Lukestide medical service; the only time in the year her surgeon father, Maurice Bennett-Jones, attended church. Similarly my father, a regular worshipper, took us as a family to services related to the world of education. Only since those days in the 1950s has the outreach ministry of cathedrals to the fringe and seekers been recognized and developed more widely elsewhere. In contrast to all that Liverpool offered, I have become aware of a current canon precentor whose starting point is that the cathedral is a monastic foundation with the congregation present as bystanders at the community's worship. Without such an outrageous statement that or something like it has long been the inference to be drawn from many cathedrals.
>
> In the days before computers and copiers made bespoke orders of service commonplace, at the Cathedral orders of service were published for each of such acts of worship so that the fringe worshipper was at ease with the liturgy rather than stumbling though a complex book. The service papers' high standard of production invited the worshipper to keep and treasure both it and the occasion they had experienced.
>
> We each recall the Christmas tree and holly bough services. Susan

recalls her first experience aged about 8, being taken by her grandmother who lived at 5 Gambier Terrace. Again, the "all-age" agenda we took for granted has only later been addressed by the church at large.

The driver behind the colour, roles and scale of movements was the creation of an inspirational ambience for both the committed and the fringe rather than the adoption of traditions too arcane for all but the initiated.[18]

Only a small number of Dwelly services for other cathedrals have I been able to identify; for example, Lang's enthronement at Canterbury, Bell's enthronement in Chichester, Thanksgiving for the King's Recovery at Westminster Abbey, and the Consecration of Cairo Cathedral. The references quoted in the paragraph above would suggest a far wider influence. There is, I believe, enough evidence to suggest that the work of Frederick Dwelly was influential in the development of cathedral worship in the twentieth century, but not enough evidence, as yet, to indicate the extent of that influence. The natural conclusion of this study ought to move into a wider study of cathedral worship in the twentieth century in an attempt to identify the specific influence of Dwelly and the Liverpool traditions nationwide. Such a study would require residential research in all 43 cathedrals and the reporting would be likely to run to beyond 100,000 words.

This book has focused tightly on the work of one man, apart from the first chapter which began with a short survey indicating the low water mark of cathedrals in the nineteenth century. This final chapter, though short and inadequate, will indicate the immense improvement in the health and popularity of cathedrals by the start of the twenty first century. Not surprisingly, Dean Howson's *Essays on Cathedrals by various writers*[19] and Bishop Benson's *The Cathedral: Its necessary place in the life and work of the church*[20] are now balanced by recent publications similar in character, though far more positive in content: *Cathedrals Now*, edited by Iain Mackenzie,[21] *Heritage and Renewal*, The Report of the Archbishops' Commission on Cathedrals,[22] *Flagships of the Spirit*, edited by Stephen Platten and Christopher Lewis,[23] *Dreaming Spires: Cathedrals in a new age*, edited by Platten and Lewis[24] and *Spiritual Capital: The Present and Future of English Cathedrals*,[25] by the Grubb Institute and Theos.

Short but significant papers and reports were produced by individuals a decade earlier. The then Vicar of Mossley Hill, Ken Riley,[26] subsequently to be Precentor and Vice Dean of Liverpool before becoming Dean of Manchester wrote *Cathedrals – Mission-Stations or Museums?* between September 1982 and February 1983 in preparation for a clergy residential conference at Windsor. Alan Webster, at that time Dean of St. Pauls, suggested that a copy be sent to all Cathedral Deans. I was intrigued by the way in which some of Riley's statements were in direct parallel with many of Dwelly's ideas. In writing about the life of cathedrals he wrote "… we have to acknowledge that much of the activity would seem to the objective observer to have more to do with keeping the past alive – the worship and words and music of a bygone age – than to do with a vibrant faith for the present."[27] The essay was written after interviews with ten deans who were keenly aware of the time as "a Day of Opportunity for the mission of a cathedral, as never before"[28] partly because of the twenty million visitors who entered their doors each year. Change was in the air but "Cathedrals are a strange mixture of unadventurous, traditional forms, on the one hand, and bold experimental worship on the other."[29] Twenty years later in a cathedral sermon in 2004 Riley was able to say, "I dare to suggest that the creativity of which Raven wrote has now been taken up and is at the heart of English Cathedral life in general …"[30] A hundred years earlier, some of Riley's words would have been hard to substantiate but they would have

Canon Cynthia Dowdle with the Most Reverend Malcolm McMahon, Archbishop of Liverpool. Vice-Dean, Dean and Archbishop McMahon at the Service for the Beginning of the Legal Year.

been meaningful to Dwelly. "Deans are conscious that the Cathedral exists for the city and not as the private property of the Dean and Chapter, the musical establishment or an elite congregation."[31] Dwelly's ecumenical gestures which caused such problems in the nineteen thirties would have caused no stir in the eighties: "The ecumenical dimension is totally accepted by the cathedrals, and they are available for use by all kinds of groups, as well as the cathedral itself mounting ecumenical acts of worship."[32] The relevance of a form of service which was so important to Dwelly in the thirties was reiterated by Riley in the eighties: "Cathedrals ought to be about the re-interpretation of the Faith for our own day, rather than content with a mere repetition of past forms. They are the Church's shop window and, as such, nothing can exaggerate their importance."[33] "Cathedrals should be 'liturgical workshops' and use their freedom to the full, not only in experimental services for special occasions, but also in statutory worship, otherwise we shall not be ready for the challenge of tomorrow."[34]

Between March and September 1989, Canon Owen Conway, Vicar of Headingley and a member of the Cathedral's Advisory Commission for England, undertook two visits to all forty three cathedrals as part of his sabbatical leave and published his responses privately in *A Cathedral Pilgrimage – Reflections and observations on the life and work of Cathedrals in England today and in the future*.[35] This report was prepared before he was appointed as Canon Precentor at Chester but Bennett's *The Nature of a Cathedral* must have been at the forefront of his mind as he wrote. It is a wide-ranging report which cannot be examined in detail but, by and large, Conway was able to report on the healthy state of cathedrals "something of a 'success story' in the world's eyes,"[36] and "... one sees in our cathedrals a great cause for hope in the church."[37] At the start of the chapter on The Cathedral's Worship he cited some words of C. S. Lewis in his address to the Friends of Chichester Cathedral in 1954: "... whereas a poor parish church must struggle to perform faithfully the minimum essential, a cathedral should be able to perform the maximum possible."[38] Conway highlighted three concepts which were central to his notions of cathedral worship: neutrality, comprehensiveness and tradition., – three words which are clearly discernible in Dwelly's work. "Neutrality implies that the worship should involve the widest possible participation, and comprehensiveness implies the need to use the full range of liturgies the church offers. Tradition is what bears witness to the truth that the important element in worship is not what you do but how you do it. In cathedrals tradition demands that it is always well done."[39] The music of cathedral worship, so vital to Dwelly, received high praise from Conway "If excellence is to be found anywhere, it is in the consistently high standard of its cathedral choirs."[40] Liverpool was the only cathedral about whom he commented favourably on the way in which former choristers were used, just as Bennett recommended. "I noted with especial pleasure the imaginative scheme at Liverpool where the 'Cross Guild' consists entirely of ex-choristers, who are much needed and used for serving and virging duties."[41] Bennett might have had the idea but it was Dwelly who instituted what is, in the eyes of Peter Toyne, fourth Chairman of Friends of Cathedral Music, unique. Ceremonial was mentioned only briefly but that area of great Dwelly strength was highlighted by Conway as it had been by Bennett: "ceremonial should have as much care and time given to it in detail as does the music."[42]

Heritage and Renewal was a comprehensive report on the state of most of the important aspects of cathedral life. Some words from Conclusions and Recommendations are central to this study, though I had not re-read them for nearly ten years, when I approached this chapter of my study.

> At the heart of cathedral life is the daily offering of worship and praise to God. Without the warming fire of worship, these elegant buildings would be ancient monuments rather than living temples capable of inspiring the souls of men and women with glimpses of the divine. The variety of worship found in cathedrals reflects their engagement with many different aspects of the community, of which their role in national or local civic life is simply one part. So we envisage a creative approach to worship in cathedrals, in which the communication of the Christian faith has a high priority."[43]

Many of the Commission's recommendations are recorded in the form of questions, questions which would certainly have been in Dwelly's mind, and answered positively, sixty years earlier.

> In what respect is the cathedral developing an imaginative and creative approach to its worship?
>
> In what ways is the cathedral taking ecumenical initiatives in its worship?
>
> Is the cathedral encouraging the composition of new liturgical and musical material?
>
> Is the cathedral seeking to include a wide spectrum of Christian worship?

Jeremy Fletcher, Precentor at York Minster, has engaged with these questions in his chapter *Liturgy on the frontiers: Laboratories for the soul*, in *Dreaming Spires*. At one time he had been sceptical about the notion of cathedral worship being on the frontier: "Instead of being laboratories for the soul, they were shelters for the nostalgic: the liturgy was traditionally founded; the music was composed by the long dead; liturgical change hit cathedrals last, not first."[44] His increased knowledge of cathedrals and their ways modified his views: "there is more innovation than I would formerly have admitted."[45] He would have approved much of Dwelly's work half a century ago. "The defining characteristic of cathedral worship is the requirement for variety, the constant use by others, and the interaction of tradition and innovation."[46] Dwelly's special services for a wide range of secular organisations would surely have been on the frontier in Fletcher's eyes: "The frontier which cathedrals currently inhabit is that between the Church and organizations and causes working across the wider community."[47] He recognised that the "spectacle and movement" which was expected in the large spaces of cathedral had a direct influence on what might happen in much smaller churches. He would have been full of admiration for the artistry displayed by Liverpool's first dean: "It would be impossible to imagine cathedrals without *movement, visual art* and *music*. Cathedrals might well be described as places of *procession*."[48] In this his judgment is in line with that expressed by Dillistone in his unpublished article of 1981. Dwelly the liturgical artist would have been praised for showing how "the best art can be used liturgically"[49] "The same is true of music, where a commitment to excellence means the commissioning of a new work, and the training of musicians from the earliest age means a healthy flow of young people soaked in the music of the church."[50] In the thirties such people as Martin Shaw and Ralph Vaughan Williams composed commissions for the cathedral; Noel Rawsthorne produced a range of works and in 2004, to mark the year of consecration, John Tavener wrote his *Atma Mass* for Liverpool. Specially produced service sheets, pioneered by Dwelly at Liverpool, taken up by most cathedrals, are now made possible in parish churches through technological advances in printing. In his final paragraph Fletcher wrote one short sentence which might be seen as an essential element of Dwelly's genius: "Our worship will be at its most challenging when mystery and inclusion coincide."[51]

I have no evidence to suggest that Jeremy Fletcher had any direct experience of Dwelly's work but what he has observed in the worship in other cathedrals in the twenty first century exhibits features of the best of Dwelly's work part-way through the twentieth century.

Trevor Beeson[52] made only the slightest passing reference to Dwelly, though he devoted a chapter to Derrick Walters, fourth dean, but he was unequivocal in high-lighting the success of cathedrals in a way which would have been quite insupportable at the time when the Liverpool Diocese was founded. "Flagships of the spirit,' 'Shop-windows of the Church of England', 'Supermarkets of religion'. These are just three of the descriptions of England's cathedrals coined by their deans in recent years the revival of cathedral life took place during a period when the rest of the Church was in serious numerical decline. There is nothing comparable in any other part of Europe." "The cathedrals have bucked the trend and are one of the Church of England's few twentieth century success stories."[53]

Had Dwelly been a traditional liturgical scholar, his books and articles in learned journals would have presented his ideas and achievements to later generations but all his liturgical genius went into creating worship which brought a great twentieth century cathedral to life. Only after a major piece of

A view through the Cathedral looking west from the Sanctuary. The space is no longer spoiled with chairs.

A Carol Service with choir and congregation in the Central Space. .A choir procession at the start of a service.

research into the life of English Cathedrals in the twentieth century has been completed can there be any authoritative assessments of what this man gave, not just to Liverpool, but to the rest of the country.

This study began with a short examination of the Cathedral as a building and as a community: an examination essential before any consideration of the work of the first Dean and his influence on the character of worship established in the building. A highly significant feature was the amount of freedom enjoyed by the chapter of the new Cathedral, unencumbered by medieval statutes. The first Dean did not inherit too many fixed expectations from his diocese and new Cathedral community.

Architecturally, the Cathedral was unique and broke new ground. From the start it was the largest cathedral in Britain, the work of a very young architect who was permitted to let his designs evolve over the whole course of the building programme. An architectural freshness and experiment would later be followed and accompanied by liturgical freshness and experiment. From the earliest days people have commented on the vast space which is Liverpool Cathedral and Scott spoke about this in a BBC broadcast on 16 July 1943 and later published in *Liverpool Cathedral Bulletin*:

> Although, as I have said, the design has been continually revised, it has always possessed certain characteristics, one of which was aptly described recently by an American officer, who called it 'Space Gothic'. What he meant can be understood by anyone standing inside the building and looking around, when he will see only wall surfaces, with no rows of detached columns and arches forming the open arcades usually found in cathedrals and churches. Why I adopted this treatment I do not know, except that I like vast modeling surfaces. I doubt if any artist uses his conscious reasoning; he obeys a sub-conscious urge, feels rather than thinks his way forward.[54]

There is a clear parallel with Dwelly's liturgical artistry here: he "continually revised" as can be seen by an examination of the service papers. This feeling rather than reasoning is central to Dwelly's artistry. Raven commented on Dwelly's difficulty "in explaining the reasons for his intuitive judgments".[55] Scott provided his friend Dwelly with vast uninterrupted space and Dwelly learned how to use this space powerfully, particularly for human movement.

In 1975 Canon Chancellor Basil Naylor considered the adequacy of the Cathedral as it neared completion, for old and new forms of Anglican Liturgy:

> As our understanding of worship extends into many new areas of thought and action, we become more and more aware of the value of space. One of the great misfortunes of the past has been the misuse, often choking, of space in places where Christians meet and worship. Here we have all the space we need. But space (on earth at least) always has a context. One of the glories of our Cathedral is its superbly designed space whose worthy use demands wisdom, imagination and skill.[56]

Naylor was aware of the changing demands being made "new shapes, patterns and forms of worship are being developed to meet the demands of a new era." He was grateful for the far-sighted vision of the architect who had "the vision, the art and the skill; to create in a traditionally shaped building a vast space where sight and movement can be unimpeded. Within the space worship areas can be composed and furniture arranged or removed to suit whatever form each act of worship is designed to take."[57] From the records we know that Dwelly was a dynamic, imaginative and effective priest before coming to Liverpool Cathedral but his greatest achievements were inspired by and created within Giles Scott's great building.

Limitations on length meant that only a single chapter could be devoted to Dwelly's early life and ministry but it is important to take account of those years as the foundations for his Cathedral achievements. Theologically his mysticism and modernism are traceable from early manhood. The significance of modernist and mystic, Ralph Inge, has been reported in Dwelly's eventual decision to offer himself for ordination. His dynamism, enthusiasm, powers of leadership and organization, his artistry and his warm humanity shone clearly from his early days at Windermere, through Cheltenham, Southport and eventually the Cathedral. Evidence of his contribution to the wider church are to be found in his work for the National Mission, the Life and Liberty Movement, liturgical experiment and Prayer Book revision. His interest in music and the arts in worship linked him with the ideas and practices of Percy Dearmer.

Dwelly was an experienced priest aged 43 when he was invited to design the service of consecration, probably the most influential service of his life. This service brought him a residentiary canonry early in 1925. The archive correspondence reveals the range of clergy who asked for his advice on the devising of a wide range of services all over the country. His central involvement in the installation of Cosmo Lang as Archbishop of Canterbury was a notable achievement. Within Liverpool Cathedral, first as a canon and then as Sub-Dean, all his organisational and artistic abilities poured forth in a wide range of special services as well as in the standard daily and weekly services which began to make innovative and imaginative use of Scott's building. His achievement over eight years made it clear that he was the obvious choice as the first Dean.

The central chapters of the book contain examination of a wide range of Dwelly "special" services together with comments upon his work by a range of people lay and ordained. The cooperation with Charles Raven, academic theologian, and Frederick Dwelly, the imaginative, dynamic liturgist, led to the Cathedral being seen as the "research" Cathedral of the Anglican Communion. It was a Cathedral established to serve its diocese in ways appropriate to the needs of those who laboured to build it. Raven's *Liverpool Cathedral: An impression of its early years*[58] indicated the theological foundations in liberal modernism and that the Cathedral's theology was free from "archaic dogmatic shackles and ecclesiastical burdens".[59] Raven's book encapsulates the ideas which were central to the Cathedral's whole being: the ideas fundamental to the thinking and planning of the first Dean. Raven wrote of Cathedral worship: "its ceremonial, its music, its services must enable modern folk to experience worship."[60] This is what Dwelly services were designed to do.

Worship in Liverpool Cathedral was inclusive, appealed widely to the local community, and the great special services were very well-attended. There was clear feeling that there were strong links between the building and the services celebrated within it. The Dean of Chichester had written, "The rediscovery of an inspiration that had been potent in the past, and its adaptation to modern life. That is the keynote of Sir Giles Scott's great building. It is the keynote of the uses to which it has been put."[61] Dwelly's uses of the vast spaces for meaningful movement was an important feature and remains so today. In a letter to the writer in September 2007, the Very Rev. Mark Boyling stressed the importance of movement as an essential ingredient made possible by what he called "unity" of space despite the building's obvious sections. Both Mark Boyling and Noel Rawsthorne have spoken of the vital importance of music, performed to the highest standard and integrated into the sweep of the service and not used as an addition or interlude.

The excellence of the Liverpool tradition was widely known and received high praise from two Archbishops in respective sermons. Cyril Garbett stated "… your services hold a place of their own in the Anglican Communion",[62] while William temple declared that "Liverpool Cathedral has won a distinctive place

Bishop Paul Bayes knocking on the West Door of the Cathedral before his installation in November 2014.

in the life of our church, not only by its splendid beauty, but by the varied expression which it has already given to Christian aspiration and worship."[63] At the times of his retirement and death, Dwelly's achievements were reported in sermons and in the media and the words of Clifford Martin, his Diocesan Bishop, attempt to sum up the total achievement. "Liverpool Cathedral is known throughout the world. It would, however, be an empty shell were it not for the uplifting services of worship which have brought life and colour, dignity and glory into it. The man behind these services has been the Dean."[64]

Dwelly's human qualities were as important as his liturgical skill and administrative ability. "He drew people more than any man I have ever known."[65] "His affection was without limit, and those who were his friends know the lengths to which he would go to bring comfort and happiness to those who needed him. His was a love which overflowed ..."[66] "But above all he possessed a genius for friendship, the capacity really to care and passionately to help the folk who came to him and with whom he was brought into contact."[67]

Dwelly's influence on the worshipping life of the Cathedral was not ended by his retirement and subsequent death. In his letter to the Cross Guild in 1955 he acknowledged their understanding of his work and their determination to keep it alive: "it will be safe in your hands",[68] and his old friend Bishop George Bell had written in the same year, "I am sure your work will live."[69] Bishop Christopher Chavasse wrote, "The great matter is that you have achieved 'immortality', and now will live in worship in this Cathedral."[70] Basil Naylor declared that he had been aware of Dwelly's presence when he was appointed because the whole Cathedral community "had the tradition almost built in to them."[71] Although he did not work with Dwelly, Naylor seemed to have an instinctive understanding of what was fundamentally important in Dwelly's work: creating imaginative, memorable services, relevant to the lives of those present.

Edward Patey was quite unlike Dwelly in personality, yet what he achieved in the Cathedral is in direct parallel with Dwelly's achievements thirty years earlier. Patey acknowledged the inherent dangers of "cutting loose" from past heritage and being "imprisoned" or "paralysed" by it. Patey and his Chapter were able to strike a sound balance and as Bishop Gordon Bates wrote in 2004, "... because Dwelly had always been creative it gave those who followed him the chance to be creative and innovative as well."[72] Patey acknowledged the close connections between Liverpool and Coventry as new communities "not tied to the past or paralysed by tradition." In a sermon he said, "A new Cathedral is an empty shell until the builders have created life and purpose and vision within it. Pre-eminently Cathedrals must be places where great worship is offered.

There must be continual experiment if Cathedral worship is not to become a mere fossilization of the past."[73] Patey and Naylor did not abandon the great Dwelly seasonal services which still proved relevant and popular but they broke new ground in a new age knowing that they were keeping faith with the Dwelly tradition.

Creativity, imagination, design, language, poetry, symbolism, music, human movement within a large space – the hall mark of a Dwelly service were discernible in Ken Riley's work during the Walters era. Riley, invited to preach at the Centenary Service in 2004, quoted some of Raven's pronouncements about worship in the Cathedral and declared their relevance seventy years later. "It is that freshness, that creative searching for the appropriate word, worship and service for each generation which has delivered Liverpool Cathedral from becoming a cocoon of nostalgia. And I dare to suggest that the creativity of which Raven wrote has now been taken up and is at the heart of English Cathedral life in general ..."[74] Both Riley and Boyling, late-twentieth century Precentors, have discerned the essence of the Dwelly Liverpool tradition in services in other great Cathedrals in the twenty first century.

The short final chapter is intended to balance some of the negative ideas in the first chapter – that cathedral life was moribund, strangled by tradition and lacking in freshness and relevance. Bishop John Inge's comment that "Cathedrals are the success story of the Church of England in the latter part of the twentieth century"[75] sums up the radical change. In line with its title, this book has focused upon worship in Liverpool Cathedral though with many references to the belief that Dwelly's influence spread far more widely through churches and cathedrals. In one sense, this study is incomplete because there has been no attempt to examine worship in other Cathedrals. There is a need for a comprehensive examination of worship in Cathedrals during the twentieth century. Such a study would reveal to what extent Frederick Dwelly and the Liverpool tradition extended beyond the bounds of the diocese.

During the fifteen years when I worked full-time in the Cathedral, I encountered thousands of visitors and listened to their comments as they responded to the building. I could not number the people who, on entering the massive space were almost without words and simply said, "Wow!" I remember the long conversation with an American tourist who said, "I've been in cathedrals all over the world but I've never seen anything like this." I took a middle-aged gentleman, formerly dressed in a dark suit and, as I took from his conversation, well educated, out onto the Corona Gallery high above the central space. He gripped the parapet and said quietly, "My God," and then apologised for his response though his words could not have been more apposite. The first chapter of this book and the first sentence quoted Betjeman's response, "Liverpool Cathedral is one of the great buildings of the world," and the enthusiasm of visitors would seem to support his claim.

The memorial to architect Giles Gilbert Scott is inlaid in the floor in the centre of the Central Space. A great many visitors seem to know something about Scott – even if it is only that he designed the famous red telephone box. Interested visitors ask about him and about the whole history of the building.

The memorial to the first Dean is a life-sized carving for which sculptor Edward Carter Preston used the death mask he had taken. Rarely did visitors ask questions about this liturgical genius and most people have never heard of Frederick Dwelly, even though it had been Dwelly's great special services which had brought life to Scott's "empty shell". One of the saddest questions I faced, on more than one occasion, was "Do you still have services here?"

Despite what I judge to be incontrovertible evidence of Dwelly's influence on Cathedral worship in Liverpool and beyond, his name is almost unknown. He was an artist whose medium was public worship rather than the wood, stone and glass of an architect. His art was to create significant acts of worship and the evidence is to be found in the service papers and the living tradition in Liverpool. Living even though hardly any of the Liverpool Cathedral community are old enough to remember Dwelly.

Shortly after his retirement having served twenty five years as Director of Music, I asked Organist Professor Ian Tracey whether he was aware of the Dwelly legacy in the worship in the Cathedral and his answer was emphatically positive. He began his comments by stressing Dwelly's belief in the power of drama in music, movement and the spoken word, all powerful tools to give the worshipper "glimpses of transcendence". Nothing must ever distract a member of the congregation whose sense of worship might be most intense for a few minutes at any time during the service. The entry processions are famous and described by Francis Jackson, one-time organist at York Minster, as "beginning in little dribbles and then advancing in great waves" all designed to match the grandeur and scope and size of the space. At Liverpool Cathedral the service always commences with the very first appearance of the advancing procession and not with the first words or music from the stalls. In Ian Tracey's words, "The Holly Bough is a typical example of his love of theatre, not at the end or the beginning of the service, but in the centre, the entry of the bishop into a darkened cathedral, behind a bough bedecked with candles and holly, accompanied by probationers carrying small Christmas trees, the Cross Guild bearing lights into the darkness and the congregation and the great organ performing some great climactic carol – a total overwhelming of all the senses

– visual, musical, aesthetic and perhaps spiritual – true worship or worthship."

Tracey's words put me in mind of the great processional Advent service, From Darkness to Light in which the whole length of the building, unfinished in Dwelly's day, is used. At the start the whole Cathedral is in darkness as Choir and Cross Guild with music and candles carry the light from the west doors right through to the Sanctuary until the whole Cathedral is flooded in light. Precentors Nicholas Frayling and Ken Riley developed this service whose popularity increases year after year.

Not surprisingly, the Dwelly musical tradition is strong: there have only been three organists in the whole life of the Cathedral and Ian Tracey was taught by Noel Rawsthorne who had been taught by Goss Custard. The improvisation style during the entry procession was developed because Dwelly instructed Goss that the organ should crescendo throughout as the procession grew in intensity because he believed this swelling of sound could be a moment of inspiration for the worshipper. Dwelly commissioned new music: a tradition which continues. Ian Tracey is not old enough to have known Dwelly but he feels himself part of the tradition: "I have tried to keep that beacon which FWD lit in my predecessors in some way alive.

Most of my work on the writing of this book was completed before the publication in 2012 of the research project undertaken by Theos and The Grubb Institute entitled *Spiritual Capital: the Present and Future of English Cathedrals.*[76] Although I read the report carefully soon after its publication, I did not consider calling upon some of its findings in my study, possibly because there was no specific reference to Liverpool Cathedral. However, on reading the report again now, I realise that many of the findings are in stark contrast to many of the derogatory comments about Cathedrals quoted in my first chapter.

I am not attempting to make any false claims that the first Dean of Liverpool

Cathedral musicians, past and present, after the service to commemorate the sixtieth anniversary of Noel Rawsthorne's appointment as organist. Front row: Noel Rawsthorne, Ronald Woan. Back row: Ian Tracey, David Poulter, Daniel Bishop, Ian Wells.

The tradition continues: John Lloyd, the longest serving member of the Cross Guild having joined the choir in 1938, Charlotte Kennerley, her first day in a cassock at the age of 7 in 2014, Lydia Heyes, former Girls' Choir member and now an active member of the Cross Guild

was responsible for the changed attitudes towards English Cathedrals but I believe there are parts of my research that indicate what a forward-looking Dean Frederick William Dwelly was. Many of the features of Cathedral life and worship in Liverpool in the 1930s are now standard across the country and clearly observable in the six Cathedrals at the heart of the Theos and Grubb Institute research: Canterbury, Durham, Leicester, Lichfield, Manchester and Wells.

In his Foreword, the Dean of Lichfield wrote, "Cathedrals are places of huge creativity, and their potential both within the Church and within society needs to be considered and carefully evaluated." Dwelly's creativity in Windermere, Cheltenham, Southport and above all in Liverpool Cathedral was famous and the words of Bishop Gordon Bates come to mind: "… because Dwelly had always wanted to be 'creative' it gave those who followed him the chance to be creative and innovative as well. Had it not been for the 'Dwelly legacy' then the liturgy and ethos of Liverpool Cathedral might just have been as uninspiring and pedestrian as many other Cathedrals in the country." Ken Riley's judgment is also relevant: "… the creativity of which Raven wrote has now been taken up and is at the heart of English Cathedral life in general." After Dwelly's retirement in 1955, Charles Raven had written, "Ever since its consecration in 1924 Liverpool Cathedral has stood for an imaginative, vital appropriate presentation of Christian faith and worship, for a worthy commemoration of national and local events, for a generous and scholarly treatment of theological and moral issues, and for magnificent music and deeply impressive ritual. It has thus become a unique centre of relevant, intelligent and aesthetic worship."

The breadth of appeal of Cathedral worship was an important feature of Dwelly's influence: the special services for a wide range of secular bodies; services which had a strong appeal beyond the Church of England and even beyond the Christian Church. Dwelly had been breaking new ground but *Spiritual Capital*[77] indicates how other Cathedrals have followed his lead: "cathedrals reach out to the general public, not just those who are part of the Church of England"; "cathedrals have a particular capacity to connect spiritually with those who are on or beyond the Christian 'periphery'"; "cathedrals have a broad reach appealing to the religious and non-religious, and to everyone in between"; "a place for interfaith and ecumenical dialogue"; "cathedrals had good or very good relationships with people who come to special services".

The report revealed how many people recognised cathedrals as sacred space and it highlights four factors which enabled the visitor to experience the sacred: architecture and sense of continuity; the music and choirs; the welcome and the pattern of worship. Clearly all these factors are relevant to all cathedrals and have been for many years. They were all factors which were meaningful to the first Dean. In the opening paragraph of this book I wrote, "it is argued that his [Dwelly] was a liturgical genius commensurate with the architectural vision of Giles Gilbert Scott, the Cathedral Architect." The two men became great friends and Dwelly was constantly striving to use the building effectively in the performance of the liturgy. This experiment with the building is still discernible today. Dwelly recognised the importance of music in the Cathedral and with the financial support of Francis Nielson and the musical expertise and professional skills of Edgar Robinson, Henry Goss Custard, Noel Rawsthorne and Ronald Woan, Dwelly established Liverpool Cathedral as a centre of musical excellence. The size of Liverpool Cathedral could make it a daunting building for visitors, but Dwelly's establishment of the College of Interpreters flourishes today with the current team of voluntary guides. Much of this book has focused on the patterns of and style of worship established by Dwelly, now nurtured and developed to ensure that the services have current relevance.

I no longer live in the Liverpool Diocese and do not worship regularly in the Cathedral but for fifteen years I had been a member of staff and for over twenty years I attended daily Choral Evensong. Having been engaged in the writing of this book for over five years, I search in myself for my personal responses to my experiences in Dwelly's great Cathedral as I contemplate some of the features of Cathedral quoted at the head of this chapter, especially variety, constant use by others, the interaction of tradition and innovation, huge creativity.

I find it hard to limit my choice of events and experiences and I know that if I were to write this next week some of my choices would be different:

After the great musical celebrations of Advent and Christmas, saying Evening Prayer in the Sanctuary with the Dean on Christmas Day.

Verging Morning Prayer and Holy Communion a few hours after my father's death.

The Hillsborough Memorial Service: the Cathedral filled to capacity with chairs all the way back to the west doors.

The Royal and Naval pageantry of Battle of the Atlantic services.

Singing the *Saint Matthew Passion* and being engulfed by the profound silence after Christ's death.

Six hundred children shouting 'Alleluia' at the tops of their voices then frozen in stillness to listen to the nine and a half second reverberation.

Re-enacting part of the Passion story with children and hearing a little girl say "It's as if I was there at the Crucifixion."

Watching the reactions of children as thousands of yellow tissue paper flower petals floated down from the Corona Gallery and filling the central space like snow.

A week every summer when John Moore's University graduation ceremonies filled the Cathedral for two ceremonies each day.

Children from local primary schools in the Toxteth area presenting their dances before a congregation of parents most of whom had never been in a Cathedral before.

Fifty six symphony concerts in the Cathedral when the Liverpool Philharmonic Hall was closed for a whole season.

Music, dance, gymnastics, judo as a thousand children welcomed the Queen to the Cathedral.

Benjamin Britten's *War Requiem* and Paul Macartney's *Liverpool Oratorio*.

Performances of *Murder in the Cathedral* when the first knight rode into the Cathedral and right through the audience on a horse.

I was glad to *Lord now lettest thou they servant depart in peace.*

During rehearsal for the Liverpool Passion Play. Mark Lewis as Jesus and the repentant thief on the cross
Opposite The end of the Ascension sequence from the Passion Plays

This year I have had a series of meetings with Simon Macaulay, Liturgy Department Manager, a man born over a quarter of a century after Dwelly's death. Though he never knew the first Dean, he has upheld all the high standards of Dwelly yet, as Dwelly did, was constantly seeking to refine aspects of worship with Altar frontals, vestments, layout of furniture and the design of production of service papers.

My final comments have to relate to my time in the Cathedral during Holy Week 2014 when Choral Evensong was celebrated beautifully at 5.30 followed

after a short break by performances of *Whom do you Seek? The Liverpool Passion Plays*. The plays were created by and presented by the Overcrofters, the Cathedral's youth group, predominantly former choristers. The scripts were written by Mark Lovelady and Daniel Bishop and Daniel Bishop, Associate Organist and former chorister, was the director. In the introduction to the script they wrote, "The free performances combined drama, liturgy, music, and used the whole Cathedral, guiding audience members around the great space of the building to watch – and at many points even to be part of – the re-enactment of Christ's passion ..." For centuries Christians have, in various ways, re-enacted or 'made real again' the events of Christ's Passion, death and resurrection – anamnesis (the past being brought into the present) and we do it every time we celebrate the Eucharist by remembering through the Eucharistic Prayer the same events we are re-enacting in the Passion Plays. *The Liverpool Passion Plays* were presented by an organization, unique amongst Cathedrals, founded by the first Dean. Dwelly's imagination, creativity and concern for words, movement and music shone through fifty seven years after his death. As Dwelly had been inspired by Scott's unfinished Cathedral, so had the Overcrofters in the completed building.

At the head of this chapter, Jeremy Fletcher wrote, "The defining characteristics of cathedral worship is the requirement for variety, the constant use by others, and the interaction of tradition and innovation" and in Adrien Dorber's words "Cathedrals are places of huge creativity." Both Fletcher and Dorber would surely have been delighted by the events in Liverpool during Holy Week.

The Cross Guild were at the heart of the performance and the whole venture was sponsored by another of Dwelly's creations – The Friends of the Cathedral. As their Chairman, Alan Matthews, wrote, "We are delighted to be associated with this venture so that once again it is possible for all who wish to attend to do so without paying any admission charge. The plays are seen as part of the Cathedral's mission ..."

The performances drew large and varied audiences. The young actors played their parts with great integrity and without histrionics, the music was imaginatively chosen and well-performed, the architectural resources of the building were sensitively exploited: the performances were searingly powerful. If proof were needed that Dwelly's influence was discernible over half a century after his death, it was to be found in Liverpool Cathedral in Holy Week.

On Sunday 21 December 2014, I sat in a reserved seat on the front row of the congregation – the best seat I had ever had – to participate in *From Crib to Cross: The Holly Bough Carol Service*. As I sat and waited for the start of the service, I realized that I had attended my first Holly Bough service – in a seat near the back – sixty years ago, when Dwelly had been part of the great procession. At the start of the 2014 service, Canon Myles Davies, Vice Dean and Precentor, greeted the congregation and reminded everyone that the service had been created originally by Dean Dwelly. The note on the service paper stated in words what was made clear later in the choreography of the whole service. "The Holly Bough procession begins near the Christmas Crib and comes to rest at the foot of the Cross, which is the focal point of the reredos above the High Altar." The service was no faded copy of a dead ritual from the past. Dwelly's original idea remained the inspiration and model for the current service, in the spirit of his best work, though there were significant and powerfully meaningful changes. Dwelly had to work in a truncated and unfinished Cathedral and there was no Christmas Crib at the west end during his time. David Poulter's deployment of the choral resources was admirable. Lay Clerks, Boys, Girls and Probationers all participated at appropriate times and sections of the choir processed and sang from different positions through the length of the Cathedral.

Liturgy and architecture complemented each other in a service which was overwhelmingly powerful. If any evidence was needed to support the first paragraph of *Apologia* at the beginning of this book, it was there in this service as it was in all the services from Advent to Epiphany. "The book argues that Dwelly was responsible for establishing the style of public worship in Liverpool Cathedral, and way beyond, and that his influence is still discernible over fifty years after his death. It is argued that his was a liturgical genus commensurate with the architectural vision of Sir Giles Scott, the Cathedral Architect."

It is not surprising that over fifty years after Dwelly's death his name is unknown by most worshippers even in Liverpool Cathedral: he was an innovative, imaginative liturgical genius determined always to devise a service which was memorable and relevant to a particular congregation at a particular time and for them he created the "special service". However, I do believe that it is important for people with an interest in Anglican worship in the twentieth century, particularly those concerned with Cathedral worship, to explore the extensive influence of Liverpool's first Dean. A collaborative venture supported by cathedral Chapters and archivists across the country to examine developments in Cathedral worship would be a valuable and illuminating exercise. Dean Dwelly of Liverpool: Liturgical Genius might then receive the recognition he deserves.

Postscript

Simon Macaulay

THE CONTINUED INFLUENCE of Dean Dwelly in the worship and liturgical practices of Liverpool Cathedral cannot be disputed. Indeed, it could be argued that in recent years some ideas which he formed in the 1920s, '30s and '40s have begun to find fuller expression in the Cathedral. The Church of England, and more especially the Diocese of Liverpool, during that period Dwelly served as Canon and then Dean, was liturgically and doctrinally quite a different place from that which exists today. Some of Dwelly's more 'advanced thinking', which might have challenged congregations and clergy alike, now seems acceptable, even ordinary. Dwelly's ideas on how colour and vesture could heighten the worship of Liverpool's new Cathedral did not all find full expression during his tenure, but the use of liturgical colour, vestments and movement in worship are now largely embraced by the broader Church, and increasingly at the Cathedral. Dwelly's legacy in the liturgical life of the Cathedral is founded not only on those practices which began in his time and under his influence but also in the things which he imagined but never realised.

In devising distinctive forms of liturgy and dress for the Cathedral, Dwelly did not work alone. Sir Giles Gilbert Scott, Edward Carter Preston and Canon Charles Raven, among others, all influenced and contributed to the 'Liverpool use'. However, the influence of one other man in particular cannot be underestimated. The Revd Professor Canon Percy Dearmer, Vicar of Saint Mary the Virgin, Primrose Hill and latterly Canon of Westminster Abbey, was perhaps the most significant Anglican liturgical scholar of his day. Dearmer was a friend and was instrumental in advising Dwelly in matters of liturgy, colour and vesture. He was of the catholic tradition but was keen to eschew the practices of the Roman Catholic Church which he saw as eroding distinctive English Catholic traditions. In this regard he had an ally in Dwelly who was no party man, but sought to draw on the best liturgical influences both ancient and modern, whilst remaining loyal to the English heritage of the Church of England. Liverpool as a Diocese seems now, in 2014, to be more at ease with the breadth of 'churchmanship' which it encompasses but in Dwelly's time the

Diocese of Liverpool was avowedly evangelical. However, Dwelly's liturgy cannot be pinned down to such narrow definitions. From 1924 onwards Dwelly and Dearmer worked together on the production of *Songs of the Spirit* (published as *Songs of Praise*), a new hymn book which did not conform to the party lines of churchmanship which were perceived to exist in other hymnals. Dwelly wrote of Dearmer: "When the differences on 'Church before Party' happened, P. D. took the line that we can sing people into putting Church before Party even if we cannot teach it. He maintained that the religion of the people is the religion of hymns – we must have Songs of the Spirit."

That Dwelly and Dearmer were of one mind in such matters is clear from Dearmer's letter to Dwelly written following discussions on revision of *Songs of Praise*: "I am delighted to find how much our minds work together. So many criticisms had been met in my revising, and all are good."

Dearmer's first visit to Liverpool Cathedral was in October 1926. According to Dearmer's wife, Nan: "Percy was delighted with Liverpool Cathedral and with the development of services there. He was very happy when he was consulted from time to time on various matters concerning it … Percy preached in the Cathedral and took part in consultations with Canon Dwelly over dress and ceremonial. The Dean tells me that the distinctive vergers' gowns and the many cloaks worn on processional occasions were all devised with Percy's help and advice."

Correspondence from Dearmer to Dwelly is preparation for the 1932 edition of Dearmer's 'Parson's Handbook' sheds light on the intended colour sequence for the Cathedral. Writing in July 1927:

> My Dear F. W.,
> I enclose yet another copy (the 4th Nan has typed!) revised of the colour sequence. I found various little verbal things and then Eeles came round and suggested certain important points. Do you mind omitting blue for Passiontide? We both think this is rather fundamental as between Rome and England. Of course we know that all your evangelicals are Roman as far as they go, but still we think they ought not to be.

There were to be more revisions of the colour sequence before it was published; and the one which came into use at the Cathedral differed further. While based on the suggestions in the correspondence between Dearmer and Dwelly it was far simpler, omitting some of the more interesting suggestions (for example, cerise with stars for Epiphany). However, in the last few years some of those things planned for in Dwelly's time but never implemented have been introduced. One such example is the introduction of a Lenten white frontal for the High

Altar bearing symbols of the passion, which is used through the weeks of Lent up until Passion Sunday. The striking simplicity of this new frontal is at once both modern and ancient, and is in accord with the pre-Reformation 'Lenten array' of the English church, rather than purple, the more common Roman use for that season. While Dwelly was undoubtedly ecumenical in his outlook, he was none the less fiercely loyal in following only those liturgical practices which conformed with English precedent and Anglican thought. Writing in 1933, in answer to an enquiry about the robes of the clergy and choir at Liverpool Cathedral, Dwelly expressed his disdain for certain 'Roman' forms of vesture and a preference for the 'purity' of the fourth century:

> I will explain as briefly as I can exactly what the robes of Liverpool Cathedral are. The robes are influenced by two things: architecture and surroundings. The severity of the Cathedral architecture called for straight lines and flowing outline, the stone (Woolton red sandstone) and the limed oak demanded a harmony of colour not to be found in the ordinary black-and-white. We are compelled to weave our own cloth to obtain the exact degree of colour required, and for our designs we went back to the purity of the ornaments of the IV century … never at any time did we use the cotta. This last is a Roman innovation, discredited by their best liturgiologists, and foreign to the English Church.

While Dwelly was able to clad his clergy in distinctive choir dress – fur edged almuces lined with the Cathedral's russet fabric, and very full surplices – there were to be no Eucharistic vestments reflecting the different colours of the liturgical year, as outlined in the scheme devised by him and Dearmer. Splashes of colour were provided in the green of the vergers' robes and the choir music folders and the russet and gold of the crucifer's tunicle, but Dwelly had to use other means to convey the distinctive flavour and 'colour' of the seasons (for example a processional cross of flowers at Eastertide). Handwritten notes in the Cathedral archive give a tantalising hint at his desire for a more ceremonial Holy Communion service which he interestingly refers to as a "Choral Eucharist":

> Robes Eeles likes various colours for robes – agrees with the existent shapes …

> … chanters at Choral Eucharist before ministers, doesn't like before choir

> Cross Supporters … doesn't like banners …

> Collecting gown – very quiet. Simple vergers. Dark colour … E doesn't like capes. Capes suggest R.C. priest.

Colour More gold Vestments! Cantors robes – alright as they are … wear copes as the colour of the day – match frontal.

Chanters at Choral Eucharist. R.C. have them at Evensong but NOT at high mass

… belong to festivals

Quando chorus regularit [sic] – staves originally to control the 'Chorus'.

Here we see Dwelly's hope to have 'copes of the colour of the day' which matched the altar frontal, a gospel procession proceeded by the processional cross and, maybe most surprisingly, 'gold vestments'. None of these would have been acceptable in a diocese as liturgically 'low' and evangelical as Liverpool was. Increasingly, however, the 'party' associations of such things are diminishing. Stoles of the appropriate liturgical colour have been used more and more at the Cathedral from the 1960s onwards, and now it is the norm for them to be used at celebrations of the Eucharist, rather than choir dress which would have been used in Dwelly's time. The gospel procession at the Eucharist, to which Dwelly's notes make reference, has been a normal part of the Cathedral's liturgy since the time of Canon Basil Naylor. Gold festal copes have been part of the clergy's liturgical wardrobe since the mid 1980s, and recently a set of purple and blue copes has been commissioned for Advent use. Perhaps most significantly a full set of Eucharistic vestments matching the Advent copes have also been acquired. These will be supplemented with full sets of vestments for each of the seasons of the Church year.

With rich liturgical resources such as *Times and Seasons* available to the present day Church, much of the liturgical colour and seasonal textual variation in worship has found official form, outside the experimental innovations and borrowings of former times. The worship at Liverpool Cathedral is still distinctive and innovative, designed, as all good liturgy should be, to suit the space in which it is offered. The great spaces of the Cathedral call for movements and colour and, thanks to Dwelly's innovation, we continue to have both in abundance. The processional Advent Service of Darkness to Light, taking as its inspiration the service at Salisbury Cathedral, uses the Cathedral to great effect; choir and clergy moving first from west to east symbolising the coming of Christ as foretold in the Old Testament, and then moving from east to west, symbolising the second coming. The Carol services throughout Advent and Christmas have evolved, each with a particular flavour. It is at these services that the Cathedral welcomes some of its largest congregations, but there is still space for pageant and movement. The annual Holly Bough Carol service, with its procession of holly and candles moving from the crib to the crucifixion scene at the high altar, speak of Christ's journey from Crib to Cross with a powerful simplicity. The changing moods of the liturgical seasons now find a fuller expression than Dwelly might have known, but it is a tradition still inspired by his time at the Cathedral which affords us such a distinctive liturgical language. The Cathedral's green, russet and gold hued robes, worn by members of the Cross Guild and vergers, are taken out of use during Lent and Passion-tide, unbleached rochets being worn in their place. This, together with simple Lenten white frontal gives worship during this season a quiet and contemplative air. Then at Easter, as well as the seasonal gold of the chapter copes, the green, russet and gold of the vergers and Cross Guild return – splashes of vibrant colour adding to the paschal festivity.

Dwelly's hope for a Cathedral which eschewed badges of party and Churchmanship and embraced the best in liturgy and vesture from the ancient traditions of the early Church is increasingly realised. However, Dwelly's legacy is not something ossified in the practices of the past. He was an innovator and change was the lifeblood of his worship. Not change for its own sake, but the blending of the familiar with the new, and the comfortable and challenging. I hope and believe that the worship of Liverpool Cathedral continues, in the best tradition of Dwelly, to be ancient and modern, challenging and familiar, and in that way to give a glimpse of the God who is at once immanent and transcendent.

Dean Dwelly of Liverpool: Liturgical Genius.

Notes

Apologia

1 Peter Kennerley, *The Building of Liverpool Cathedral* (Preston 1991).
2 Peter Kennerley, *Frederick William Dwelly: First Dean of Liverpool* (Lancaster 2004).

Chapter One: The establishment of a new cathedral in Liverpool

1 Liverpool Cathedral Committee, *Liverpool Cathedral Bulletin* No. 99 (Liverpool 1976), p. 183.
2 Edwin Smith and Olive Cook, *English Cathedrals* (London 1989), p. 239.
3 Stanford Lehmberg, *English Cathedrals* (London and New York 2005).
4 Tim Tatton-Brown, *Great Cathedrals of Britain* (London: BBC Books 1989).
5 Ramsey Muir, *A History of Liverpool* (Liverpool 1907), p. 8.
6 Joseph Sharples, *Liverpool* (New Haven and London 2004), p. 10.
7 Nikolaus Pevsner, *South Lancashire* (Harmondsworth 1969), p. 155.
8 Quentin Hughes, *Seaport* (Liverpool 1964), p. 104.
9 Sharples, *Liverpool*, p. 18.
10 Canon Stewart report at The Town Hall Meeting, June 1901.
11 *The Graphic* magazine 1877, cited David Lewis, *The Churches of Liverpool* (Liverpool, 2001), p. 6.
12 Archbishops' Commission on Cathedrals, *Heritage and Renewal* (London 1994), p. 187.
13 Ibid., p. 190.
14 Ibid., p. 191.
15 Ibid., p. 192.
16 Ibid., p. 194.
17 Ibid., p. 196.
18 Lehmberg, *English Cathedrals*, p. 271.
19 Philip Barrett, *Barchester: English Cathedral Life in the Nineteenth Century* (London 1993).
20 J. S. Howson, *Essays on Cathedrals by various writers* (London 1872), p. 5.
21 Harvey Godwin in ibid., pp. 6, 7.
22 Gore Ousley in ibid., p. 215.
23 E. W. Benson, *The Cathedral: Its necessary place in the life and work of the church* (London 1878).
24 Frank Bennett, *The Nature of a Cathedral* (London 1925), p. 16.
25 Church Assembly and SPCK, *Report of the Cathedrals' Commission* (London 1927).
26 Ibid., p. 228.
27 Ibid., p. 304.
28 Ibid., p. 189.
29 Ibid., p. 101.
30 Owen Chadwick, *The Victorian Church*, 2nd edn (London, 1970, 1972), p. 366.
31 Church Assembly, *Report of the Cathedrals' Commission* (1927), p. 227.
32 Chadwick, *The Victorian Church*, p. 373.
33 Barrett, *Barchester: English Cathedral Life*, p. 311.
34 Chadwick, *The Victorian Church*, p. 390.
35 Sir James Picton, *Memorials of Liverpool* (London 1873), p. 174.
36 Michael Smout, ed., *A Portrait of the First Four Bishops of Liverpool* (Liverpool 1985), p. 1.
37 Francis James Chavasse, Letter to the

Diocese (Liverpool, 21 June 1901).

38 Liverpool Cathedral Committee, *The Town Hall Meeting* (Liverpool 1901), p. 20.

39 Ibid., pp. 20, 21.

40 Ibid., p. 18.

41 Ibid., p. 21.

42 Pevsner, *South Lancashire*, p. 175.

43 Hughes, *Seaport*, p. 134.

44 Sharples, *Liverpool*, p. 68.

45 Ibid., p. 70.

46 Cathedral Committee, *Report* (Liverpool 1904).

47 Kennerley, *The Building of Liverpool Cathedral*.

48 By the Authority of the Cathedral Committee, Liverpool Cathedral, *The Story of the Past, the Need of the Present, the Dream of the Future* (Liverpool 1904).

49 Sarah Crew, *Visionary Spires* (London 1986), p. 107.

50 Giles Scott in *Cathedral Souvenir, Liverpool Daily Post and Echo* (1904), p. 6.

51 Gavin Stamp in 'A Catholic church in which Everything is Good and Genuine' in *Ecclesiology Today* (May 2007), p. 64.

52 Ibid., p. 64.

53 Giles Scott in *Cathedral Souvenir, Liverpool Daily Post and Echo* (1904) p. 14.

54 John Betjeman in *Liverpool Cathedral Bulletin* No. 13 (Liverpool 1976), p. 183.

55 Paul Johnson, *Cathedrals of England Scotland and Wales* (London 1990), p. 194.

56 Giles Scott in *The Morning Post* (Liverpool 19 July 1924).

57 Ibid.

58 Liverpool Cathedral Committee, *Liverpool Cathedral Bulletin* No. 98 (Liverpool 1975), p. 151.

59 Sir Giles Scott, B.B.C. broadcast 16 July 1944 reprinted *Liverpool Cathedral Bulletin* No. 66 (Liverpool 1944), p. 79.

60 Johnson, *Cathedrals of England Scotland and Wales*, p. 196.

61 Sir Giles Gilbert Scott, Liverpool Cathedral Committees, *Liverpool Cathedral Bulletin* No. 6 (Liverpool 1944), p. 79.

62 Basil Naylor in The Cathedral Committee, *Liverpool Cathedral Bulletin* No. 98 (Liverpool 1975), p. 150.

63 Sir Giles Scott in *Liverpool Cathedral Bulletin* No. 66 (Liverpool 1944), p. 80.

64 Charles Raven, *Liverpool Cathedral, An impression of its early years* (London 1933), p. 9.

65 Ibid., p. 11.

66 Ibid., p. 10.

67 John Peart-Binns, Albert Augustus David Liberal Autocrat in Smout, *Four Bishops of Liverpool*, p. 52.

68 Ibid., p. 38.

69 Raven, *Liverpool Cathedral*, p. 19.

70 Lehmberg, *English Cathedrals*.

71 Kennerley, *The Building of Liverpool Cathedral*.

Chapter Two: The development of a priest

1 Robert Dwelly, handwritten statement, date uncertain.

2 Mrs Evelyn Hounsell, letter to Peter Kennerley, 1993.

3 *Chard Parish Magazine*, August 1927.

4 Canon Harston Morris in *Emmanuel Messenger*, 1957.

5 Euens, Rev. F. L., In Memoriam Caroline Dwelly, *Good Shepherd Parish Magazine*, March 1928.

6 Charles Raven, Sermon in Liverpool Cathedral, December 1960.

7 Unidentified newspaper article, April 1898.

8 Prebendary G. H. W. Mallett in *The Chard and Illminster News*, 12 July 1941.

9 F. W. Dwelly, *Diary of my Holiday in London*, handwritten, 1897.

10 Ibid.

11 Ibid.

12 F. W. Dwelly, unsent post card, 14 July 1917.

13 Anonymous obituary notice, origin unknown, May 1957.

14 F. W. Dillistone, *Charles Raven* (London 1957) p. 143.

15 F. W. Dwelly, *Summer Holidays 1903*, handwritten journal.

16 Ibid.

17 Ibid.

18 Ibid.

19 Ibid.

20 Ibid.

21 Charles Raven, Sermon in Liverpool Cathedral, December 1960.

22 F. W. Dwelly, *Summer Holidays 1903*, handwritten journal.

23 M. M. Scarr, letter to Peter Kennerley, 1990.

24 *Yale News*, 4 March 1925.

25 William Ralph Inge, *Truth and Falsehood in Religion* (London 1906).

26 Adam Fox, *Dean Inge* (London 1960), pp. 84, 85.

27 Inge, *Truth and Falsehood in Religion*, p. 15.

28 Ibid., p. 16.

29 James Crewdson, open letter, 9 July 1910.

30 Inge, *Truth and Falsehood in Religion*.

31 Rev. E. J. Nurse in *Westmorland Gazette*, 17 December 1910.

32 "Looker On" in unidentified Cheltenham journal, 22 January 1916.

33 Article in *The Cheltenham Echo*, 1955.

34 Edna Banks, letter to F. W. Dwelly, 24 June 1955.

35 *The Gloucester Echo*, 30 December 1915.

36 *Cheltenham Chronicle and Gloucester Graphic*, 12 February 1916.

37 F. A. Iremonger, *William Temple* (London 1948), p. 220.

38 Ibid., p. 223.

39 Carolyn Scott, *Dick Sheppard* (London 1977).

40 *The Times*, 20 June 1917.

41 Albert Augustus David, letter To F. W. Dwelly, 4 October 1923.

42 Nan Dearmer, *The Life of Percy Dearmer* (London 1941).

43 Donald Gray, *The 1927–28 Prayer Book Crisis*, 2 vols (Norwich: SCM Canterbury Press 2005, 2006).

44 Ibid., vol. 1, p. 28.

45 F. W. Dwelly in *Emmanuel Messenger*, date unknown.

46 Lambeth Conference encyclical letter, 1908.

47 Ed. F. B. Macnutt, *The Church in the Furnace* (London 1917).

48 Ronald Jasper, *The Development of Anglican Liturgy 1661–1980* (London 1989), p. 99.

49 F. W. Dwelly, *Acts of Devotion* (London 1916).

50 Jasper, *The Development of Anglican Liturgy*, p. 98.

51 Dwelly, *Acts of Devotion*.

52 Ibid., p. 14.

53 F. W. Dwelly in *The Emmanuel Messenger*, 1919.

54 Ibid.

55 J. A. Lee, *In Emmanuel's Land* (Southport 1998), p. 22.

56 Ibid.

57 Southport newspaper, unidentified.

58 Jasper, *The Development of Anglican Liturgy 1661–1980*.

59 *A New Prayer Book* (London 1923), p. 4.

60 Stanley Morison, *English Prayer Books* (London 1945)

61 *A New Prayer Book* (London 1923).

62 Ibid.

63 Ibid.

64 Ibid.

65 F. W. Dwelly, *Emmanuel Messenger*, December 1923.

66 *Emmanuel Messenger*, February 1924.

67 *Emmanuel Messenger*, July 1921.

68 Kennerley, *Frederick William Dwelly*, p. x.

Chapter Three: Consecration

1 *Church Times*, July 1924.

2 *Catholic Times*, 19 July 1924.

3 Charles Raven, *Liverpool Diocesan Leaflet*, 1955.

4 *Church Times*, 25 July 1924.

5 *The Church of England Newspaper*, 25 July 1924.

6 Albert Augustus David, information sheet to diocesan clergy, 11 June 1924.

7 Nicholas Basson, B.A. dissertation, Liverpool John Moores University, 1996.

8 F. W. Dwelly, note to his parents, 19 July 1924.

9 J. W. Tyrer, Liverpool Diocesan Service Book Commission, *The Sources of the Liverpool Cathedral Consecration Service*, undated.

10 Morison, *English Prayer Books*.

11 *Sunday Times*, 20 July 1924.

12 *Church Times*, 25 June 1924.

13 J. P. Baker, letter to F. W. Dwelly, 18 July 1924.

14 Dillistone, *Charles Raven*, p. 144.

15 *Manchester Guardian*, July 1924.

16 *The Form and Order of the Consecration of the Cathedral Church of Christ in Liverpool*, 19 July 1924.

17 Clifford Martin, *Liverpool Diocesan Review*, 1955.

18 Dillistone, *Charles Raven*, p. 144.

19 Clifford Martin, *Liverpool Diocesan Leaflet*.

20 F. W. Dillistone, unpublished article to mark the centenary of Dwelly's

birth, 1981.

21 *The Form and Order of the Consecration of the Cathedral Church of Christ in Liverpool*, 19 July 1924.

22 Ibid.

23 Ibid.

24 Ralph Dawson, *Emmanuel Messenger*, June 1957.

25 *The Form and Order of the Consecration of the Cathedral Church of Christ in Liverpool*, 19 July 1924.

26 Ibid.

27 Ibid.

28 Ibid.

29 *Church of England Newspaper*, 25 July 1924.

30 *Sunday Times*, 20 July 1924.

31 *Church Times*, 19 September 1924.

32 Cosmo Lang letter to F. W. Dwelly, 22 July 1924.

33 Mervyn Haigh letter to F. W. Dwelly, undated but soon after 19 July 1924.

34 Albert Augustus David letter to F. W. Dwelly, 27 July 1924.

35 Randall Davidson, letter to F. W. Dwelly, 1 December 1924.

Chapter Four: Canon Dwelly

1 Raven, *Liverpool Cathedral*, p. 7.

2 Randall Davidson, Letter to F. W. Dwelly, 1 December 1924.

3 F. J. Chavasse letter to F. W. Dwelly, 1 December 1924.

4 *The Church Times*, December 1924.

5 J. P. Baker letter to F. W. Dwelly, 30 November 1924.

6 Charles Raven letter to F. W. Dwelly undated, but clearly end of November beginning of December 1934.

7 F. W. Dwelly sermon in St. John the Divine New York.

8 H. B. Washburn, Dean Episcopal Theological School, Cambridge, MA. to F. W. Dwelly 3 March 1925.

9 Dillistone, *Charles Raven*, pp. 147, 148.

10 Chadwick, *The Victorian Church*, p. 39.

11 Mervyn Haigh letter to F. W. Dwelly, 2 November 1925.

12 Cosmo Lang, cited Kennerley, *Frederick William Dwelly*, p. 100.

13 G. K. A. Bell letter to F. W. Dwelly, 5 December 1928.

14 Cosmo Lang letter to F. W. Dwelly, 5 December 1928.

15 G. K. A. Bell letter to Albert Augustus David, cited Kennerley, *Frederick William Dwelly*, p. 101.

16 F. W. Dwelly, Art and Worship, lecture notes 5 March 1928.

17 Ibid.

18 Ibid.

19 Ibid.

20 Ibid.

21 Ibid.

22 Ibid.

23 Ibid.

24 Ibid.

25 Ibid.

26 Ibid.

27 Ibid.

28 G. K. A. Bell letter to F. W. Dwelly, 30 April 1929.

29 Ibid.

30 Cosmo Lang letter to F. W. Dwelly, 1 May 1929.

31 F. W. Dwelly letter to Cosmo Gordon Lang, undated, presumed May 1929.

32 First Lord of the Treasury letter to F. W. Dwelly, 1929.

33 *A New Prayer Book* (London 1923).

34 Dearmer, *The Life of Percy Dearmer*, p. 298.

35 Dearmer, P., Shaw, M., Vaughan Williams, R. , eds, Preface to *Songs of Praise*, revised edition (London 1931).

36 Liverpool Cathedral Committee, *Liverpool Cathedral Bulletin*, September 1929, p. 42.

37 *The Diocese of Liverpool The Fiftieth Year* 1930.

38 Albert Augustus David in the Town Hall, 12 July 1930.

39 *The Church Times*, July 1930.

40 Ibid.

41 Judith Blezzard, Holst and Vaughan Williams Manuscripts in Liverpool Cathedral in *Transactions of the Historic Society of Lancashire and Cheshire*, Vol. 139, 1990.

42 J. Meyrick-Roberts, unidentified newspaper report, October 1926.

43 Martin Shaw letter to F. W. Dwelly, undated (early 1930s).

44 Service paper. *Kinship of the Sea*, 9 February 1930.

45 Martin Shaw, *Up to Now* (London 1929), pp. 176, 177.

46 Cited in Penelope Curtis, 'The Sculptural Scheme in the Anglican Cathedral: Sculpting to Order?' in Penelope Curtis, ed., *Patronage and Practice – Sculpture on Merseyside* (Liverpool 1989), p. 94.

47 Ibid., p. 94.

48 Joseph Sharples in 'From Signwriter to Cathedral Sculptor' in Ann Compton, *Edward Carter Preston* (Liverpool 1999), p. 40.

49 Ibid., p. 29.

50 Sharples in 'From Signwriter to Cathedral Sculptor', p. 40.

51 Alex Bruce, *Cathedral Open and Free: Dean Bennett of Chester* (Liverpool 2000), p. 122.

52 Trevor Beeson, *The Deans* (London 2004), p. 126.

53 Ibid.

54 Bennett, *The Nature of a Cathedral*.

55 Ibid., pp. 6, 7.

56 Ibid., p. 16.

57 Ibid., p. 15.

58 Ibid., pp. 21, 22.

59 Ibid., p. 70.

60 Ibid., p. 31.

61 Ibid., p. 40.

62 Ibid., p. 40.

63 Ibid., p. 31.
64 Ibid., p. 37.
65 Patrick David letter to Peter Kennerley, 2002.
66 Mary Raven letter to Peter Kennerley, 2002.
67 Diana Luck letter to Peter Kennerley, 2002.

Chapter Five: The establishment of the deanery

1 John Peart-Binns, Albert Augustus David The Liberal Autocrat in Smout, *Four Bishops of Liverpool*.
2 F. W. Dwelly, handwritten note on single sheet, 2 July 1931.
3 John Peart-Binns, Albert Augustus David The Liberal Autocrat in Smout, *Four Bishops of Liverpool*, p. 41.
4 "Dick" Sheppard letter to F. W. Dwelly 25 July 1931.
5 Bernard Chavasse letter to F. W. Dwelly undated.
6 Grace Chaffey letter to F. W. Dwelly 26 July 1931.
7 A. F. S. Harding letter to F. W. Dwelly undated.
8 Bishop of Fulham in letter to F. W. Dwelly 31 July 1931.
9 Arthur Thornhill in letter to F. W. Dwelly July 1931.
10 Haveloch Davidson in letter to F. W. Dwelly July 1931.
11 Nichol Grieve in letter to F. W. Dwelly.
12 *The Post and Mercury*, 21 July 1931.
13 William Temple, read by Chapter Clerk in the Chapter House, October 1931.
14 Albert Augustus David in *The Times*, 5 October 1931.
15 Thompson Elliott *The Daily Post*, 10 October 1931.
16 Albert Augustus David, letter to clergy, October 1931.
17 Ibid.
18 A. Duncan-Jones in the *Manchester Guardian*, 9 October 1931.
19 Dearmer, *The Life of Percy Dearmer*, p. 273.
20 F. W. Dillistone, *The Language of Movement*, unpublished article to commemorate the birth of F. W. Dwelly, 1981.
21 T. J. B. in an unidentified newspaper article.
22 Albert Augustus David, sermon in Liverpool Cathedral, 4 October 1931.
23 Charles Raven, *Liverpool Cathedral an Impression of its Early Years* (London 1933).
24 Ibid., p. 7.
25 Ibid., p. 14.
26 H. D. A. Major, *English Modernism* (London 1927), pp. 6, 7.
27 Ibid., p. 18.
28 Ibid., p. 136.
29 Inge, *Truth and Falsehood in Religion*, p. 5.
30 Major, *English Modernism*, p. 11.
31 Roger Lloyd, *The Church of England in the Twentieth Century* (London 1950), p. 34.
32 Charles Raven, *The Eternal Spirit* (London 1926), p. 33.
33 Horton Davies, *Worship and Theology in England 1900–1965* (Princeton 1965), p. 135.
34 Raven, *Liverpool Cathedral*, pp. 10, 11.
35 Ibid., p. 21.
36 Ibid., pp. 17, 18.
37 Ibid., pp. 19, 20, 21.
38 Ibid., p. 22.
39 Ibid., p. 22.
40 Ibid., p. 23.
41 Ibid., p. 24.
42 Ibid., p. 24.
43 Ibid., p. 25.
44 Ibid., p. 26.
45 Ibid., pp. 29, 30.
46 Ibid., p. 31.

47 Ibid., pp. 33, 34.
48 Statement after College of Counsel Meeting, 16 November 1932.
49 Ibid., Professor J. Myres.
50 Ibid., G. K. A. Bell.
51 Ibid., John Masefield.
52 General J. C. Smuts, Address in the Cathedral, 20September 1931.
53 John Masefield, Address in the Cathedral, October 1931.
54 Letter from Patrick David to Peter Kennerley, 1999.
55 W. R. Matthews, *Memories and Meanings* (London 1969), p. 158.
56 John Peart-Binns, Albert Augustus David The Liberal Autocrat in Smout, *Four Bishops of Liverpool*, p. 51.
57 Dillistone, *Charles Raven*, p. 160.
58 Albert Augustus David in Cathedral service, July 1924.
59 *East Anglian Times*, 3 November 1924 (The Bishop had begun his episcopate in Suffolk).

Chapter Six: Controversy

1 Matthews, *Memories and Meanings*, p. 158.
2 Joe Riley, *Today's Cathedral* (London 1978), p. 104.
3 Lawrence Redfern, *The Inquirer*, cited by Alec Ellis, *Lawrence Redfern – a Memoir* (Liverpool 1968), p. 36.
4 Lawrence Redfern, Letter to F. W. Dwelly, 1933.
5 Roger Markham, letter in *Liverpool Daily Post and Echo*, 25 October 1933.
6 H. W. Peacock, letter in *Liverpool Daily Post and Echo*, 27 October 1933.
7 UNITY, letter in *Liverpool Daily Post and Echo*, 27 October 1933.
8 E. Dawson, in *Liverpool Daily Post and Echo*, 27 October 1933.
9 C. Ernest Procter, Letter in *Liverpool Daily Post and Echo*, date uncertain but between 26 and 30 October 1933.

10 J. B. Lancelot, Letter in *Liverpool Daily Post and Echo*, 1 November 1933.
11 Adrian Hastings, *A History of English Christianity 1920–1990* (London 1986), p. 252.
12 Ibid., p. 253.
13 Riley, *Today's Cathedral*.
14 Lord Hugh Cecil, letter to Archbishop William Temple.
15 Letter from Albert Augustus David to Hugh Cecil published in *The Liverpool Echo*, 5 January 1934.
16 Albert Augustus David, sermon in the Cathedral, 7 January 2004, reported in *The Daily Post*.
17 Ibid.
18 Eric Rigby-Jones in *Liverpool Daily Post*, 4 January 1934.
19 Hensley Henson before Northern Convocation 1934.
20 Hensley Henson, sermon in Liverpool Cathedral reported in *Liverpool Courier*, 28 July 1924.
21 Albert Augustus David in *Diocesan Review* 1934.
22 Raven, *Liverpool Cathedral*.
23 Gordon Bates letter to Peter Kennerley 2003.
24 John H. Harris, letter To F. W. Dwelly.
25 "Dick": Sheppard in *The Quiver*, 1934.
26 Ibid.
27 Ibid.
28 Charles Raven, letter to F. W. Dwelly, January 1934.
29 Letter from Charles Raven to F. W. Dwelly (undated).
30 Letter from Charles Raven to F. W. Dwelly, date uncertain.
31 Letter from F. W. Dwelly and C. E. Raven read from the pulpit in Liverpool Cathedral, 17 June 1934.
32 Ibid.
33 Ibid.
34 L. P. Jacks, letter to Raven and

Dwelly, read from the pulpit of the Cathedral, 17 June 1934.

35 Ibid.

36 Albert Augustus David letter to diocesan clergy 1934.

37 Chapter Minutes, 6 June 1937.

38 F. W. Dwelly letter to Rev. J. T. Wilkinson.

39 Alan Wilkinson, *Dissent or conform? War, Peace and the English Churches 1900–1945* (London 1986), p. 69.

40 John Peart-Binns, Albert Augustus David The Liberal Autocrat in Smout *Four Bishops of Liverpool*, p. 69.

41 Ibid., p. 41.

42 Dillistone, *Charles Raven*, p. 41.

Chapter Seven: The liturgical artist

1 Cyril Garbett in Liverpool Cathedral Committee, *Liverpool Cathedral Bulletin* Vol. 6 (1945), p. 102.

2 University of Liverpool Orations Delivered at the Conferment of Honorary Degrees, 2 July 1954.

3 *The Church of England Newspaper*, 1931.

4 Liverpool Cathedral Service Paper, 27 March 1932.

5 Ibid.

6 Wilkinson, *Dissent or Conform?*, p. 69.

7 Colin Dunlop Letter to F. W. Dwelly, 18 May 1932.

8 Ibid.

9 Ibid.

10 Ibid.

11 Morison, *English Prayer Books*, pp. 118, 119.

12 Ibid., p. 120.

13 Ibid.

14 Ibid., p. 120.

15 Rear-Admiral W. S. Chalmers, *Max Horton and the Western Approaches* (London: Hodder and Stoughton, 1954).

16 Liverpool Cathedral service paper, 1943.

17 Ibid.

18 Ibid.

19 Ibid.

20 Ibid.

21 Royal Air Force Service paper, 1943.

22 Ibid,

23 Morison, *English Prayer Books*, p. 132.

24 *Solemn Entry in Time of War* service paper, July 1941.

25 Clifford Martin, *Liverpool Daily Post*, May 1957.

26 Ibid.

27 *Installation of Clifford Arthur Martin as Fourth Bishop of Liverpool* service paper, September 1944.

28 Ibid.

29 Ibid.

30 Ibid.

31 Nichol Grieve letter to F. W. Dwelly, 1935.

32 Note by anonymous Free Church minister, February 1937.

33 J. T. Wilkinson, letter to Free Church Ministers, 16 April 1937.

34 J. T. Wilkinson, letter to Albert Augustus David, 25 May 1937.

35 J. T. Wilkinson, article in an unidentified newspaper.

36 *Merseyside Free Church Centre Annual Secretaries' Report* 1937.

37 Chapter Minute Book, 6 June 1937.

38 Note from an unidentified Methodist minister.

39 Howard Marshall article in *The Listener*, 14 April 1937.

40 Ibid.

41 Ibid.

42 Ibid.

43 Ibid.

44 Ibid.

45 Clifford Arthur Martin letter to Alan Topping, January 1976.

Chapter Eight: "The first human milestone"

1 W. J., one of a series of typed

accounts of war time Cathedral incidents. No one had yet been able to identify W. J. but he/she must have been a part of the Cathedral community.

2 Sir Max Horton's speech when accepting the Freedom of the City of Liverpool.

3 Colin Dunlop, letter to F. W. Dwelly, December 1952.

4 F. W. Dillistone, letter to Alan Wilkinson, September 1983.

5 F. W. Dillistone, letter to Alan Wilkinson, December 1986.

6 F. W. Dillistone, *The Language of Movement*, 1981, unpublished article to commemorate the centenary of Dwelly's birth.

7 Alan Wilkinson letter to F. W. Dillistone, 1982.

8 Alan Wilkinson in letter to F. W. Dillistone, 31 August 1983.

9 F. W. Dillistone letter to Alan Wilkinson, 5 September 1983.

10 Ibid.

11 Albert Augustus David sermon in Liverpool Cathedral, 29 March 1949.

12 Eda David letter to Christine Wagstaffe, June 1955.

13 Francis Nielson letter to Christine Wagstaffe, September 1954.

14 F. W. Dwelly letter to Cross Guild, 16 June 1955.

15 J. S. Bezzant letter to Christine Wagstaffe, 19 June 1955.

16 Colin Dunlop letter to F. W. Dwelly, 27 June 1955.

17 W. R. Matthews letter to F. W. Dwelly, 27 June 1955.

18 George Bell letter to F. W. Dwelly, 27 June 1955.

19 Bernard Chavasse letter to F. W. Dwelly, undated.

20 H. Gresford Jones, letter to F. W. Dwelly, 20 June 1955.

21 Anonymous Editorial in *The Liverpool Cathedral Choristers' Guild Magazine*, Autumn 1955.

22 Christopher Chavasse in *Liverpool Cathedral Choristers' Guild Magazine*, 1955.

23 Cathedral Executive Committee, July 1955.

24 Edna Banks letter to F. W. Dwelly, 24 June 1955.

25 Eda David letter to Christine Wagstaffe, 21 June 1955.

26 Clifford Martin letter to Christine Wagstaffe. 19 June 1955.

27 Lionel Jacobs letter to Christine Wagstaffe, June 1955.

28 Clifford Martin, *Liverpool Diocesan Leaflet*, October 1955.

29 Clifford Martin, unidentified source.

30 Charles Raven, *Liverpool Diocesan Leaflet*, October 1955.

31 Charles Raven, *The Guardian*, May 1957.

32 Harston Morris sermon, reprinted *Emmanuel Messenger*, June 1957.

33 Charles Raven, *Liverpool Diocesan Leaflet*, 1955.

34 Clifford Martin, *Liverpool Diocesan Leaflet*, 1955.

35 Anonymous article in *Liverpool Daily Post*, June 1955.

36 Ibid.

37 Charles Raven, *The Guardian*, May 1957.

38 Anonymous writer in *The Guardian*, 1957.

39 Clifford Martin, *Liverpool Diocesan Leaflet*, 1957.

40 V. Spencer Ellis, *Liverpool Diocesan Leaflet*, 1957.

41 *Liverpool Echo*, 9 May 1957.

42 Harston Morris, sermon reprinted in *Emmanuel Messenger*, June 1957.

43 Ralph Dawson, *Emmanuel Messenger*, June 1957.

44 Gerald Ellison sermon in Liverpool Cathedral, 11 December 1960.

45 Charles Raven sermon in Liverpool Cathedral, 11 December 1960.
46 Christopher Chavasse letter to F. W. Dwelly, 20 June 1955.

Chapter Nine: Dwelly tradition: death mask or spirit

1 Riley, *Today's Cathedral*, p. 86.
2 Ibid., p. 86.
3 Ibid., p. 95.
4 Ibid., p. 95.
5 Ibid., p. 87.
6 Ibid., p. 91.
7 The Cathedral Committee, *Liverpool Cathedral Bulletin*, 85 December 1963, p. 74.
8 Myles Davies, Sermon in Liverpool Cathedral, November 2006.
9 Ian Tracey letter to Peter Kennerley, December 2006.
10 Myles Davies sermon in Liverpool Cathedral, November 2006.
11 Ian Tracey letter to Peter Kennerley, December 2006.
12 Ibid.
13 Ibid.
14 Edward Patey, *My Liverpool Life* (London 1983), p. 3.
15 Ibid., p. 4.
16 Ibid., p. 6.
17 Ibid., p. 5.
18 Edward Patey, cited in Riley, *Today's Cathedral*, p. 8.
19 Patey, *My Liverpool Life*, p. 47.
20 Edward Patey, cited in Riley, *Today's Cathedral*, p. 7.
21 Patey, *My Liverpool Life*, pp. 14, 15.
22 Ibid., p. 47.
23 Morison, *English Prayer Books*, p. 132.
24 Patey, *My Liverpool Life*, p. 68.
25 Gordon Bates, Letter to Peter Kennerley, 2004.
26 Patey, *My Liverpool Life*, p. 58.
27 Ibid., p. 59.
28 Ibid., p. 59.
29 Ibid., p. 70.
30 Ibid., pp. 24, 25.
31 Ibid., pp. 26, 27.
32 Consecration Service, 1924 and Completion Service, 1978.
33 Ibid.
34 Words spoken by F. W. Dillistone in the Completion Service, 1978.
35 Stuart Blanch sermon, Completion Service, 1978.
36 *The Telegraph*, 26 October 1978.
37 Beeson, *The Deans*, pp. 218, 219.
38 Derrick Walters, cited Kennerley, *The Building of Liverpool Cathedral*, p. 203.
39 Ibid., p. 203.
40 Peter Toyne cited Kennerley, *The Building of Liverpool Cathedral*, Centenary Edition (Lancaster 2004), p. 260.
41 Rupert Hoare in Cathedral Centenary service paper, 19 July 2004.
42 Ken Riley, sermon in Liverpool Cathedral 19 July 2004.
43 Ibid.
44 Gordon Bates, letter to Peter Kennerley, 2004.

Chapter Ten: Cathedrals are the success story of the Church of England

1 Lehmberg, *English Cathedrals*, p. 271.
2 Raven, *Liverpool Cathedral*.
3 John Inge, 'Cathedrals Outreach and Education' in Stephen Platten and Christopher Lewis, *Dreaming Spires? Cathedrals in a new age* (London 2006), p. 31.
4 Mervyn Haigh letter to F. W. Dwelly, 1928.
5 George Bell letter to F. W. Dwelly, 1929.
6 Cosmo Lang letter to F. W. Dwelly, 1929.
7 *Manchester Guardian* 1931.
8 William Temple 1931.
9 *Church of England Newspaper* 1931.
10 Cyril Garbett, sermon 1945.

11 Clifford Martin, *Liverpool Diocesan Leaflet*, 1955.

12 Christopher Chavasse, *Liverpool Cathedral Choristers' Guild Magazine*, 1955.

13 Gerald Ellison sermon in Liverpool Cathedral, 1960.

14 Edward Patey cited Kennerley, *The Building of Liverpool Cathedral*.

15 Ken Riley sermon in Liverpool Cathedral, 2004.

16 John Wayne letter to Peter Kennerley, 13 April 2007.

17 Jonathan Bailey letter to Peter Kennerley, 21 April 2007.

18 Ibid.

19 Howson, *Essays on Cathedrals*.

20 Benson, *The Cathedral*.

21 Iain Mackenzie, *Cathedrals Now: Their use and place in society* (Norwich 1996).

22 *Heritage and Renewal*, The Report of the Archbishops' Commission on Cathedrals (London: Church House Publishing, 1994).

23 Stephen Platten and Christopher Lewis, *Flagships of the Spirit* (London 1998).

24 Platten and Lewis, *Dreaming Spires?*.

25 *Spiritual Capital: The Present and Future of English Cathedrals* (The Grubb Institute and Theos, 2012)

26 Ken Riley, *Cathedrals – Mission Statements or Museums?* Unpublished paper 1983.

27 Ibid.

28 Ibid.

29 Ibid.

30 Ken Riley sermon in Liverpool Cathedral 2004.

31 Riley, *Cathedrals – Mission Statements or Museums?*.

32 Ibid.

33 Ibid.

34 Ibid.

35 Owen Conway, *A Cathedral Pilgrimage – Reflections and Observations on the life and work of Cathedrals in England today and in the future* (Leeds 1989).

36 Ibid.

37 Ibid.

38 Ibid.

39 Ibid.

40 Ibid.

41 Ibid.

42 Ibid.

43 Archbishops' Commission on Cathedrals, *Heritage and Renewal* (London 1994), p. 173.

44 Jeremy Fletcher, Litany on the Frontiers: Laboratories for the Soul, in Platten and Lewis, *Dreaming Spires?*, pp. 40, 41, 47, 52.

45 Ibid.

46 Ibid.

47 Ibid.

48 Ibid.

49 Ibid.

50 Ibid.

51 Ibid.

52 Beeson, *The Deans*, p. 233.

53 Ibid.

54 Giles Gilbert Scott in *Liverpool Cathedral Bulletin* Vol. V pp. 79, 80.

55 Charles Raven, sermon December 1960.

56 Basil Naylor in *Liverpool Cathedral Bulletin*, Vol. XIII pp. 150, 151.

57 Ibid.

58 Raven, *Liverpool Cathedral*.

59 Major, *English Modernism*, pp. 6, 7.

60 Raven, *Liverpool Cathedral*, p. 11.

61 R. Duncan Jones, 9 October 1931.

62 Cyril Garbett sermon.

63 William Temple sermon.

64 Clifford Martin, *Liverpool Diocesan Leaflet*, 1955.

65 W. Harston Morris, *Emmanuel Messenger*, 1957.

66 Gerald Ellison, sermon in Liverpool Cathedral 1960.

67 Charles Raven, sermon in Liverpool Cathedral 1960.

68 F. W. Dwelly in *Liverpool Cathedral Choristers' Guild Magazine*, 1955.

69 George Bell letter to F. W. Dwelly, 1955.

70 Christopher Chavasse letter to F. W. Dwelly, 1955.

71 Basil Naylor, in *Liverpool Cathedral Bulletin* No. 98 (1975).

72 Gordon Bates letter to Peter Kennerley, 2004.

73 Edward Patey sermon.

74 Ken Riley sermon in Liverpool Cathedral 2004.

75 John Inge, 'Cathedrals Outreach and Education' in Platten and Lewis, *Dreaming Spires?*.

76 Theos and The Grubb Institute, *Spiritual Capital: the Present and Future of English Cathedrals*.

77 Ibid.

Bibliography

Published Sources

Archbishops' Commission on Cathedrals, *Heritage and Renewal* (London: Church House Publishing 1994)

Barrett, Rev. Philip, 1993, *Barchester: English Cathedral Life in the Nineteenth Century* (London: SPCK 1993)

Basson, Nicholas, *Record and Examination of the Life and Work of Frederick William Dwelly*, BA dissertation (Liverpool: John Moores University 1998)

Bennett, Very Rev. Frank, *The Nature of a Cathedral* (London 1925)

Benson, Rt. Rev. E. W., *The Cathedral: Its necessary place in the life and work of the church* (London: John Murray 1878)

Beeson, Very Rev. Trevor, *The Deans* (London: SCM Press 2004)

Blezzard, Judith, Holst and Vaughan Williams Manuscripts at Liverpool Cathedral in *Transactions of the Historic Society of Lancashire and Cheshire*, Vol. 139 (1990)

Bruce, Alex, *Cathedral Open and Free: Dean Bennett of Chester* (Liverpool: Liverpool University Press 2000)

Chadwick, Owen, *The Victorian Church*, 2nd edn (London: A. & C. Black 1970, 1972)

Chadwick, Owen, *Michael Ramsey: A Life* (London: Oxford University Press 1990)

Compton, Ann, *Edward Carter Preston* (Liverpool: University of Liverpool Art Gallery 1999)

Conway, Rev. Owen, *A Cathedral Pilgrimage – Reflections and Observations on the life and work of Cathedrals in England today and in the future* (Leeds: Private Publication 1989) #

Crew, Sarah, *Visionary Spires* (London: Waterstone and Co. 1986)

Curtis, Penelope, *Patronage and Practice Sculpture on Merseyside* (Liverpool: National Museums and Galleries on Merseyside 1989)

Davies, Horton 1965, *Worship and Theology in England 1900–1965* (Princeton 1965)

Dearmer, Nan, *The Life of Percy Dearmer* (London 1941)

Dearmer, Rev. Percy and Shaw, Martin, *Songs of Praise* (London: Oxford University Press 1925)

Dillistone, Very. Rev. Dr. Frederick, *Charles Raven* (London: Hodder and Stoughton 1975)

Dwelly, Rev. F. W., *Acts of Devotion* (London: SPCK date uncertain, 1916?)

Dwelly, Very Rev. F. W. (attributed), *Services for Broadcasting* (London: BBC 1931)

Ellis, Dr. Alec, *Lawrence Redfern – A Memoir* (Liverpool: private publication 1968)

Fletcher, Rev. Jeremy, Litany on the Frontiers; Laboratories for the Soul, *Dreaming Spires?* Platten and Lewis (London: SPCK 2000)

Fox, Adam, *Dean Inge* (London: John Murray 1960)

Gray, Rev. Dr. Donald, *The 1927–28 Prayer Book Crisis*, Vol. 1, 1 and 2 (London: The Alcuin Club 2005, 2008)

Grubb Institute and Theos, *Spiritual Capital: The Present and Future of English Cathedrals* (Theos and the Grubb Institute, 2012)

Hastings, Adrian, *A History of English Christianity 1920–1990* (London: SCM 1986)

Howson, Very Rev. J. S., *Essays on Cathedrals by various writers* (London: John Murray 1872)

Hughes, Quentin, *Seaport* (Liverpool: The Bluecoat Press 1964)

Inge, Rt. Rev. Dr. John, Cathedrals, outreach and education, in *Dreaming Spires?* Platten and Lewis (London: SPCK 2006)

Inge, Rev. W. R., *Truth and Falsehood in Religion* (London 1906)

Inge, Rev. W. R., *Christian Mysticism* (London: Methuen 1899)

Iremonger, Rev. F. A., *William Temple* (London: Oxford University Press 1948)

Jacks, Rev. Dr. L. P., Raven, Rev. Dr. Charles and Dwelly, Very Rev. F. W., *Two Letters* (London: Oxford University Press 1934) *

Jasper, Rev. Ronald, *The Development of Anglican Liturgy 1661–1980* (London: SPCK 1989)

Johnson, Paul, *Cathedrals of England Scotland and Wales* (London: Wiedenfeld and Nicholson 1990)

Kennerley, Peter, *The Building of Liverpool Cathedral* (Preston: Carnegie 1991)

Kennerley, Peter, *The Building of Liverpool Cathedral* Centenary Edition (Lancaster: Carnegie 2004)

Kennerley, Peter, *Frederick William Dwelly: First Dean of Liverpool* (Lancaster: Carnegie 2004)

Lewis, David, *The Churches of Liverpool* (Liverpool: The Bluecoat Press 2001)

Lee, J. A., *In Emmanuel's Land* (Southport: private publication 1998)

Lehmberg, Stamford, *English Cathedrals* (London and New York: Hambledon and London 2005)

Lloyd, Roger, *The Church of England in the Twentieth Century* (London: Longmans Green and Co. 1950)

Mackenzie, Iain M. (ed.), *Cathedrals Now: Their use and place in society* (Norwich: The Canterbury Press 1996)

Macnutt, Rev. F. B., *The Church in the Furnace* (London: Macmillan 1917)

Major, Rev. H. D. A., *English Modernism* (London: Cambridge University Press 1927)

Matthews, Very Rev. W. R., *Memories and Meanings* (London: Hodder and Stoughton 1969)

Morison, Stanley, *English Prayer Books* (London: Cambridge University Press 1945)

Muir, Professor Ramsey, *A History of Liverpool* (Liverpool: The University Press 1907)

Patey, Very Rev. Edward, *My Liverpool Life* (London and Oxford: Mowbray 1983)

Peart-Binns, John, Albert Augustus David Liberal Autocrat in Smout, Rev. M, *The four Bishops of Liverpool* (Liverpool 1985)

Pevsner, Nikolaus, *South Lancashire* (Harmondsworth: Penguin Books 1969)

Picton, Sir James, *Memorials of Liverpool* (London: Longmans Green and Co. 1873)

Platten, Very Rev. Stephen, and Lewis, Very Rev. Christopher, *Flagships of the Spirit* (London: Darton Longman and Todd 1998)

Raven, Rev. Dr. Charles, *The Eternal Spirit* (London: Hodder and Stoughton 1926)

Raven, Rev. Dr. Charles, *Liverpool Cathedral: An impression of its early years* (London: Oxford University Press 1933) *

Riley, Joe *Today's Cathedral* (London: SPCK 1978)

Scott, Carolyn, *Dick Sheppard* (London: Hodder and Stoughton 1977)

Smith, Edwin and Cook, Olive, *English Cathedrals* (London: Herbert 1989)

Smout, Rev. Michael, ed., *A Portrait of the First Four Bishops of Liverpool* (Liverpool: Diocesan Centenary Committee 1985)

Sharples, Joseph, From Signwriter to Cathedral Sculptor in Compton, A., *Edward Carter Preston* (University of Liverpool 1999)

Sharples, Joseph, *Liverpool* (New Haven and London: Yale University Press 2004)

Shaw, Martin, *Up To Now* (London: Oxford University Press 1929)

Tatton-Brown, Tim, *Great Cathedrals of Britain* (London: BBC Books 1989)

Temple, Rt. Rev. William, Introduction, in *A New Prayer Book* (London: Oxford University Press 1923)

Vidler, Rev. Dr. Alec R., *Essays in Liberality* (London: SCM Press 1957)

Wilkinson, Rev. Alan, *Dissent or Conform? War, Peace and the English churches 1900–1945* (London: SCM Press 1986)

Articles, Papers, unpublished sources and correspondence
References are marked with their location as follows: * Dwelly archive, # Author's papers, + Cathedral archives.

Anonymous, Notes from Free Church Minister (February 1937)*

T. J. B., Article in unidentified newspaper (undated)*

Bailey, Rt. Rev. Jonathan, Letter to Peter Kennerley (21 April 2007) #

Bailey, Rt. Rev. Jonathan, Email to Peter Kennerley (26 May 2007) #

Baker, Rev. J. P., Letter to F. W. Dwelly (18 July 1924) *

Baker, Rev. J. P., Letter to F. W. Dwelly (30 November 1924) *

Banks, Edna, Letter to F. W. Dwelly (24 June 1955) *

Bates, Rt. Rev. Gordon, Letter to Peter Kennerley (2004) #

Bell, Rt. Rev. George, Letter to F. W. Dwelly (6 December 1928) *

Bell, Rt. Rev. George, Letter to F. W. Dwelly (5 December 1928) *

Bell, Rt. Rev. George, Letter to F. W. Dwelly (17 May 1929) *

Bell, Rt. Rev. George, Letter to F. W. Dwelly (1929) *

Bell, Rt. Rev. George, Letter to F. W. Dwelly (27 June 1955) *

Bezzant, Rev. J. S., Letter to Christine Wagstaffe (19 June 1955) *

Blanch, Archbishop Stuart, Sermon in Liverpool Cathedral (25 October 1978) +

Fulham, Bishop of, *Letter* to F. W. Dwelly (31 July 1931) *

Catholic Times, Liverpool Protestant Cathedral (19 July 1924) *

Cathedral Committee, *Liverpool Cathedral, The story of the Past, the Need of the Present, The Dream of the Future* (Liverpool 1904) +

Cathedrals' Commission Report (Church Assembly and SPCK 1927)

Report of the Cathedrals' Commission (London: Church Assembly and SPCK 1927)

Church Assembly, *Report of the Cathedrals' Commission* (London 1927)

Cathedral Souvenir: Royal Visit to Liverpool (Liverpool Daily Post and Echo 1904)*

Cecil, Hugh, Letter to William Temple (1933) *

Chard Parish Magazine, August 1927, *Robert Dwelly, 1843–1927* *

Chaffey, Grace, *Letter* to F. W. Dwelly (26 July 1931) *

Chavasse, Rt. Rev. Francis James in *A Cathedral for Liverpool* (Cathedral Committee 1901) +

Chavasse, Rt. Rev. Francis James, Letter to F. W. Dwelly ( ) *

Chavasse, Rt. Rev. Christopher, Letter to F. W. Dwelly (20 June 1955) *

Chavasse, Rt. Rev. Christopher, *Dean Dwelly* in Liverpool Cathedral Choristers Guild Magazine (September 1955) *

Chavasse, Bernard, undated, Letter to F. W. Dwelly *

Cheltenham Chronicle and Gloucester Graphic, Valedictory services (12 February 1916) *

Cheltenham Echo (1955) *

Church of England Newspaper, Liverpool Cathedral Consecrated (25 July 1924) *

Church of England Newspaper (1931) *

Church Times, The Cathedral's Popularity (19 September 1924) *

Church Times, Liverpool Cathedral Consecration Ceremonies (25 July 1924)*

Church Times (July 1929) *

College of Council, Minutes (16 November 1932) *

Crewdson, James, Typed statement from church warden, Windermere (9 July 1910) *

David, Rt. Rev. Albert Augustus, Letter to F. W. Dwelly (4 October 1923) *

David, Rt. Rev. Albert Augustus, Information sheet for diocesan clergy (11 June 1924) *

David, Rt. Rev. Albert Augustus, *The Consecration of Liverpool Cathedral* (11 July 1924) *

David, Rt. Rev. Albert Augustus, Letter to F. W. Dwelly (27 July 1924) *

David, Rt. Rev. Albert Augustus, Letter to George Bell (6 December 1928)*

David, Rt. Rev. Albert Augustus, Letter to Diocesan Clergy (1931) *

David, Rt. Rev. Albert Augustus, Letter to Sir Frederick Radcliffe (17 April 1931) *

David, Rt. Rev. Albert Augustus, Letter to *The Times* (5 October 1931) *

David, Rt. Rev. Albert Augustus, *The Liverpool Echo* (5 January 1934) *

David, Rt. Rev. Albert Augustus, Sermon in Liverpool Cathedral (4 October 1931) *

David, Rt. Rev. Albert Augustus, Sermon, *Liverpool Daily Post* (8 January 1934) *

David, Eda, Letter to Christine Wagstaffe (June 1955) *

David, Eda, Letter to Christine Wagstaffe (21 June 1955) *

David, Eda, Letter to Christine Wagstaffe (24 August 1955) *

David, Patrick, Letter to Peter Kennerley (12 January 1999) #

Davidson, Havelock, Letter to F. W. Dwelly (1931) *

Davidson, Archbishop Randall, Letter to F. W. Dwelly (2 December 1924) *

Davies, Rev. Myles, Sermon in Liverpool Cathedral (December 2006) #

Dawson, E., Letter in *Liverpool Daily Post* (27 October 1933) *

Dawson, Rev. Ralph, F. W. Dwelly Vicar 1916–1925 in *Emmanuel Messenger* (Southport June 1957) *

Dearmer, Rev. Percy, Letter to F. W. Dwelly (June 1927) *

The Diocese of Liverpool in the Thirtieth Year, information leaflet (1930) *

Dunlop, Rev. Colin, Letter to F. W. Dwelly (18 May 1932?) *

Dunlop, Rt. Rev. Colin, Letter to F. W. Dwelly (December 1952) *

Dunlop, Rt. Rev. Colin, Letter to F. W. Dwelly (27 June 1955)*

Dillistone, Very Rev. Dr. Frederick, Letter to Alan Wilkinson (September 1983) *

Dillistone, Very Rev. Dr. Frederick, Letter to Alan Wilkinson (13 April 1983) *

Dillistone, Very Rev. Dr. Frederick, Letter to Alan Wilkinson (4 September 1983) *

Dillistone, Very Rev. Dr. Frederick, *The Language of Movement*, unpublished article

(1981) *

Dillistone, Very Rev. Dr. Frederick, Letter to Alan Wilkinson (1986) *

Dillistone, Very Rev. Dr. Frederick, Letter to Alan Wilkinson (5 December 1986) *

Duncan-Jones, Very Rev. R. S., Liverpool Cathedral this Week, *The Manchester Guardian* (9 October 1931) *

Dwelly, F. W., *Diary of my Holiday in London*, unpublished MS (1897) *

Dwelly, F. W., *Summer Holidays*, unpublished MS (1903) *

Dwelly, Rev. F. W., Post Card (14 July 1917) *

Dwelly, Rev. F. W., Letter to his family (19 July 1924) *

Dwelly, Rev. F. W., Emmanuel Church, Peace Day, Letter to congregation (Undated) *

Dwelly, Rev. F. W., Sermon in St. John the Divine, New York (1925) *

Dwelly, Rev. F. W., *Art and worship*, lecture script (March 1928) *

Dwelly, Rev. F. W., Letter to Cosmo Lang (15 May 1925) *

Dwelly, Rev. F. W., Service notes for the Archbishop (15 May 1929) *

Dwelly, Rev. F. W., Note (2 July 1931) *

Dwelly, Rev. F. W., Letter to Rev. Karl Reiland (11 May 1933)

Dwelly, Very Rev. F. W. & Raven, Rev. Dr, Letter to Dr Jacks, Sermon read in Liverpool Cathedral by Canon Arthur Davey (17 June 1934) *

Dwelly, Very Rev. F. W., Letter to John Wilkinson (19 September 1938) *

Dwelly, Very Rev. F. W., Letter to Anthony Eden (9 June 1955) *

Dwelly, Very Rev. F. W., Letter to the Cross Guild (18 June 1955) *

Dwelly, Robert, handwritten statement, date uncertain *

East Anglia Times (3 November 1924) *

Ellison, Rt. Rev. Gerald, 1960, Memorial Sermon (December 1960) *

Emmanuel Church Parish Magazine (Southport 1919)

Emmanuel Messenger (Southport July 1921)

Emmanuel Messenger (Southport December 1923)

Emmanuel Messenger (Southport 1924)

Euens, Rev. F. Leonard, In Memoriam Caroline Dwelly, *The Good Shepherd Parish Magazine* (March 1928) *

Form and Order of the Consecration of the Cathedral Church of Christ in Liverpool, service paper (19 July 1924) *

Frye, Geoffry, Letter to F. W. Dwelly (9 May 1929) *

Garbett, Archbishop Cyril, Sermon printed in *Liverpool Cathedral Bulletin* No. 67 (9 June 1945) +

The Gloucester Echo, F. W. Dwelly Leaving Cheltenham (30 December 1915) *

Gresford-Jones, Rt. Rev. H., Letter to F. W. Dwelly (20 June 1955) *

Grieve, Rev. Nichol, Letter to F. W. Dwelly (10 August 1931) *

Grieve, Rev. Nichol, Letter to F. W. Dwelly (1935) *

Harding, A. F. S., Letter to F. W. Dwelly (July 1931) *

Harris, John H., letter undated *

Harston-Morris, Rev. W., Tribute to Frederick William Dwelly, *Emmanuel Messenger* (June 1975) *

Haigh, Rev. Mervyn, Letter to F. W. Dwelly (2 November 1928) *

Haigh, Rev. Mervyn, Letter to F. W. Dwelly (22 July 1924) *

Harding, A. F. S., Letter to F. W. Dwelly (10 August 1931) *

Harston Morris, Rev. W. E., *Emmanuel Messenger* (1957)
Henson, Rt. Rev, Hensley, cited *Liverpool Daily Post* (8 June 1934) *
Hoare, Rt. Rev. Rupert, Cathedral service paper (19 July 2004) +
Hounsell, Mrs Evelynn, Letter to Peter Kennerley (1993) #
W. J., typed note (6 May 1941) *
Jacobs, Rev. Lionel, Letter to F. W. Dwelly (21 June 1955) *
Kinship of the Sea, service paper (9 February 1930) +
Lang, Archbishop Cosmo, Sermon at Consecration Service (19 July 1924) *
Lang, Archbishop Cosmo, Letter to F. W. Dwelly (22 July 1924) *
Lang, Archbishop Cosmo, Letter to F. W. Dwelly (5 December 1928) *
Lang, Archbishop Cosmo, Letter to F. W. Dwelly (December 1928) *
Lang, Archbishop Cosmo, Letter to F. W. Dwelly (1 May 1929) *
Lancelot, Rev. J. R., Letter in *Liverpool Daily Post* (1 November 1933) *
Liverpool Cathedral Committee, *Liverpool Cathedral*, Liverpool (1901) +
Liverpool Cathedral Chapter Minutes (6 June 1937) +
Liverpool Cathedral Committee, *Liverpool Cathedral Bulletin* Nos. 1–100 (1925–1978) +
Liverpool Cathedral Choristers' Guild Magazine (Autumn 1955) *
Liverpool Cathedral Service Paper (27 March 1932) *
Liverpool Cathedral *Installation of Clifford Arthur Martin as Fourth Bishop of Liverpool* (September 1944) +
Liverpool Daily Post, Cathedral Issue (4 January 1934) *
Liverpool Courier (28 July 1924) *
Liverpool Daily Post, Letter 'Unity' (27 October 1933) *
Liverpool Daily Post, Letter 'A Unitarian in Liverpool Cathedral' (27 October 1933) *
Liverpool Daily Post, Anglican Ban on Unitarians (8 June 1934) *
Liverpool Daily Post, A Tribute to Dr. Dwelly (October 1955) *
Liverpool Echo, The Creative Genius of Dr. Dwelly (October 1957) *
Liverpool Post and Mercury, The Significance of the Cathedral (21 July 1931) *
"Looker On", article in anonymous Cheltenham journal (January 1916) *
Luck, Diana, Letter to Peter Kennerley (8 January 1999) #
Mallett, Rev. G. H. W., *Chard and Illminster News* (December 1941) *
Manchester Guardian (21 July 1924)*
Markham, Rev. Roger, Unitarian Preacher at Liverpool Cathedral, in *Liverpool Daily Post* (25 October 1933) *
Marshall, Howard, The church in Action, in *The Listener* (14 April 1937) *
Martin, Rt. Rev. Clifford, F. W. Dwelly in *Liverpool Diocesan Leaflet* (1955) *
Martin, Rt. Rev. Clifford, Letter to Christine Wagstaffe (19 June 1955) *
Martin, Rt. Rev. Clifford, Dr. Dwelly Maker of Magnificence, *Liverpool Daily Post* (May 1957) *
Martin, Rt. Rev. Clifford, Letter to Alan Topping (January 1976) *
Masefield, John, address in Liverpool Cathedral (October 1931) *
Matthews, Very Rev. W. R., Letter to F. W. Dwelly (27 June 1955) *
Merseyside Free Church Centre Annual Secretaries' Report (1937?) *
Methodist Minister, note unidentified (1937)*
Meyrick-Roberts, J., unidentified newspaper article (October 1926) *
Naylor, Rev. Basil, in *Liverpool Cathedral Bulletin* No. 98 (Liverpool 1975) #

Nurse, Rev. E. J., in *The Westmorland Gazette* (17 December 1910)

Peacock, H. W., Unitarian in Cathedral Pulpit, *Liverpool Daily Post* (27 October 1933) *

Proctor, Rev. C. Ernest, Cathedral Services, in *Liverpool Daily Post* (26 October 1933) *

Radcliffe, Sir Frederick, Letter to Albert Augustus David (20 July 1924) *

Raven, Rev. Dr. Charles, Letter to F. W. Dwelly (1 December 1924)*

Raven, Rev. Dr. Charles, Letter to F. W. Dwelly (January 1934) *

Raven, Rev. Dr. Charles, Letter to F. W. Dwelly (Undated) *

Raven, Rev. Dr. Charles, An Old Friend's Appreciation, in *Liverpool Diocesan Leaflet* (1955) *

Raven, Rev. Dr. Charles, Dr. Frederick W. Dwelly, in the *Guardian* (1957) *

Raven, Rev. Dr. Charles, Sermon in Liverpool Cathedral (December 1960) *

Raven, Mary, Letter to Peter Kennerley (10 January 1999) #

Redfern, Rev. Lawrence, Letter to F. W. Dwelly (undated) *

Rigby-Jones, Eric, *The Times* (4 January 1934) *

Riley, Rev. Ken, *Cathedrals – Mission Stations or Museums?* Private paper (1983) #

Riley, Very Rev. Ken, Cathedral Centenary Service Sermon (19 July 2004) #

Seaborne, Professor Davies, *Orations Delivered at the Conferment of Degrees*, Liverpool University (2 July 1954) *

Scarr, M. M., Letter to Peter Kennerley #

Scott, Giles, *The Morning Post* (19 July 1924) *

Scott, Sir Giles, broadcast published in the *Liverpool Cathedral Bulletin* No. 66 (Liverpool 1944) +

Shaw, Martin, Letter to F. W. Dwelly (Undated) *

Sheppard, Rev. "Dick", Letter to F. W. Dwelly (25 July 1931) *

Sheppard, Rev. "Dick", Unitarians in Liverpool Cathedral, *The Quiver* *

Solemn Entry in Time of War (July 1941) +

Smuts, General J. C., Address in Liverpool Cathedral (20 September 1931) *

Spencer, Rev. V. Ellis, Frederick William Dwelly, *Liverpool Diocesan Leaflet* (July 1957)*

Stamp, Gavin, A Catholic Church in which everything is genuine and good, in *Ecclesiology Today*, Issue 38 (May 2007)

Sunday Times, Modern Pageantry and Mediaeval Ritual (20 July 1924) *

Temple, Archbishop William, Greeting from the Primate, *Chapter Documents* (1931) +

Temple, Archbishop William, Sermon in Liverpool Cathedral (1949) *

Thompson-Elliott, Canon, *The Daily Post* (10 October 1931) *

Thornhill, Rev. Arthur, Letter to F. W. Dwelly (1931)*

The Times, Movement for Reform (20 June 1917) *

The Times (5 October 1931) *

Toyne, Professor Peter, Memorial Sermon, Dean Walters (2000) #

Ian Tracey, Letter to Peter Kennerley (December 2006) #

Ian Tracey, Letter to Peter Kennerley (17 October 2007) #

Tyer, Rev. J., 1924, Liverpool Diocesan Service Book Commission, Sources of the Liverpool Consecration Service (1924) *

'Unity', *Liverpool Daily Post and Echo* (26 October 1933) *

W. J., Diary / Journal (6 May 1941) *

Washburn, Rev. H. B., Letter to Frederick William Dwelly (3 March1925) *

Wayne, Rt. Rev., Letter to Peter Kennerley (March 2007) #

Wayne, Rt. Rev., Letter to Peter Kennerley (13 March 2007) #

Wilkinson, Rev. J. T., Letter to Free Church Ministers (16 April 1937) *

Wilkinson, Rev. J. T., Letter to Albert Augustus David (25 May 1937) *

Wilkinson, Rev. J. T., Christian Unity. Remarkable Service in Liverpool Cathedral (undated) *

Wilkinson, Rev. Alan, Letter to F. W. Dillistone (1982) *

Wilkinson, Rev. Alan, Letter to F. W. Dillistone (31 August 1983) *

Wilkinson, Rev. Alan, Letter to Frederick Dillistone (1 December 1986) *

Yale News, Canon Dwelly is Speaker in Dwight Hall To Night. Fights Unreality in Religion. (4 March 1925) *